MW01644885

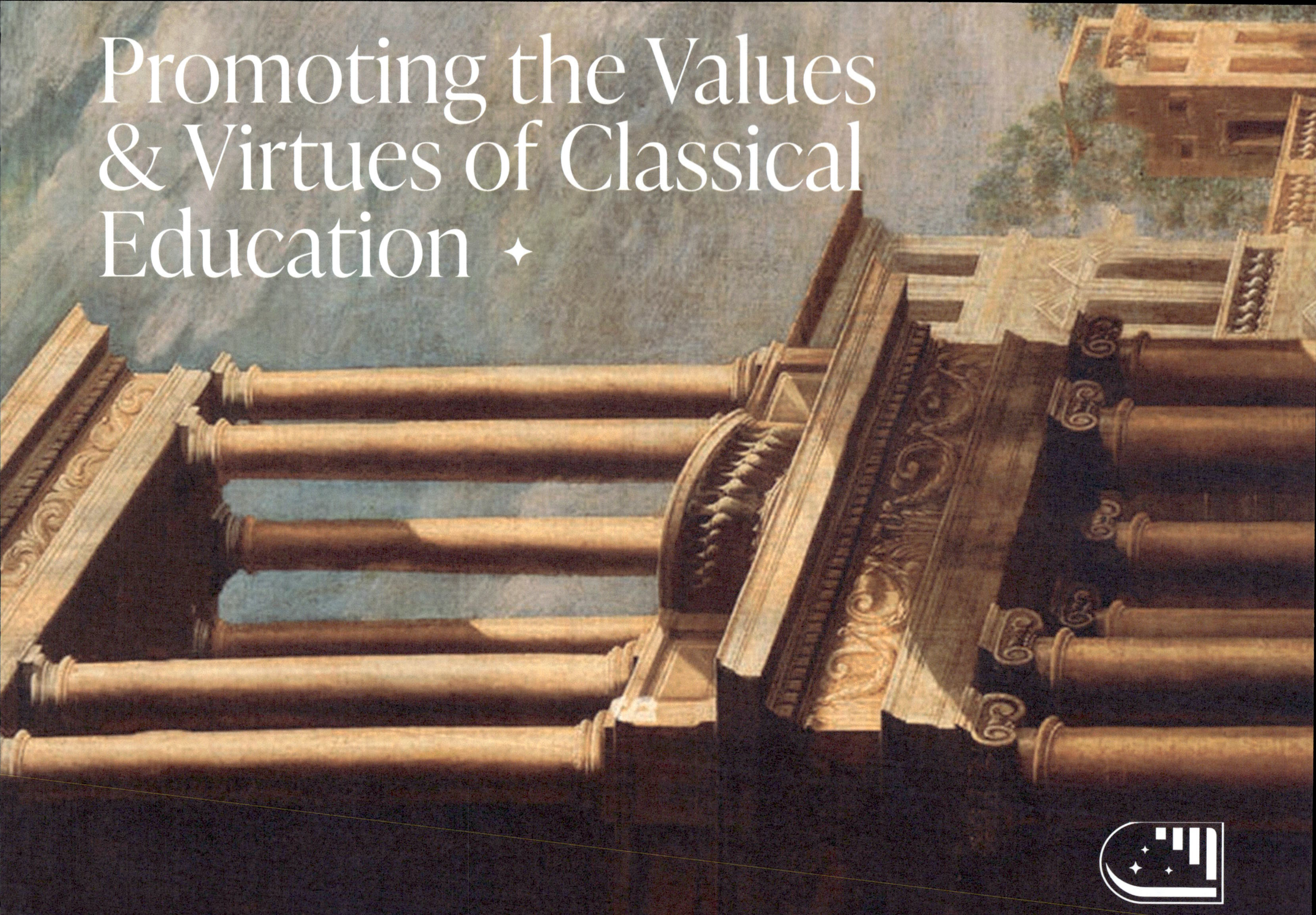
Promoting the Values
& Virtues of Classical
Education

The Greeks

Volume IV: *The Thales Canon*

Winston Brady

Thales Press Raleigh, North Carolina

This book is the property of:

Thales Canon: Volumes I-VI.

***Thales Canon: Volume IV*: The Greeks** was published in Raleigh, North Carolina for use in Thales Academy, a network of low-cost, high-quality private schools in North Carolina, South Carolina, Tennessee, and Virginia.

First Edition. Written by Winston Brady, Director of Thales Press. Editing provided by Wesley Hoag, Sarah Forrest, Will Begley, and Keller Moore.

 For an answer key, assessments, and other supplementary resources, please email thalespress@thalesacademy.org

Copyright 2023 by Thales Press.

Cover photo is *Achilles and Ajax Playing Dice*, a vase from 530 BC; the photo in the Table of Contents is of the Theatre of Dionysus in Athens and was taken by Kieran Everett.

Table of Contents

THE LIBRARY AT ALEXANDRIA

The photo for each section of the Thales Canon will always be a library because the study of history requires reading and study, the kind of work best done in a library like that pictured here.

Section I
The Greeks

CHAPTERS

THE ACROPOLIS / ATHENS

Photo by Mostafa Meraji

CHAPTER

Minos & Mycenae

ROADMAP

- Read a story from Greek mythology about the wars between the Greek gods, the creation of mankind, the stealing of fire, and the myth of Pandora's box.
- Learn about the landscape of the Greek world and its relationship to Greek history and culture.
- Learn about Minoan Crete and take a *closer look* at the Palace at Knossos.
- Read about the world of Mycenae and its warriors, its palace culture, and its sudden disappearance from the Mediterranean world.
- Study the archaeology of Minoan Crete, ancient Troy, and Mycenae and think about what we can learn from the treasures of the historical past.
- Learn more about Greek mythology and the Greek pantheon of gods and goddesses.

THALES OUTCOME
Nº 9

A Cooperative and Contributive Team Member *exemplifies an engaged and contributive member of a group to achieve the best results.*

The world of the Late Bronze Age was characterized by dynamic city-states, courageous leaders, and international, farflung trading routes. With the civilizations of Minoan Crete and Mycenaean Greece, the Greeks have finally entered into the story of ancient history—albeit with different results based on how well they can interact and get along with others.

The Creation (and Misery) of Man / Hesiod's *Works and Days*

Description: This creation story comes from the poet **Hesiod**, who lived sometime in the century from 750 to 650 BC. He wrote two works that provide many of the more famous stories we know from Greek mythology: the *Theogenoi*, or the "Wars of the Gods," and *Works and Days* about the creation of man and of man's difficult existence on earth. The selection below comes from *Works and Days* and goes from the creation of the universe to the appearance of evil in the world.

Hesiod's *Works and Days*

01 In the beginning was **Chaos**, a vast, swirling, endless void. Out of Chaos came Erebus and Night, and from Night came Aether and the Day. Gaia, the earth, came forth from Chaos too, and Gaia gave birth to Uranos, the heavens. Then, with **Uranos, Gaia** produced that first race of deathless gods—first the **Titans**, that powerful race that included Oceanus and Iapetus, Phoebe and Mnemosyne, goddess of memory, and Cronos, he who would one day rule over everything that came before him. Tartarus, that great black realm to which the cruelest of mortals are imprisoned, came forth also. And Gaia and Uranos gave birth to monsters, the dreaded Cyclopes with their one bulging eye and the **Hecatoncheires**, savage gods equipped with a hundred hands.

02 Uranos feared his children, feared they would one day rise against him and take his place as ruler of the cosmos. So he took his children and buried them deep inside Gaia. Gaia herself, their mother, could not stand for this, and she gave her son **Cronos** a scythe to deal with Uranos as he deserved. So Cronos attacked his father, mutilating him and casting his parts across the sea. The blood from mutilated Uranos fell into the sea and from the foam arose **Aphodrite**, goddess of love and desire.

CRONOS & HIS SCYTHE

An illustration of the Titan Cronos and the scythe he used to attack his father, Uranos.

03 Then Cronos, the god of time and the harvest, now ruled. He, with his Titan-bride Rhea, now had their own children, deathless gods like Demeter and Hestia, Hera and Hades, and Poseidon. And Cronos, fearing his children would usurp him much as he had usurped his father, decided his children would not see daylight: he consumed each one, eating them whole and imprisoning them inside his own deathless form.

04 Rhea, like Gaia, could not stand to see her children treated so. She decided to betray Cronos, gave him a stone to eat instead of Zeus, their last child, and hid the infant god on **Mount Ida** where Zeus could grow up safe from the jealous gaze of Cronos. And when Zeus came of age, he waged war against Cronos and all the Titans, war the likes of which the cosmos had never seen. Zeus freed the monsters imprisoned within dark Tartarus. Zeus bought the Cyclopes' strength with the privilege of making his weapons should they fight for him. From that time forth to this day, the Cyclopes make the light-

Vocabulary & Annotations

Hesiod
A Greek poet from the very end of the Greek Dark Ages. Hesiod's *Theogeny* and the *Works and Days* provide us with much of our knowledge of Greek mythology. .

Chaos
A primordial god in Greek mythology. These gods do not have the same kind of personality that deities in the Greek pantheon like Zeus and Hera posssessed.

Uranos, Gaia
Uranos is the heavens and Gaia is the earth. Herein, a union of the heavens and the earth produce the first race of gods, the Titans.

Titans
If we think of the Greek gods as succeeding generations of gods, then the Titans are the second. They are noted for their strength.

Hecatoncheires
Their name means literally "the hundred-handed ones."

Cronos
Gaia hid Cronos, who mutilitated Uranos. The same conflict between father and son likewise occurred between Cronos and his son, Zeus.

Aphrodite
The Greek goddess of love and desire. She technically has two different origin stories; the other states she was a child of Zeus.

ning bolts that Zeus hurls in fury. And the Hecatoncheires, imprisoned inside Tartarus, were glad to put their hundred hands to good use, casting whole mountains at Cronos until finally Zeus and his army triumphed over savage Titans.

05 Thus, Zeus, the noblest and wisest of all the gods yet to be born, now ruled the cosmos. He freed his siblings from their torment inside the guts of Cronos and set about to rule the universe he had taken by force. Demeter cared for the harvest and saw that the earth would produce fruit; Hestia cared for the hearth and the warm embers that make life bearable. Zeus and his brothers Poseidon and Hades cast lots to see what elements they would command: Zeus won the skies and the heavens, which were, of course, most fit for him. Poseidon the earth-shaker won the seas and everything in them, and Hades, who always had in him a pitiless streak, won the Underworld, the realms of Tartarus and all the lands of the dead to which all men go and from which none may escape.

PROMETHEUS' PUNISHMENT / ZEUS, KING OF THE GODS

Prometheus stole fire from Mount Olympus as a way of helping mankind and punishing Zeus.

06 The cosmos was now at peace—that is, until **Prometheus**, a Titan also spared from Zeus' wrath, took clay and formed it into something new: **man**. Prometheus made man to walk like the gods, upright and on two legs, and not crawl along the ground like the savage beasts.

07 Then Prometheus and Zeus quarreled. Prometheus tricked Zeus at a great banquet amongst the gods, giving Zeus an offering that looked fit for the king of Olympus. But Prometheus' gift was mostly animal bones, not the rich fat and meat whose aroma pleased the gods. Zeus, angry, punished Prometheus by punishing mankind: Zeus denied to man the gift of fire. For

THE GREEK WORLD & GREEK MYTHOLOGY

Greek mythology has a number of fantastic monsters but are often set in the real world of the Greeks.

without fire, mankind was forced to eat meat raw like any other savage beast; nor could they make tools needed to improve their lives and raise themselves still further above the wretched beasts.

08 Prometheus, angry at proud Zeus, took pity on mankind. He stole from Olympus the gift of fire and brought it down to man, carrying the sacred embers in a **fennel stalk**. And thus mankind now had fire and the means by which they could raise themselves above the level of beasts. Man could cook his food and shape new tools that made working the ground easier still—but man could also make weapons, new and cruel blades with which to bring down suffering upon themselves they had not known before.

09 Zeus' fury knew no bounds, punishing the crafty titan Prometheus and proud mankind alike. Prometheus he bound on the Caucasus mountains, chaining him upon a high crag and setting an eagle to feast each day on the liver of Prometheus. The titan was immortal and thus regrew a new liver each day for Zeus' hungry eagle to feast upon.

10 But what punishment would be most fitting for mankind? Zeus sent every form of suffering and hardship upon the race of men who dwell upon the earth, and he did it by the following means. Zeus made a new creation—like man but different, a woman whose beauty, grace, and every refinement mirrored that of gods like Aphrodite and Athena and the other deathless gods who rule from Mount Olympus.

11 Hephaestus made the creature; Aphrodite gave it her charm and beauty; Athena taught her every household art and skill Athena herself knew;

Vocabulary & Annotations

Mount Ida
A mountain in modern-day Turkey.

Prometheus
In Greek, Prometheus' name means "fore-thought." He is a Titan whom Zeus spared from destruction and imprisonment.

...fennel stalk
A fennel is an onion-like plant; the husk-like outer covering can be used to transfer the embers of a fire.

Hellespont
The Hellespont is a strait that separates Europe from Asia; today, it is known as the Dardanelles.

Peninsula
A *peninsula* is a piece of land surrounded on three sides by water and is thus "almost an island".

Peloponnese
A large peninsula in southern Greece that contained the prominent cities of Sparta, Argos, and Corinth.

Isthmus
An isthmus is a land bridge that connects two larger land areas. The isthmus of Corinth and the isthmus of Panama are two of the most significant such land bridges.

and Hermes, god of craftsmen and thieves, gave to her a portion of his wily spirit. The woman Zeus named **Pandora**, for all the gifts she received from the goddesses who dwell on high. And then Zeus gave Pandora to Epimetheus, the brother of Prometheus, as a gift, along with a wedding present: a box bearing the simple words DO NOT OPEN.

12 Could Pandora keep from opening the box? Could Epimetheus keep her from giving into her curiosity? Could he keep from looking inside the box, the last gift the deathless gods had given to her? No, Pandora could not: She opened the box and let loose every form of suffering and misery Zeus had in store for mankind: plagues and famines, wars and strife, jealousy and hatred set between man and man.

13 By the time Pandora closed the lid, all that was left inside was hope. Hope remained, but now all the earth and the sea were full of every kind of evil that Zeus who rules the heavens and hurls the lightning has in store for man. Nor is there any way to escape the will of Zeus.

Reading Comprehension Questions

1. The selection above comes from the Greek poet Hesiod, adapted from two poems entitled the *Theogony* and *Works and Days*. Describe the plot of this creation story.

2. What themes describe the "origins" of the gods, from Chaos and Erebus to the Olympians?

Reading Comprehension Questions

4. Why did Prometheus make mankind? Why did Zeus deny to man the gift of fire? Why did Prometheus steal it?

5. Why is fire at once a blessing and a curse for mankind?

6. Who is really at fault for all the misery and hardship set loose upon mankind?

The Greeks & the Greek World / Introduction & Geography

THE NAME *GREECE* for Greece is not entirely accurate. For the Greeks called themselves **Hellenes** and their land **Hellas**. Yet, a tribe who called themselves the *Greeks* settled in southern Italy around the eighth century BC. There, they came in contact with the Romans, and the Romans mistook the name of their tribe for that of the entire race and all the people like these Greeks who lived across the Adriatic Sea. The Romans then referred to all the people who spoke a language and shared customs similar to that of the Greeks as *Greeks*. When the Romans conquered Greece in the second century BC, the name stuck.

The peoples living in the geographical region they called Hellas (but we call Greece) enjoy a history that dates back thousands of years. The Greeks were a part of the dynamic world of **the Late Bronze Age** in the thirteenth and the twelfth centuries BC. The Greek mainland had its own system of palace centers at Mycenae, Tiryns, and Pylos, and these and other cities participated in the Club of Great Powers, although it was not an equal to kingdoms like the Egyptians or the Hittites. Phoenician ships traded Tyrian purple, copper, tin, and other valuable commodities for perfume and foodstuffs made in Greek cities like Tiryns and Pylos.

The ancient Greeks have long influenced the course of Western civilization. They have maintained such an influence today because they are responsible for a large number of *firsts*—at least, the people of other historical eras first came to know these events through the Greeks. For example, we have the first significant epic poems with Homer's *Iliad* and the *Odyssey*.

An epic poem is a long, narrative poem that focuses on struggles of universal importance; these epic poems detail the heroic tales of Greek warriors fighting at the city of Troy sometime around the twelfth century BC. While Homer's *Iliad* and *Odyssey* are not the first epic poems—that honor goes to *Gilgamesh* from ancient Sumer—they did influence every other epic poet that came after Homer, whereas *Gilgamesh* was lost for centuries.

Another first was the **city-state**. Technically, ancient Sumer invented the city-state but the ancient Greeks developed and refined the institution, which the Greeks called the **polis**. Thinkers and leaders of later historical eras, particularly the Renaissance of the fifteenth century and the Enlightenment of the eighteenth, credited the Greeks with first introducing the city-state to them (although this isn't accurate). In addition, the first significant schools of philosophy and the beginnings

The ancient Greeks provided so many meaningful contributions to the Western tradition and of the unique freedoms we enjoy today, but we should not idealize ancient Greece—they had many of their own flaws, as we will soon see.

THE WORLD OF THE GREEKS
Image from Google Earth

of democratic institutions all first came to Western European civilization and indeed across the world through Greek philosophers like Socrates, Plato, and Aristotle, Greek thinkers such as these thought about the deep issues of the human condition—what is justice? what is the good life? how should I live—but they could only go so far in their answers concerning the nature of the good life.

The Hebrew and Christian Bible introduced many categories of philosophical and scientific thought; later, the Christian church and medieval scholastics imparted answers to the questions of good and evil, justice and injustice, and other significant questions Greek philosophers and thinkers could not answer by themselves either.

And, for all the elements of Greek civilization we may like and find admirable, the Greeks still made many mistakes we do not wish to repeat. Without the idea of the *imago dei*, the idea that all people are made in God's image, the Greeks did and practiced many things we find reprehensible. So, there are as many things to praise about the Greeks as there things to avoid.

In this section, we will look at the geography of Greece and how the mountains, valleys, and seas helped influence Greek culture. Then, we will turn to the first civilizations in Greek history: Minoan Crete and Mycenaean Greece.

The Geography of Ancient Greece

The Greeks are one of the most significant civilizations to arise out of the Mediterranean world. The **Mediterranean Sea** laps against the shores of modern-day countries like Spain, Israel, France, and Egypt, but it also has a series of smaller seas or "arms" within it. These include the Ionian, Aegean, and Adriatic seas, smaller bodies of water within the Mediterranean. Over

Vocabulary

Hellenes
The name the Greeks used to refer to themselves.

Hellas
The word *Hellas* and *Hellenes* is actually the word the Greeks used to refer to themselves and their culture. The word *Greek* is a misnomer that was popularized by the Romans.

The Late Bronze Age
The Late Bronze Age refers to the last thousand or so years of the Bronze Age, characterized by huge trading networks and international diplomacy. The Bronze Age lasted until approximately 1200 BC, when the period collapsed suddenly and without warning.

City-State
A city-state is an independent commercial center responsible for drafting and maintaining its own laws, infrastructure, military, and other services we might expect of modern-day states.

Polis
The Greek word for *city-state*.

Mediterranean Sea
From the Latin for "in the middle of the land", the Mediterranean Sea is the principal body of water for the ancient world. The Mediterranean is surrounded by the modern-day countries of Spain, France, Tunisia, Egypt, and Israel, among others.

time, as the Greeks became master shipbuilders and navigators, the Greeks sailed these wine-dark seas and established colonies and trading posts far away from the Greek mainland. In general, trade helps a society to flourish, but for the Greeks, it was an absolute necessity: the Greek mainland is not well suited for intensive agriculture, with only an estimated thirty percent of the country containing suitable farmland. For the Greeks to obtain basic foodstuffs and other goods that they could not produce in large enough quantities at home, trade was a necessity.

Greece, meanwhile, is a mountainous region, crisscrossed by valleys and rivers. Many Greek villages are relatively close to the sea, allowing them to trade with peoples across the Mediterranean. Or those peoples could bring their goods to the Greeks, and that relatively easy access to the sea made it easy for goods and technology to come to the Greek mainland. One notable example is the Phoenician alphabet, brought to the Greeks by sailors from Tyre and elsewhere, which became the basis for the later Greek alphabet.

Within Greece, those mountains and rivers separated one Greek village from another. Over time, as villages came together or villages conquered and absorbed their rivals, these villages developed into city-states, large urban cities surrounded by the farmland upon which they depended for foodstuffs and other resources. Mountains and rivers separated these city-states from each other, allowing each of them to develop a unique identity.

People living in Athens thought of themselves as Athenians, people in Sparta as Spartans, and so on. But that separation was not so great that they could not share ideas and customs. Ancient Greek had a number of dialects, but each dialect was relatively similar to each other. As a result, Greeks from Corinth could still trade with and communicate with Greeks from Athens and other city-states when they needed to do so.

GREEK COUNTRYSIDE / CRETE

Greece's scenic beauty may have encouraged Greek literature and poetry, its landscape being so beautiful it invites contemplation, reflection, and joy (photo by Stepan Unar).

Today, Greece is part of the Balkans, a region that encompasses the southeastern corner of Europe. In the ancient world, Greek civilization was split into two halves, separated by the Aegean Sea. First, we have the region of **Ionia** on the west coast of Asia Minor. These cities included the commercial centers of Miletus, Ephesus, and Halicarnassus, the hometown of the historian Herodotus. Such cities were initially founded by colonists from mainland Greece, and they became wealthy by acting as middle men between larger kingdoms of the Near East and their Greek-speaking cousins to the west.

Connecting Asia Minor to the Greek mainland was the **Aegean Sea**. The Aegean was named for Aegeus, the father of the Greek hero Theseus who, when he thought his son Theseus had died fighting the Minotaur, cast himself into the sea below. The Aegean Sea has over one hundred and fifty islands varying in size and importance. Some islands had great religious significance to the Greeks, such as the island of Delos that, in Greek mythology, was the birthplace of the gods Apollo and Artemis. The Aegean Sea flows into the Mediterranean Sea and is connected to the Black Sea by the **Hellespont**, the straits that today are known as the Dardanelles.

The second half of the Greek world is the Greek mainland. On mainland Greece, we have a number of regions

THE GREEK MAINLAND / 1200S BC

Dark Ages settlements at places like Sparta, Corinth, and Athens became large, flourishing city-states in Archaic Greece and Classical Greece.

dominated by a particular *polis* or city-state. Such regions include Attica, with its principal city of Athens; Boeotia, with its principal city of Thebes; and Laconia, with its city of Sparta. Sparta sits on a **peninsula** named the **Peloponnese**, named for Pelops, the son of Tantalus in Greek mythology.

The Peloponnese was connected to Boeotia and Attica via a narrow land bridge called an **isthmus** dominated by the city of Corinth. Further to the north lies Mount Olympus, the highest mountain in Greece and said to be the home of the Greek gods. Lastly, the regions of Thessaly, Macedon, and Thrace sat on the edge of the Greek world, sharing many of its customs and traditions as that of their Greek customs to the south.

These regions were large and contained fertile farmland and vital natural resources. But they were also geographically spread out and lacking the kind of urban centers that made the rest of Greece economically prosperous.

Greek civilization and culture flourished on the mainland, in and among the *poleis* of Athens, Sparta, and Corinth. But it did not start there. Instead, the first great flourishing of Greek culture appeared on Crete, an island separating the Aegean world from the rest of Mediterranean and loomed large in Greek mythology.

Vocabulary

Ionia
The west coast of Asia Minor that had been colonized by Greek city-states.

Aegean Sea
The sea of the Greek world, populated with Greek islands, criss crossed with Greek trading routes, and filled with stories of Greek gods and heroes.

Hellespont
The Hellespont is a strait that separates Europe from Asia; today, it is known as the Dardanelles.

Peninsula
A *peninsula* is a piece of land surrounded on three sides by water and is thus "almost an island".

Peloponnese
A large peninsula in southern Greece that contained the prominent cities of Sparta, Argos, and Corinth.

Isthmus
An isthmus is a land bridge that connects two larger land areas. The isthmus of Corinth and the isthmus of Panama are two of the most significant such land bridges.

Reading Comprehension Questions

1. For what firsts are the Greeks primarily responsible? What institutions and ideas did we receive from the Greeks?

2. How did Greek geography influence Greek culture and customs?

3. Describe the world of the Greeks using the terms Aegean, Attica, Peloponnese, and Ionia.

Minoan Crete / 1700 to 1550 BC

CHRONOLOGICALLY, MOST STUDIES of ancient Greece begin with the island of **Crete**. With its palace at Knossos, the history of Crete, as we understand it, began around 2000 BC. The culture of Minoan Crete flourished from 1700 to 1375 BC, although Minoan Crete seemed to decline circa 1550 BC. During this time when Crete was a part of the dynamic, international trading networks during the Late Bronze Age. The palace at Knossos boasted culture and wealth comparable to that of Egypt and Babylon during the same period.

To help differentiate this period in Greek and Near Eastern history, this period is often identified as **Minoan Crete**, named for King Minos of Greek mythology. In Greek mythology, **King Minos** built a massive labyrinth underneath his palace where he kept a monstrous half-man, half-bull named the Minotaur, with *tauros* being Greek for "bull". If you know the story, Minos fed Athenian teenagers to the Minotaur until Theseus killed the savage beast. Given the long shadow that Greek mythology has cast over the Western tradition, the designation *Minoan Crete* helps us to understand this era in Greek history and differentiate from other eras in Greek history.

MINOTAUR / HALF-MAN, HALF-BULL

The monster known as the Minotaur lived beneath the palace at Crete; the above is black-figure kylix pottery and was made 560-550 BC.

We have relatively little writing from Minoan Crete. The Minoans used a writing system called **Linear A** that remains largely undecipherable, and thus our knowledge of this Bronze Age civilization is rather limited. Perhaps a priestly king ruled the Cretans, a figure who controlled the economy and acted as a representative between the gods and the Cretan people. Unlike other parts of Greece, Crete has relatively good land for farming, with fertile plains scattered throughout the island. Crete's location in the eastern Mediterranean and its

Minoan Crete became fabulously wealthy during the Bronze Age. They operated as a kind of "middle man" between the civilizations of Egypt, Phoenicia, and the various palace cultures dotting mainland Greece. Yet, despite their sophistication, Minoan civilization mysteriously disappeared around 1550 BC.

Vocabulary

Crete
An island in the eastern Mediterranean that supplied convenient ports for their wealthy trading partners like Egypt and Phoenicia.

Minoan Crete
The name given to a period in Greek history during the Late Bronze Age when the island of Crete was independent and wealthy.

King Minos
In Greek mythology, Minos was the king of Crete. He built a labyrinth beneath his palace, where he kept a cruel beast called the Minotaur.

Linear A
The writing system of Minoan Crete that remains largely indecipherable today.

Knossos
The chief city of Minoan Crete, famous for its palace.

Fresco
A fresco is a type of painting done on wet plaster, so that the painting and plaster dry together. The word is Italian for *fresh* since the painting must be done relatively quickly before the plaster has a chance to dry.

PLAN OF THE PALACE OF KNOSSOS.

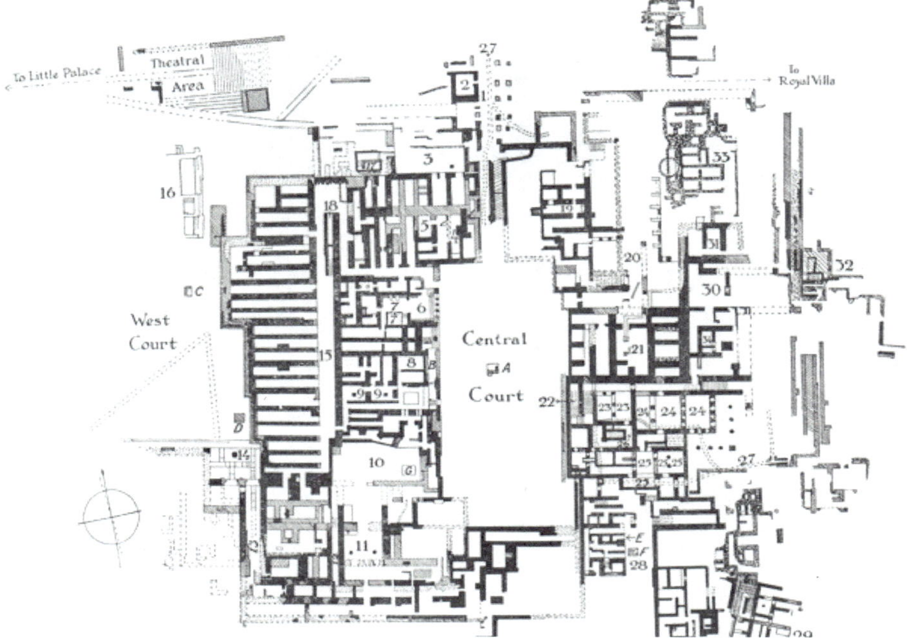

THE PALACE OF KNOSSOS / DIAGRAM
Image from Brown University

natural harbors made it an excellent site for overseas trade, particularly with wealthier neighbors like Egypt and Phoenicia. Their principal city was at Knossos, which had a port and a massive palace used to entertain guests. To an extent, the ruins looked enough like a palace that the first archaeologists assumed it was the same structure from the story of Theseus and the Minotaur.

The best primary source we have of Minoan Crete is that of the ruins themselves, found at the famous palace of **Knossos**. The palace itself is large and elaborate, decorated with **frescoes** that show scenes of youths leaping over bulls, dolphins, and strange creatures from mythology.

Moreover, the frescoes bear influence of Minoan contact with Egypt and the rest of the Near East. The use of fresco as an art form, a type of painting done on wet plaster, is found at the palace at Avaris in Egypt and Medinet Habu, amongst other locations.

Given that these frescoes at the ruins at Knossos present some of the best evidence we have from Minoan Crete, let's take a closer look at them now.

Reading Comprehension Questions

1. Where is Crete located? How did its location contribute to its prosperity?

2. How did Crete operate within the network of Bronze Age palaces?

3. What myths surround the island of Crete? What might the famous labyrinth have been?

A Closer Look at the Palace of Knossos

Instructions: The Palace at Knossos is particularly famous for its beautiful and elaborate frescoes. Carefully look at the frescoes below and asks questions about what the civilization of Minoan Crete may have looked like. Moreover, are there any scenes or activities noticeably *absent* from these frescoes? After looking at each image, answer the questions at the end of this *Closer Look* section.

BULL-LEAPING FRESCO / PALACE AT KNOSSOS

NORTH PORTICO / PALACE AT KNOSSOS

GRIFFIN / KNOSSOS

GRIFFIN IN THRONE ROOM / KNOSSOS

One of the multiple rooms with large, throne-like settings.

PITHOI STORAGE JARS

PORTICO WITH BULL FRESCO

DOLPHINS AT KNOSSOS

MINOAN WOMEN IN PROCESSION

THE PRIEST-KING (?)

Archaeologists suggest this may have been a regal, priestly figures on par with similar figures throughout the ancient Near East.

RUINS / PALACE AT KNOSSOS

Closer Look Questions

1. Describe the frescoes on the walls of the palace. What are the subjects of these paintings? What do they suggest about the people of Crete? What were they interested in?

2. What do these frescoes show about the wealth of Crete? Does Crete look t have been a wealthy, prosperous place? Did they have to be wealthy in order to produce such beautiful works of art? Why or why not?

3. Are there any paintings here that suggests the people of Minoan Crete were even interested in warfare? Anything that might have communicated their power and prestige to guests?

For teachers and teaching parents: *Minoan Crete had grown fabulously wealthy serving as a kind of "middle man" between Mycenaean Greece and New Kingdom Egypt. But, they were not a warrior culture and seemingly did not focus on fighting, building naval ships, or anything that may have helped them defend themselves from attack—like the one we will examine in the next section!*

Mycenae & Mycenaean Greece / ~ 1550 to 1177 BC

THE QUESTIONS ON THE previous page implied something terrible was about to happen to Minoan Crete. Think of the Assyrians and the decorations they had at their palaces: images of warfare, sieges, and burning and looting towns. The Assyrians hoped to communicate to anyone visiting Nineveh the Assyrians were strong, warlike, and merciless, with any resistance to the Assyrian Empire being foolish and misguided. Minoan Crete, meanwhile, seemed to communicate a very different message to one group of visitors coming from the Greek mainland, people who saw only that Crete was both wealthy and defenseless. Minoan Crete went into decline circa 1550 BC for reasons largely hidden from contemporary historians, but one theory is that invaders from mainland Greece came and conquered the island of Crete.

Those people were the Mycenaeans, named for their home city of **Mycenae**. Mycenae's name may have come from its legendary founder, a Greek hero named Perseus. Perseus is more famous for slaying Medusa, a monster who turned anyone who looked at her to stone, but Perseus also founded and named Mycenae. The name *Mycenae* comes from the Greek word for "a mushroom," although it is also used to refer to the cap of a sword. (So yes, we can call Mycenaean Greece *the Mushroom Kingdom*!) Like the Minoans, the Mycenaeans operated trade networks across the Aegean. Those networks brought the Mycenaeans into contact with Crete and the palace culture at Knossos. But, unlike the Minoans, the Mycenaeans were strong, hardy warriors.

Mycenaean Greece looms large in Greek mythology and the stories of the Greek poet Homer. Homer's *Iliad* tells story of the Mycenaean king Agamemnon and his Greek allies sent a thousand ships against the city of Troy on Asia Minor. The Greek poet **Homer** composed his poems sometime in the Greek Dark Ages, and immortalized the struggle of the Greeks and the Trojans, and of the Greeks' decade-long effort to take the city of Troy. The exploits of the Mycenaeans and their Greek allies may be the stuff of legend, but in real, historical fact the Mycenaeans extended their influence throughout the Aegean through trade and, at times, through warfare. One theory is that the Mycenaeans conquered the wealthy but vulnerable island of Crete around 1550 to 1450 BC. Presumably, the warlike Mycenaeans recognized they could conquer the relatively weaker Cretans and add them to the large amount of territory that Mycenae already controlled on the Greek mainland.

Through trade and warfare, Mycenae dominated mainland Greece during the Late Bronze Age. Because the deeds of Mycenae are celebrated in the works of Homer, our study of Mycenae becomes much harder: where do we separate fact from fiction? What really happened at Mycenaean Greece that we as historians can study, from which we may gain meaningful insights?

Vocabulary

Mycenae
The Greek city of Mycenae, located near the isthmus of Corinth. Mycenae flourished during the Late Bronze Age in the thirteenth to the eleventh centuries BC.

Homer
The blind poet and author of the oral poems the *Iliad* and the *Odyssey*, two epic poems about the events in and around the Trojan War. He was born in the eighth century BC.

Tiryns and Pylos
Tiryns and Pylos were two of the most prosperous cities in Greece during the Late Bronze Age.

Acropolis
The highest part of a Greek city that contained a citadel and supplies capable of withstanding a siege.

Linear B
The writing of ancient, Mycenaean Greece.

THE ACROPOLIS / ATHENS
An acropolis is the highest location in a Greek city, with the Athenian acropolis being the most famous; photo by Constantinos Kollias.

The city of Mycenae sits on the Peloponnesian peninsula, near the isthmus of Corinth. Mycenae was a powerful Bronze Age civilization in their own right, with a palace culture similar to that of other ancient Near Eastern civilizations. Mycenaean cities included the larger cities of **Tiryns and Pylos**, as well as smaller cities like Athens and Sparta, although these cities would become more significant in later periods of Greek history. Archaeological evidence suggests relatively little fighting took place between palaces on the Greek mainland, so they may have been friendly towards each other on account of bonds of kinship and trade. Or, they may have been conquered by Mycenae generations earlier and had long accepted Mycenaean dominance.

The best historical evidence of Mycenaean Greece are the ruins of the cities they built. Typically, each city followed a similar layout. At the center of a Mycenaean city was a fortified palace, which housed the Mycenaean nobility and the bureaucrats needed to help them manage the local economy and trade both inside and outside of Greece. They normally included a citadel built atop an **acropolis** that was at the highest part of the city (the prefix *acro* means "highest"). The acropolis was built in the highest position inside the city so that the city's defenders had a suitable location to defend themselves against an attacking army. Most Mycenaean cities were surrounded by walls and other fortifications. The walls themselves were so large that later Greeks gave them the names Cyclopean Walls, because the walls were so large they could only have been built by the Cyclopes, monsters in Greek mythology. Inside Mycenaean cities was a large, fortified palace, built in a style similar to that of the Minoans on the island of Crete.

Some Mycenaean cities, such as Pylos in Greece, had a population of upwards of 100,000 people. The Mycenaeans maintained a group of skilled, educated bureaucrats who recorded commercial transactions across Greece in a script known as **Linear B**. Unlike its earlier predecessor, Linear A, we can decipher Linear B, the script of Mycenaean Greece, thanks to the work of an English classicist named Michael Ventris (1922-1956). Ventris was actually an architect by training—not an academic or a classicist—but his intellectual curiosity led him to pour over stone tablets containing the strange writing of Linear B; he slowly but surely deciphered the writing after he guessed that Linear B was an earlier form of Greek. The last piece of the puzzle was the identification of the Greek word *tripod*, written in Linear B and placed just below a drawing of a tripod. That particular insight gave Ventris enough information to crack the rest of the code of the Linear B script.

Scholars used their knowledge of Linear B to reconstruct parts of daily life in Mycenaean Greece. Commercial records showed the likes of luxury goods like copper and tin for making bronze, exotic goods like ivory and amber, raw materials like dyes and spices, and manufactured goods like wines, ceramics, and clothing being imported into various Mycenaean cities. The city of Pylos had upwards of 600 slaves attached to the palace grinding grain or weaving clothing at one time (Pomeroy).

TREASURY OF ATREUS (LEFT) / INSIDE A THOLOS TOMB (RIGHT)

Atreus was the legendary founder of Mycenae and the father of Agamemnon; the tholos tomb is from the island of Sardina

Such records are also found in the *tholoi* tomb of Mycenaean Greece. Derived from the Greek word for *beehive*, each **tholos tomb** (plural *tholoi*) was deep beehive-like structures dug deep into the Greek countryside and outfitted with bricks and timbers to support its weight. Each *tholos* tomb served as the grave site for Mycenaean kings and the warrior nobility, outfitted with weapons and luxury goods. One can chart the reach of Mycenaean trade routes by the kinds of goods found in a *tholos* tomb at a certain date. While

Vocabulary

Tholos Tombs
From the Greek word for *beehive*, these tombs were the grave sites of Mycenaean kings.

Wanax
The Mycenaean word for *king*.

Sea Peoples
While their exact identity remains uncertain, the *Sea Peoples* is a catch-all term to the various groups of people that invaded kingdoms around the ancient Near East.

The Dorians
A race of people claiming descent from the Greek hero Heracles; they may have invaded mainland Greece at the end of the Bronze Age.

Greek Dark Ages
The Greek Dark Ages lasted from 1100 to 750 BC, or from the end of the Mycenaean civilization to the rise of Athens, Sparta, and other prominent city-states of Archaic Greece. The centuries in between saw a notable lack of writing and literary documents which accounts for the period's "darkness."

Archaic Greece
A period in Greek history from approximately 750 BC to the invasion of the Persian Empire in 480 BC. During this period, the city-states of Athens, Sparta, and Thebes, among others, became especially prominent.

most of these *tholoi* tombs were robbed, the ones that were not have elaborate grave gifts, including weapons and jewelry.

But the most famous part of Mycenaean culture was its warriors. At the head of each Mycenaean city was the **wanax**, the Mycenaean word for *king*. Based on goods found in *tholoi* tombs, the Mycenaeans fought in armor made of bronze, leather, and helmets made of boars' tusks. They carried a large shield made of ox-hide and bronze plates and shinguards, and they fought with spears, arrows, bows, and short thrusting swords and daggers. The Mycenaeans had access to chariots, but in the rocky hillsides of Greece these chariots would not have been very useful aside from a mobile command platform in battle. Due to close proximity with the sea, the Mycenaeans conducted raids against Aegean islands like Cyprus, Rhodes, and Crete, as well as the mainland of Asia Minor. Such raids may have been the basis for the epic poems of the *Iliad* and the *Odyssey*.

But like the rest of the ancient Near East, Mycenae was destroyed during the collapse of the Bronze Age. Circa 1200 BC, raiders, often referred to as the **Sea Peoples**, invaded mainland Greece as they invaded the rest of the Mediterranean world. They may have destroyed Mycenae and its network of palaces, but there is also evidence that these fortified palaces were destroyed by an earthquake.

Greek sources such as the esteemed historian Thucydides (460-400 BC) say that this invasion came at the hands of the Dorians. The **Dorians** lived in northern Greece near Thessaly, claiming to be the descendants of the Greek hero Heracles. Near the end of the Late Bronze Age, the Dorians returned to their ancestral home, the Peloponnese, conquered the region and displaced the native peoples. The archaeological records do not necessarily support this story, or at least point to a date for their invasion much later.

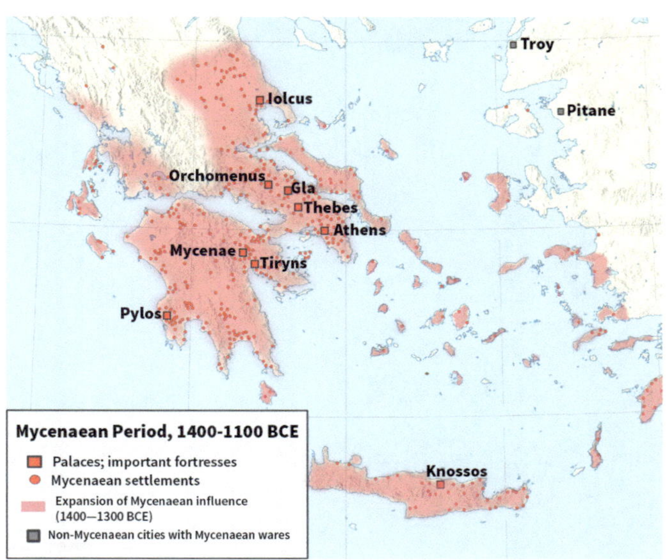

DETAILED MAP OF MYCENAEAN GREECE / 1400 BC

From here, Mycenaean Greek writing disappears, and Mycenae falls into the **Greek Dark Ages**, a period that lasts from around 1100 to 750 BC. With the collapse of the Late Bronze Age circa 1200 BC, trade routes disappeared and commercial activity plummeted. Without trade, there was no money to support scribes as they learned to read and write a complicated writing system. And without a multitude of commercial transactions, there was not the same need to pay for scribes and bureaucrats to read and write a complicated language. Without such individuals recording events and transactions, the number of primary sources from this period decreases significantly. And without written sources, we are metaphorically in the dark. Textual primary sources shed light on a historical period and without them, the Greek Dark Ages was exceedingly *dark* to us—hence, the name.

The Greeks would return to prominence in the Archaic period. During the **Archaic period**, lasting from 750 BC to the invasion of the Persian Empire in 480 BC, we see the rise of city-states like Athens and Sparta. We will turn to their story in the next chapter but first, let's take a closer look at Homer's *Iliad* and examine its complex relationship to the world of Mycenaean Greece.

Reading Comprehension Questions

1. Who were the Mycenaeans, and what do we know about them?

2. What is a *tholos* tomb?

3. What was Mycenaean culture like, based on its grave goods at its *tholoi* tombs?

4. Who were the Dorians, and what do we know about them?

A Closer Look at Archaeology & the City of Troy

HOMER'S *ILIAD* is an epic poem centered on a short period during a ten-year-long war between the Trojans and the Greeks. The story of the *Iliad* focuses on an army of Greek warriors, led by chieftains like Agamemnon, Odysseus, and Achilles, who besiege the city of Troy. The Greeks wanted to not only reclaim Helen of Sparta, a beautiful Greek princess who had been abducted by the Trojan prince Paris, but also loot the city of Troy and bring its riches back to Greece.

For centuries, historians have speculated whether or not the events of the *Iliad* actually took place and, if so, where those events occurred. The best location for the fabled city of Troy is the city of Hisarlik, located in Turkey on the coastline of the Aegean Sea. Looking at the diagram to the right detailing the archaeological site and its layers, which layer would be the best layer corresponding to the events of Homer's *Iliad*?

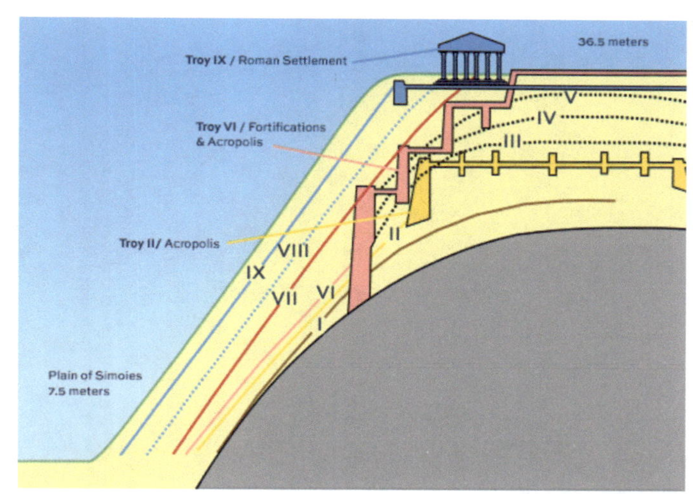

RUINS OF TROY

Layers I through IX are labeled on the diagram; (Bibi Sant-Pol)

Closer Look Questions

1. Which layer, from Troy I to Troy IX, provides the best possible candidate for the city of Troy as depicted in Homer's *Iliad*? Recall that, in archaeology, the deeper layers are from earlier periods of history. Do your best, and look at the photos on the next page as needed.

‖ **WALLS OF TROY I**

‖ **SOUTHWEST GATE / TROY II**

‖ **WALLS / TROY II**

‖ **EXCAVATED LAYERS / TROJAN SETTLEMENTS**

‖ **WALLS / TROY VI**

TROY VI & TROY IX

The walls on the right are from Troy IX

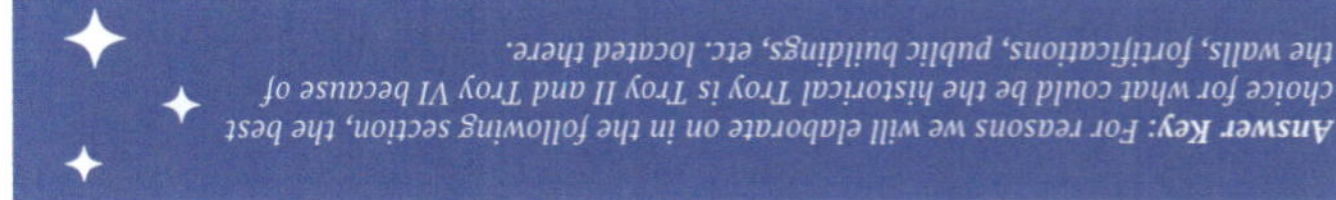

***Answer Key**: For reasons we will elaborate on in the following section, the best choice for what could be the historical Troy is Troy II and Troy VI because of the walls, fortifications, public buildings, etc. located there.*

Homer & Mycenaean Greece / ~ 800s BC

LIKE MINOAN CRETE, the best sources we have of Mycenaean Greece are its ruins. Unlike Minoan Crete, the exploits of Mycenaean Greece and its warrior-kings are celebrated in one of the most famous sources from the ancient world: Homer's *Iliad*, describing the Greeks' ten-year-long war with Troy, and the *Odyssey*, following the voyage home of the Greek hero Odysseus. However, Homer's epics are not primary sources. They are works of epic poetry celebrating the heroes of Ancient Greece; these literary works make it harder to study the time period of Mycenaean Greece.

According to the legends surrounding Homer himself, Homer was a blind poet who traveled throughout Greece, singing the songs of great heroes who lived just before the collapse of Mycenaean Greece. If Homer was a real, historical figure—and he may not have been—he lived in and around the eighth century BC. (If Homer was not a real poet, then presumably there was a group of poets who contributed to the poem as a whole. We should note that the latter option—that Homer was a group of poets and not a single genius—has its own problems as a theory, and the present author believes the *Iliad* and the *Odyssey* were the work of one poet, a genius named Homer.) Homer composed these poems orally, meaning that these works were not originally written down. Instead, Homer (or whoever the poet was) recited these poems from memory at banquets or festivals held at a temple or a fortified palace somewhere in Dark Ages Greece.

Homer's *Iliad* and *Odyssey* center on the Trojan War, a ten-year-long war the Greeks waged against the city of Troy. Troy sits on the west coast of Asia Minor near the straits of the Hellespont, and Troy grew rich through trade as ships sailed past going in and out of the Aegean Sea. With help from Aphrodite, the Greek goddess of love, a Trojan prince named Paris abducted Helen of Sparta. Helen was said to be the most beautiful woman

HOMER / EIGHTH BC
Roman copy from the second c. BC, now in the British Museum

in the world, and Paris brought her back to Troy. But Helen had a husband back home in Greece: Menelaus, king of Sparta. Menelaus enlisted the help of his brother, Agamemnon, king of Mycenae, to bring her back. And so, the beauty of Helen of Troy, formerly of Sparta, launched a thousand ships filled with Greek warriors coming to take her back and burn Troy to the ground as punishment. Homer fills the *Iliad* with epic battle scenes fought in and amongst the heroes of ancient Greece: Odysseus, Achilles, Diomedes, Ajax the Greater and Ajax the Lesser for the Greeks, and Hector, Aeneas, and Sarpedon for the Trojans. The *Odyssey*, meanwhile, follows the Greek hero Odysseus on his ten-year-long journey home from Troy.

In the eighteenth and nineteenth centuries, historians and scholars believed that the Homeric epics were largely legendary. If Homer existed at all, he made up the legends; if the *Iliad* and the *Odyssey* had any truth at all, they were gross embellishments of what were small-scale raids, not wars between rival empires. Moreover, the text of Homer's epics do not quite represent the time period in which they supposedly occur: Homer's *Iliad* and *Odyssey* take place during the Late Bronze Age, but they do not describe Bronze Age fighting. Battle scenes are not the large-scale pitched battles between rival empires such as at the Battle of Qadesh; instead, the battle scenes look more like duels fought between one side's champion against another. Then, when Homer describes warfare and weaponry, Homer describes elements of Dark Ages Greece with which Homer himself was more familiar. The weapons, armor, and other elements of war seem taken from the Greek Dark Ages when Homer lived, as opposed to the Late Bronze Age when heroes like Achilles and Hector walked the earth. So did the events of the Trojan War, the material composing the most celebrated poems in Western literature, take place in any meaningful way?

One German businessman and adventurer loved the Homeric epics so much, he set out to prove the events they depicted were true—or, at least, that the events were more true than most people believed. Heinrich Schliemann lived from 1822 to 1890, and as a boy, he loved the Greek epic poems the *Iliad* and the *Odyssey*. As an adult, he traveled around Greece and the Ottoman Empire in modern-day Turkey. At the time, the Ottoman Empire controlled Asia Minor and thus access to the sites where the events of the Trojan War would have happened which Schliemann was sure they had. Schliemann traveled around Greece and Turkey to sites that, based on the Homeric epics, were the most probable locations for the events described in the *Iliad*. The

HEINRICH SCHLIEMANN / 1822 - 1890
German archaeologist

most significant of these sites Schliemann discovered were located at Mycenae and at Hisarlik in modern-day Turkey. From 1870 to 1890, Schliemann discovered archaeological ruins and artifacts, all of which he probably too quickly identified as belonging to heroes from the *Iliad*. More importantly, though, he discovered at Hisarlik the ruins of what most archaeologists confirm are the ancient city of Troy.

The Ruins of Troy

At Hisarlik stands a mound about 100 feet in height. Within this mound are the *strata*, or layers, of previous settlements. Within this mound, Schliemann and his associate Wilhelm Dörpfeld uncovered nine layers. Each layer corresponds to a distinct period of settlement, and each settlement they labeled Troy I through Troy IX. The layers associated with the world of the Late Bronze Age are Troy VI and Troy VII, with evidence of walls 15 feet thick and 17 feet high. Troy VI seems to have been destroyed by an earthquake and thus does not confirm

Homer's grand epics. But Troy VIIa and VIIb has evidence of destruction by firing and looting, with houses crowded around the town's central fortress and storage jars filling up every conceivable amount of space in those towns. Presumably, if the city was under siege for a long period of time, their inhabitants would build their dwellings closer to the fortress for protection and devote considerable space for storing and preserving food. That some houses contained unburied human remains indicates the city may have been sacked, and the presence of Mycenaean pottery implies the sackers were the Mycenaean. Renowned University of Cincinnati archaeologist Carl Blegen identified the site and this layer as Troy VIIa. Troy VIII and IX, meanwhile, are later Greek and Roman settlements (Britannica).

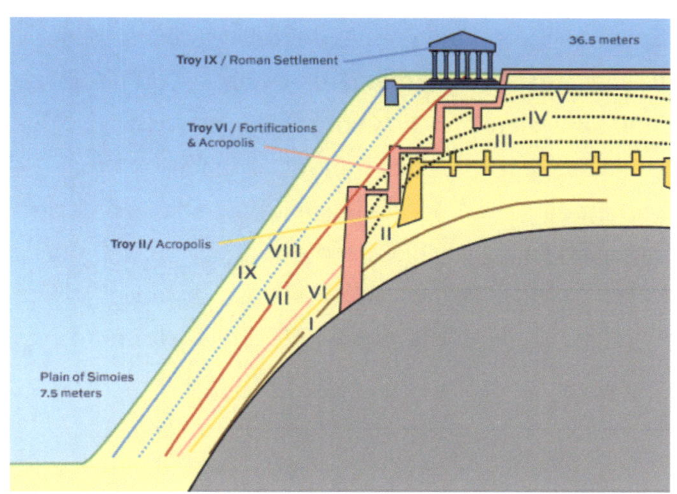

RUINS OF TROY

Layers I through IX are labeled on the diagram, with earlier settlements being at the bottom of the mound; diagram by Bibi Sant-Pol.

The Palace at Mycenae

The other major site that Schliemann excavated was Mycenae, located in Greece near the isthmus of Corinth. Schliemann's discoveries at Mycenae may be more significant than those he made at Hisarlik. Schliemann was probably too quick to identify objects he found at Mycenae as having belonged to famous kings like Agamemnon and others. When Schliemann discovered an object of great value—the death mask to the right, for instance—Schliemann identified it as having belonged to Mycenae's most famous king, even though there was no way of proving whose face may have lain beneath so precious an object. In fact, such a mask may predate the life of Agamemnon by three centuries. Among the other ruins at Mycenae are the Cyclopean Walls, walls so large that only the mythical monsters known as the Cyclops could have built them.

AGAMEMNON'S DEATH MASK

Discovered by Schliemann in 1876 and gave its name, but the mask dates to 1500 BC

Schliemann's discoveries did not necessarily confirm every detail about the Iliad and the Odyssey. He may have jumped to conclusions about the death mask of Agamemnon and other relics from Greece's vaulted past and made assumptions that cannot possibly be proven, but he did prove that Homer's work contains important seeds of historical truth. That is, the critics who said that Homer's Iliad is entirely myth with no basis in fact are also wrong. That great cities once stood at the far western tip of Asia Minor or on a remote corner of the Peloponnesian War carry with them the possibility that Homer's great epic have some basis in fact and that, perhaps, his great heroes in some way, shape, or form walked the earth. Schliemann's enthusiasm, determination, and willingness to travel great distances to find the truth are all traits we should cultivate for ourselves, too.

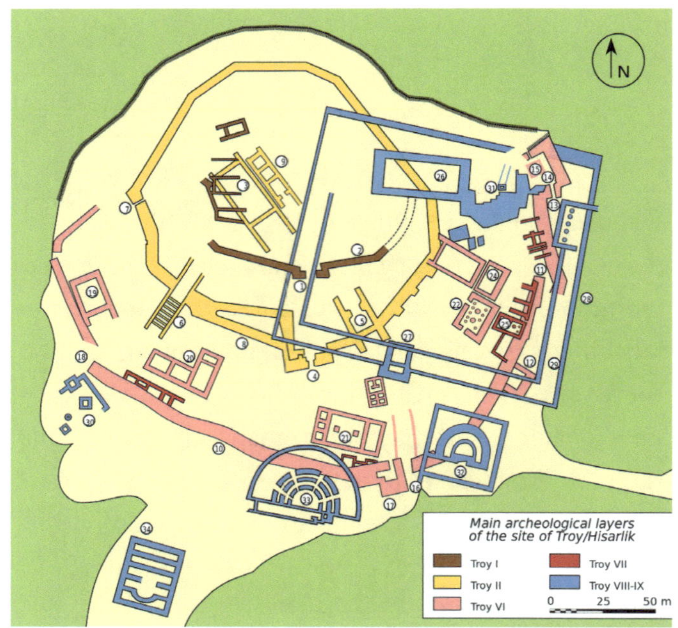

ARCHAEOLOGICAL PLAN / TROY
Image created by Bibi Sant-Pol

THE LION GATE / MYCENAE

CYCLOPEAN WALLS / MYCENAE

Closer Look Questions

1. Who was Homer and when did he live?

2. What did scholars assume about the Trojan War?

3. Who was Heinrich Schliemann and what were his major accomplishments?

4. What character traits did Schliemann have we should try and follow? What were some of his flaws and errors that we should try to avoid?

A Closer Look at the Greek Pantheon

THE WORD PANTHEON means *all the gods* and typically refers to the preeminent, ruling deities in a mythological tradition. The Sumerian pantheon included gods and goddesses like Enlil, Enki, and others, whereas the Egyptians worshiped Osiris, Isis, and Ra as the most significant gods in their pantheon. In this *Closer Look*, we will examine the pantheon of gods and goddesses in Greek mythology.

Greek mythology has captivated readers for thousands of years. The tale of Troy, the labors of Heracles, and the strange world of gods, titans, nymphs, and monsters has provided much of the foundation for the Western canon. Much of the original Greek myths were passed down via oral tradition—a poet singing the songs of great heroes long since past at some public ceremony. Later, the poets Hesiod and Homer put these tales into verse. Hesiod wrote two poems centered on the creation and character of the Greek gods and their interaction with mankind, whereas Homer is the author of the *Iliad* and the *Odyssey*, epic poems centered on the Trojan War and the return home of one of Greek hero Odysseus. Both Hesiod and Homer lived around the eighth century BC, and they are often credited with inventing many aspects of Greek religion and mythology because of the influence their poems had on Greek culture.

But of course, the Greek understanding of the world and of the gods they believed to rule it derives, in part, from the Greek landscape. As with Mesopotamia and Egypt, much of the relationship between the gods and mankind is "seen through" the natural world around a particular society or culture. In Mesopotamia, the weather is unstable and unpredictable with frequent droughts, famines, hailstorms, monsoons, and floods. Such natural disasters led ancient Mesopotamians to believe their gods hated mankind, even that the gods created mankind to be slaves. In Egypt, the prosperity of the Nile River helped the Egyptians to conceive of the ideal of *ma'at*, seen in the balance between the Nile and the desert, the delta and the valley.

Greece is a mountainous country surrounded by seas, overshadowed by mountains, and crisscrossed by rivers and streams. The landscape seems ideal for contemplation and reflection, sitting atop a mountain or near the sea and wondering what strange creatures lived on a nearby island inside a volcano, or just beyond the horizon. Plus, the Greeks lived in the middle of the Mediterranean and amongst busy shipping lanes crisscrossing the sea from Egypt to Anatolia to Syria to Carthage and Rome. As a result, they occasionally brought in new gods and goddesses from further east if they liked them well enough. Most Greek settlements were dedicated to one Greek god or goddess in particular, with Athens and Athena being the most significant examples. Now, let's examine the members of the Greek pantheon and learn more about them.

The Greek Pantheon

God or Goddess	*Background*	*Powers, Responsibilities, & Stories*	*Photo (if applicable)*
Primordial Gods	*These gods begin with Chaos, which produces Erebus, associated with the underworld and darkness, and Night.* *Day comes forth from Night, followed by Gaia and Uranus.* *They give rise to the other gods, but they do not have much personality in and of themselves.*	The two most important of these primordial deities are Gaia, or mother earth, and Uranos (right), the personification of the heavens. The union of the earth and the heavens produces the titans, the first race of immortal deities. Uranos fears his children will overthrow him, and he stuffs his children deep inside Gaia, causing her great pain and suffering.	
The Titans	*The Titans are a race of immortal gods that ruled the universe following Uranus and Gaia.* *The titans include gods such as Oceanus, Iapetus, Phoebe, and Mnemosyne, the goddess of memory.* *Cronus, the youngest titan, overthrew his father Uranus and took over as the ruler of the Greek cosmos.*	Cronus attacked and mutilated his father, Uranos, with a sickle (hence, the sickle in the illustration to the right.) Cronus and Rhea produced children of their own, but Cronus was afraid they would overthrow him in the same way he overthrew his father, Uranos. Thus, Cronus ate his children and imprisoned them within his own stomach.	
The Olympians	*The Titans Cronus and Rhea produced children including Hera, Hestia, Poseidon, Demeter, and Hades. Zeus was the youngest, but Rhea tricked Cronus into eating a stone and thus saved Zeus from destruction and imprisonment. Zeus waged a successful rebellion against Cronus, overthrew him and the titans, freed his siblings, and took over as king of the Greek cosmos.*	Zeus led a rebellion against Cronus and the other Titans. After Zeus successfully overthrew Cronus, he freed his siblings and reorganized the cosmos, bringing to it peace and order. The Greeks believed that Zeus and his siblings lived on Mount Olympus and thus called them the *Olympians*. Later additions included Apollo, Artemis, Hermes, Athena, Ares, Aphrodite, and Hephaestus. Later, the Romans largely imported the pantheon of the Greeks into Roman society and culture.	

The Greek Pantheon (Continued)

God or Goddess	*Background*	*Powers, Responsibilities, & Stories*	*Photo (if applicable)*
Zeus	*One of the Twelve Olympians and the so-called king of the gods. Hesiod's* Theogeny *tells of us Zeus being born of the titan Cronus and Rhea. Cronus and Rhea were titans who ruled the universe, and according to Greek mythology, Cronus ate his own children to keep them from overthrowing him. In an event known as the Titanomachy, Zeus rebelled against Cronus, freed his siblings imprisoned inside Cronus' stomach, and then set about ordering the created universe.*	Zeus is the god of the rains, thunder, lightning, and the heavens, as well as being the king of the gods. Zeus is associated with animals like eagles, trees like the oak, and thunderbolts, and his children include a long list of heroes such as Heracles and gods like Apollo, Athena, and Hermes.	
Hera	*Hera is one of the original six children of Cronus and Rhea. She is the queen of the gods and the husband of Zeus, although many tales in Greek mythology speak of Zeus' unfaithfulness to Hera.*	Hera is the queen of the gods and the goddess of marriage, the family, and childbirth.	
Poseidon	*Poseidon is one of the original six children of Cronus and Rhea and thus the brother of Zeus. At the close of the Titanomachy, Zeus, Poseidon, and Hades gambled for whatever elements they would control, and Poseidon won control of the seas.*	Poseidon is the god of the sea, earthquakes, and horses. He is associated with weapons like the trident and animals like dolphins and other sea creatures, as well as horses and bulls. Like Zeus, he is the father of many Greek heroes, notably, Theseus and Orion.	

The Greek Pantheon (Continued)

God or Goddess	Background	Powers, Responsibilities, & Stories	Photo
Demeter	*Demeter is one of the original children of Cronus and Rhea and one of the most significant goddesses in the Greek pantheon, given that she ensures bountiful harvests for the world. Her most famous myth involves the abduction of her daughter Persephone by Hades. While Persephone is forced to spend time in the Underworld with Hades, Demeter is so sad she will not allow anything to grow, a time period that corresponds to the cold winter season.*	Demeter is the goddess of grain and agriculture which, to us, does not seem as exciting as thunder or the ocean. In mythology, Demeter was one of the most important deities because without Demeter's aid, the Greek world would not have enough food to survive.	
Hestia	*Hestia is one of the six children of Cronus and Rhea and is the goddess of the hearth, the central fireplace in a home that unites a family together.*	Like Demeter, Hestia has a role of great importance to civilization in general. The fireplace in a home is used for cooking food, heating the home, and helping the family to survive in a harsh and unforgiving world. But the hearth does not make for exciting stories, and Hestia would eventually give up her place on Mount Olympus to Heracles, the son of Zeus famous for his strength and prowess.	
Hades	*Hades is one of the original children of Cronus and Rhea. Hades is the king of the Underworld and thus, he is not really an Olympian.*	Often, the Underworld is associated with wealth and riches, so Hades is described as being wealthy and greedy. Hades is associated with intimidating, frightening animals such as screech owls and Cerberus, a three-headed dog who guards the Underworld.	

The Greek Pantheon (Continued)

God or Goddess	Background	Powers, Responsibilities, & Stories	Photo (if applicable)
Aphrodite	*Aphrodite has more than one birth story, but the one Hesiod tells is of Aphrodite being born from the mutilated body parts of Uranus, the god of the heavens. Cronus had rebelled against his father Uranus in the same way Zeus rebelled against Cronus. After Cronus wounded his father, he threw Uranus' body parts across the heavens, and from Uranus' blood arose Aphrodite, the Greek goddess of love, beauty, and desire.*	Aphrodite is the goddess of love, beauty, and desire and is associated with animals and plants associated with love: animals like swans, doves, and sparrows, and plants like roses and myrtles. She is also a fertility goddess, which is important in and of itself to ensure plants and animals produce more offspring. Aphrodite may have been imported from the ancient Near East since she bears a great resemblance to goddesses like Astarte and Ishtar in Canaanite and Babylonian mythology.	
Athena	*Athena is the daughter of Zeus and Metis, a goddess associated with wisdom. Zeus feared a prophecy that Metis' child would overthrow their father, so Zeus swallowed Metis and the child she was carrying.* *Still, Zeus cannot keep Athena from being born, who emerged fully developed, fully grown, fully armed from Zeus' head*	Athena is the goddess of wisdom, the household arts like weaving and sowing, and warfare. She is the patron deity of Athens, as well as the patron deity of heroes like Odysseus. She is also associated with animals that appear wise and crafty such as owls and snakes and plants like olives (she even brought olives to ancient Athens). Her nickname is *Pallas Athena,* and she carries the *aegis*, a shield that has an image of Medusa.	
Hephaestus	*Like Aphrodite, Hephaestus has several birth stories. Homer's* Odyssey *tells us that he was born crippled and lame and his mother, Hera, threw him off of Mount Olympus in a rage.* *He is the god of craftsmen, metallurgy, carpenters, tools, etc. In some myths, he is married to Aphrodite. He is crippled and lame, a condition he may have had at birth or because his mother, Hera, threw him off of Mount Olympus.*	Hephaestus is associated with volcanoes, fires, blacksmithing, hammers, tongs, etc., and other tools of the blacksmithing trade.	

The Greek Pantheon (Continued)

God or Goddess	Background	Powers, Responsibilities, & Stories	Photo (if applicable)
Ares	*The Romans held Mars in much higher esteem than did the Greeks and connected him with more honorable, heroic warfare The month of March is named after him, and Romulus and Remus are his sons.*	Ares is described as bloodthirsty, violent, and ultimately as a god who enjoys war. As the god of war, Ares is associated with animals like dogs and vultures because these animals eat dead bodies after a battle. In Greek mythology, he has a child with Aphrodite named Harmonia. In Roman mythology, he is the father of Romulus and Remus, the founders of the city of Rome.	
Hermes	*Hermes is the god of commerce and travelers, as well as of thieves, and merchants. He is also the messenger god who carries news from Mount Olympians down to earth.* *He is the son of Maia, one of the Titans, and Zeus.*	Hermes is associated with roosters and tortoises. He carries a staff called the *caduceus* which has two intertwining snakes seen on ambulances today. In Greek mythology, Hermes stole Apollo's cattle and invented the lyre to avoid getting in trouble with Apollo.	
Apollo and Artemis	Apollo and Artemis are the twin children of Zeus and a titaness named Leto. Having angered Hera, Leto had to search across the Aegean world to find a place to give birth to her twins. Leto settles on Delos, an island that will be sacred to Apollo and Artemis thereafter. Together, they slay a monster called Python that Hera sends after them and their mother, Leto.	Apollo is the god of light, gold, the sun, philosophy, and music, whereas Artemis is the goddess of the hunt, the moon, silver, and of maidens.	

The Greek Pantheon (Continued)

God or Goddess	*Background*	*Powers, Responsibilities, & Stories*	*Photo (if applicable)*
Dionysus	*Dionysus is a later addition to the Greek pantheon, a god that may have been imported from cults further east.* *Dionysus is the son of Zeus and Semele, a mortal princess. When Semele asks Zeus to show her his "true form"; Zeus' true form is a lightning bolt, which electrocutes Semele.* *Semele was carrying Zeus' child, and Zeus puts the unborn child in his thigh, where the child—Dionysus—finishes growing and developing until Dionysus is born.*	Dionysus is the god of wine, revelry, comedy, and the theatre. Later plays during the Greek Classical period depict Dionysus as punishing mortals who refuse to worship him. He is associated with grapes, panthers (he rides in a chariot drawn by panthers), and the *City Dionysia,* a series of religious festivals in Athens dedicated to Dionysus.	
Heracles Note: Heracles' Latin name *Hercules* is more commonly used when talking about this Greek hero.	*Heracles is the son of Zeus and Alcmene, a princess who lived in Mycenaean Greece. Zeus extended the time he stayed with Alcmene by demanding Helios, the god of the sun, not shine for three days, which may have given Heracles his great strength.* *Knowing that Zeus had been unfaithful (again) to her, Hera hates Heracles and sends misfortune after misfortune upon him, beginning with sending snakes to devour Heracles in his crib. Heracles strangles the snakes, demonstrating his great strength.*	Heracles is famous for his strength and noted lack of self-control. In a fit of madness sent upon him by Hera, he killed his own children. Stories of his Twelve Labors include him killing monsters like the Nemean Lion, the Hydra, and the Erymanthian Boar. He also fathered the race known as the Dorians, the mysterious group of marauders that may have invaded the Peloponnesian peninsula at the close of the Late Bronze Age.	

Closer Look Questions

1. How did the Greek landscape influence Greek mythology?

2. In a sense, from where (or from whom) does Greek mythology come?

3. What purpose is there in personifying the forces of nature, or elements of human society like warfare and marriage?

4. What do the Greek gods and goddesses tell us about human nature in general and about ourselves in particular?

ACTIVITY

Direct Instruction Review

The hardest part about history is memorizing all those facts, dates, and events. To make this process easier, we have included this short section called *Direct Instruction Review*. Direct Instruction (or DI) is a powerful pedagogical tool whereby teachers ask students a series of *call-and-response* questions, and students respond back with the aim of learning this material to *mastery*. Teacher's lines are in **bold**; student's lines in *italics*.

Where do we begin with the Greeks? *On the island of Crete!*

Where is Crete? *Crete is an island in the southern half of the Aegean Sea, so they were able to trade with the Phoenicians, the Egyptians, and the rest of mainland Greece.*

When did Minoan Crete flourish? *Minoan Crete flourished during the Late Bronze Age from 1700 to 1550 BC thanks to their trade with Egypt and Phoenicia.*

When did Crete go into decline? *For reasons unknown, Minoan Crete went into decline in 1550 BC.*

What probably happened to them? *They were probably conquered by warriors from mainland Greece.*

What cities were in mainland Greece? *Tiryns and Pylos were large cities with large, fortified palaces, but the biggest city was at Mycenae.*

And where is Mycenae? *Mycenae is located on the Peloponnesian peninsula, near the isthmus of Corinth.*

And why is Mycenae important? *Mycenae was the largest and most powerful city in Greece during the Late Bronze Age.*

And what was Mycenae like? *Like other Greek cities, Mycenae had a large fortified palace and walls so big they could only have been built by the monstrous Cyclopes.*

Do we know anything about their society? *Mycenae was ruled by a king called a* wanax, *and they traded with other large states during the Late Bronze Age.*

Why is it hard to study the history of Mycenaean Greece? *The world of the Mycenaeans was celebrated in the epic poems of Homer, namely, the* Iliad *and the* Odyssey, *making it hard to separate historical fact from celebrated fiction.*

And what was the Iliad? *The* Iliad *focuses on the Trojan War, an epic struggle between the city of Troy and Mycenae and the Greek allies of Mycenae.*

ACTIVITY

Map Practice: The Greek World

Instructions: Carefully look over the maps below, which are identical to maps provided in the rest of this chapter. However, there is one crucial difference: these maps have blanks in the place of the name of a sea, a region, or a site. Fill in the appropriate blank with the term list provided above each map.

The Mediterranean World: Western Mediterranean, Eastern Mediterranean, Black Sea, Aegean Sea, Ionian Sea, Adriatic Sea, and Tyrrhenian Sea.

The Greek World: The Bosporus, the Hellespont, Thrace, Macedon, Mount Olympus, Thessaly, Athens, the Aegean, Ionia, and Mediterranean Sea, Sparta, the Peloponnese, Miletus, and Crete.

Want to study this map online? Type in the link below or scan the QR code to access an interactive diagram: **https://bit.ly/3okSogF**

ACTIVITY

Timeline Practice / Minoan Crete & Mycenaean Greece

The hardest part about history is memorizing all those facts, dates, and events. To make this process easier, check out the timeline below—well, technically, there are *two* timelines. Some entries are missing dates, and others are missing the event that occurred on that date. With the information available from both timelines, fill in the missing blanks to get a better sense of the timeline for this chapter.

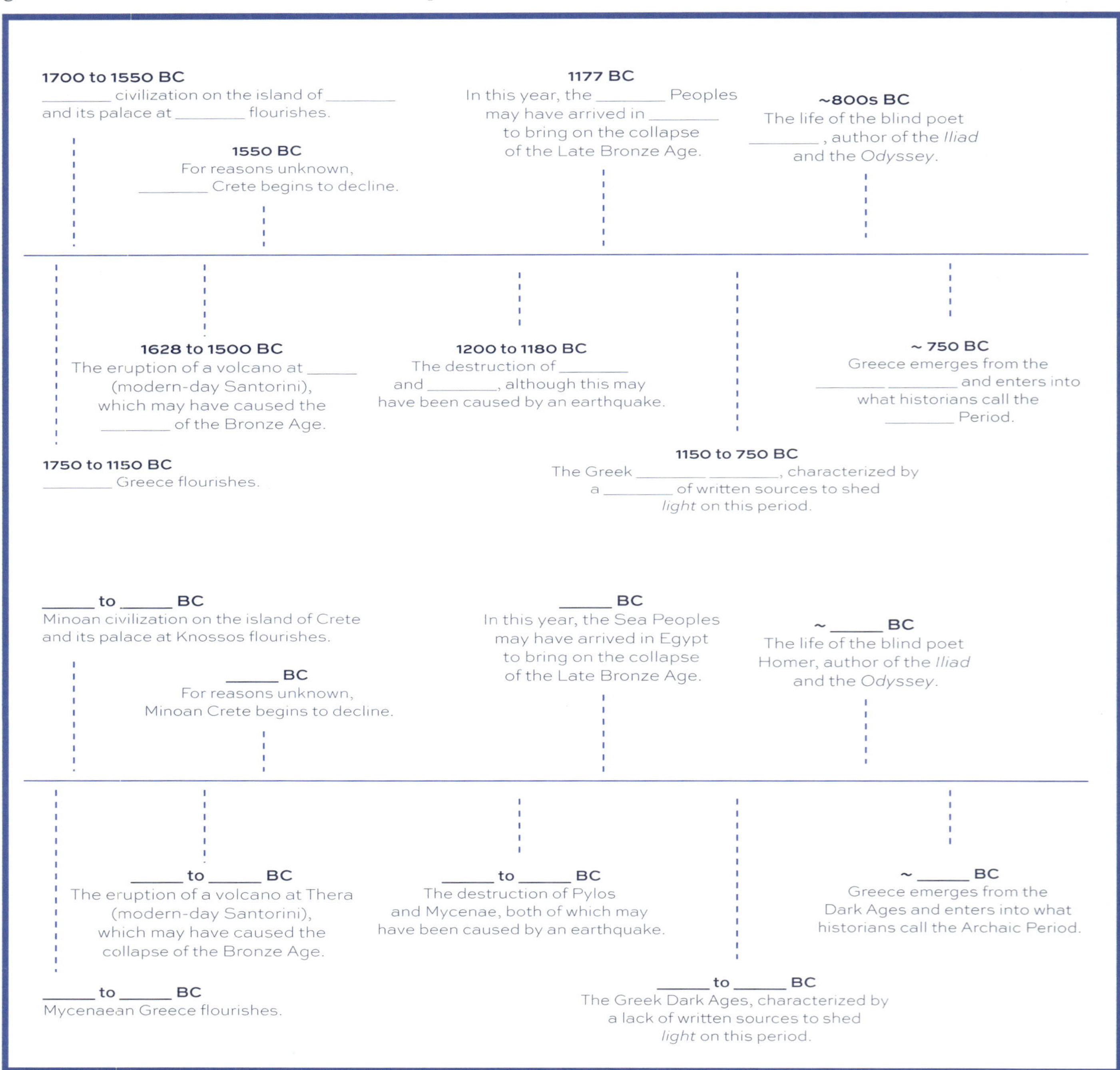

WRITING

Writing Prompt

Writing is thinking, so we will spend considerable time this year writing and thinking about history. In the space provided, write a short essay answering the question: ***Describe the world of the Mycenaeans and the Minoans. What did they focus on? What might its people have been like? How were they like the peoples of the ancient Near East, and how were they different?***

THEATER OF DIONYSUS / ATHENS

Photo by Kieran Everett

Archaic Greece

ROADMAP

- Read a primary source from the Greek historian Thucydides about the roots of Greek culture.
- Learn about Greek city-states and what makes them unique.
- Compare and contrast the founding of Corinth, Sparta, and Athens and how each of them responded very differently to the challenges before them.
- Take a *Closer Look* at ancient Greek warfare, the military formation known as the *phalanx*, and ancient Greek pottery.
- Practice our knowledge of maps and chronology, as well as our writing skills through reading comprehension questions and an essay.

THALES OUTCOME
Nº 3

One who displays Self-Reliance *evaluates one's interdependence with, independence from, and dependence on local, national, and global communities in relation to oneself.*

City-states are like the cities we know today, except they are independent. They make their own laws and build their own roads (if they have them). In this chapter, we will learn about the Greek city-states of Corinth, Sparta, and Athens and how each of them took very different paths during the Archaic period.

Primary Source Analysis / Thucydides & the Roots of Greece

Description: The Greek historian **Thucydides** lived from 460 to 400 BC. We have looked at various samples from the historian Herodotus, who is credited as the *Father of History*. We look to Thucydides, though, as the father of *scientific history*, because Thucydides was far more careful in citing sources and more exact in determining the causes and motivations behind the actions he described in his history book, which covers a devastating war between Athens and Sparta. In the opening to *The History of the Peloponnesian War*, Thucydides begins with this description of the Greek world and the peoples living in it. This text comes from Book I, Chapter 1 of Thucydides, translated by Richard Crawley.

THUCYDIDES / 460-400 BC

Thucydides & the Roots of Greece

01 For instance, the country we now called **Hellas** had in ancient times no settled population. On the contrary, people migrated from one area to another quite often, the several tribes quickly abandoning their homes should their numbers grow too large for the land to support. Without business and trade, without freedom of communication either by land or sea, and in cultivating no more of their territory than the day-to-day requirements of life merited, lacking real, settled industry, never planting their land since they could not tell when an invader might not come and take it all away, and when he did come they had no walls to stop him, thinking that the necessities of daily sustenance could be supplied at one place as well as another, they readily moved from one habitation to another.

02 As a result, they never built large cities and never attained to any other form of greatness. The richest soils were always most subject to this change of masters; such as the districts now called **Thessaly, Boeotia,** most of the Peloponnese, Arcadia excepted, and the most fertile parts of the rest of Hellas.

03 The goodness of the land favored the one class of individuals to grow more powerful than the others. In this way, groups were created that proved a fertile source of ruin. It also invited invasion. Accordingly, **Attica**, because of the poor quality of its soil, enjoyed a very remote period of freedom from faction and never changed its inhabitants. And here is no inconsiderable exemplification of my assertion that the migrations were the cause of there being no correspondent growth in other parts.

04 The most powerful victims of war or faction from the rest of Greece took refuge with the Athenians as a safe retreat; and at an early period, becoming naturalized, swelled the already large population of the city to such

Vocabulary & Annotations

Thucydides
An Athenian general and historian whose most famous work is *The History of the Peloponnesian War*, which describes a conflict fought between Athens and Sparta. Thucydides lived from 460 to 400 BC and is credited as the *Father of Scientific History*.

Hellas
The word *Hellas* and *Hellenes* is actually the word the Greeks used to refer to themselves and their culture. The word *Greek* is a misnomer that was popularized by the Romans.

Thessaly and Boeotia
These are regions in mainland Greece.

Attica
Attica is a region in mainland Greece of which Athens is the principal city.

Minos
Minos was a famous king of Crete in Greek mythology. Here, Thucydides claims that Minos controlled a navy that allowed him to project his power outwards from his palace at Knossos.

The Cyclades
The Cyclades are a chain of islands in the eastern Mediterranean.

THE GREEK MAINLAND
Four of the largest and most prominent Greek city-states; map image from Google Earth

a height that Attica became at last too small to hold them, and they had to send out colonies to Ionia.

05 It appears, therefore, that before the Trojan War, the Hellenes were too weak and too disorganized to do anything of great significance. Indeed, they could not unite for an expedition such as the Trojan War till they had gained increased familiarity with the sea. And the first person known to us by tradition as having established a navy is **Minos**. He made himself master of what is now called the Hellenic Sea, and ruled over the **Cyclades**, into most of which he sent the first colonies and thus did his best to put down piracy in those waters, a necessary step to secure the revenues for his own use.

06 For in early times the Hellenes and the barbarians of the coast and islands, as communication by sea became more common, were tempted to turn pirates, under the conduct of their most powerful men; the motives being to serve their own greed and to support the needy. They would fall upon a town unprotected by walls, and consisting of a mere collection of villages, and would plunder it; indeed, this came to be the main source of their livelihood, no disgrace being yet attached to such an achievement, but even some glory.

07 But as soon as Minos had formed his navy, communication by sea became easier. He colonized most of the islands and expelled criminals he found there. The coast population now began to apply themselves more closely to building up wealth and industry. Some even began to build themselves walls on the strength of their newly acquired riches. For the love of gain would reconcile the weaker to the dominion of the stronger, and the possession of **capital** enabled the more powerful to reduce the smaller towns to subjection. And it was at a somewhat later stage of this development that they went on the expedition against Troy.

09 What enabled **Agamemnon** to raise the armament was more, in my opinion, his superiority in strength, than the oaths of Tyndareus, which bound the suitors to follow him. The power of the descendants of **Pelops** came to

‖ THE BURNING OF TROY

be greater than that of the descendants of **Perseus**. To all this Agamemnon succeeded. He had also a navy far stronger than his contemporaries, so that, in my opinion, fear was quite as strong an element as love in the formation of the confederate expedition. The strength of his navy is shown by the fact that his own was the largest contingent, and that of the Arcadians was furnished by him. This is, at least, what Homer says, if his testimony is deemed sufficient. Besides, in his account of the transmission of the scepter, he calls him

Of many an isle, and of all Argos king.

Now Agamemnon's power and dominion was that of a land power; and he could not have been master of any except the adjacent islands (and these would not be many), but through the possession of a fleet.

10 And from this expedition we may guess the character of earlier enterprises. Now, Mycenae may have been a small place, and many of the towns of that age may appear comparatively insignificant, but no exact observer would therefore feel justified in rejecting the estimate given by the poets and by tradition of the glory and strength of Agamemnon's forces.

11 For I suppose **if Sparta** were to become desolate, and the temples and the foundations of the public buildings were left, that as time went on there would be a strong disposition with posterity to refuse to accept her fame as a true exponent of her power. And yet they occupy two-fifths of Peloponnese and lead the whole, not to speak of their numerous allies without. Still, as the city is neither built in a compact form nor adorned with magnificent temples and public edifices, but composed of villages after the old fashion of Hellas, there would be an impression of inadequacy. Whereas, if Athens were to suffer the same misfortune, I suppose that any guess from the appearance presented to the eye would make her power to have been twice as great as it is.

Vocabulary & Annotations

Capital

Capital refers to the possession of economic resources capable of producing goods at relatively low cost. A single olive tree in one's backyard is just a tree; an orchard of productive olive trees is capital.

Agamemnon

The king of Mycenae and the leader of all the Greeks assembled at Troy. Here, Thucydides argues Agamemnon was the leader because he possessed the largest fleet of ships.

Pelops

In Greek mythology, Pelops helped establish the house of Atreus, the ruling family of Mycenae. Agamemnon and Menelaus are descendants of Pelops.

Perseus

The Greeks believed Perseus, the hero who killed Medusa, also founded the nation of Persia.

...if Sparta

Thucydides observes that the city of Sparta is so simple and unimpressive that later generations will not recognize how powerful Sparta actually was.

Reading Comprehension Questions

1. Why did peoples move about so much in ancient Greece? What changes allowed Greece to become more settled and prosperous?

2. What made figures like Minos and Agamemnon so powerful?

3. What's better, a large army or a large navy? Explain your reasoning.

4. Based on your answer, who might be more powerful—Athens, with their navy, or Sparta, with their army?

Out of the Darkness / Dark Ages to Archaic Greece

THE NAME *DARK AGES* is not very helpful. We do not use the term **Dark Ages** because this period was literally dark, as if the sun refused to shine from 1150 to 750 BC. Or because the time period was one of intellectual darkness and superstition, as the Renaissance poet Petrarch called the centuries from the fall of Rome to the rise of the Renaissance *dark*. By the way, the Middle Ages were not anywhere near as *dark* as Petrarch's own time, or indeed of our own time, both of which were filled with political instability and wars of great magnitude. Petrarch's assumptions as to what makes a historical era *dark* are not entirely fair. Instead, the word *dark* in *Dark Ages Greece* refers to the lack of primary source writings, the kind of textual evidence that provides light for us to see into this era in Greek history. So what happened?

With the collapse of the Bronze Age came a collapse in trade routes. That collapse in trade routes meant that fewer commercial transactions were taking place. Without those commercial transactions—the buying and selling of land or the transport of precious metals across the sea—there was little need to pay for a class of scribes and bureaucrats to learn a complex writing system. Some material culture survived, but the primary sources that illuminated the Late Bronze Age disappeared. As a result, we simply do not know very much about the centuries from 1150 to 750 BC apart from the material culture that survived.

From archaeological evidence, we know a little about life during the Dark Ages. Most Greeks kept farming and herding, growing olives, figs, and grapes, herding goats and sheep, and making wine, cheese, and wool. Blacksmiths turned to iron as their primary building tool since they no longer had access to the copper and tin needed to make bronze. Greek craftsmen continued making pottery to store grain and wine and other goods.

Historians and archaeologists love pottery because, from an old, discarded pot, they infer many things about the time period. The type of pottery, its quality, and its abundance in archaeological sites can provide helpful clues about Greek society and the craftsmen that helped produce that pot. During the Greek Dark Ages, the pottery is of a noticeably inferior quality and not as many samples of that pottery are found. As a result, historians and archaeologists infer that the material culture, trade routes, and artistic sensibilities had all weakened significantly during the Greek Dark Ages. Less trade meant less need for large *amphora* jars to store goods, and less trade meant less money to produce pots with intricate geometric designs or scenes from Greek mythology.

The Archaic period was characterized by the steady growth of the city-state, which the Greeks called a polis. *While each city-state operated independently of others, they worshiped the same gods, traded for goods, and vied in manifold ways to make such contributions the whole Greek world would acknowledge their city-state as the best.*

Vocabulary

Greek Dark Ages
The Greek Dark Ages lasted around 1100 to 750 BC from the end of the Mycenaean civilization to the rise of Athens, Sparta, and the other prominent city-states of Archaic Greece. The centuries in between saw a notable lack of writing and literary documents which accounts for the period's *darkness*.

Basileus
The name of the *king* in ancient Greece following the collapse of the Bronze Age.

Archaic Greece
From the Greek world for *old*, this period lasted from 800 to 500 BC, characterized by the growth of its most famous city-states, Athens and Sparta.

The Olympic Games
Held in honor of Zeus, the Olympics were competitive games that brought all the Greek-speaking world together. The first Olympics were held in 776 BC.

THE GREEK MAINLAND
Four of the largest and most prominent Greek city-states; map image from Google Earth

Based on texts from later periods, we can make some inferences about changes in government and leadership. For instance, the Mycenaean *wanax* was replaced by a official called the **basileus**, a Greek term for a *king* or *chief*. The word *basileus* was an old term for a subordinate official in Mycenae, someone who handled matters on behalf of the *wanax*. Now these officials ruled those villages and districts in their own right. The *basileus* enjoyed more power now than he did in Mycenaean Greece: he would meet with a group of elders and other warriors and solicit their advice, but his vote was supreme. In this way, the *basileus* ruled like a king.

Archaic Greece

The lack in material culture would not persist for long. In and around 750 BC, as trade routes reemerged and the population increased, Greece entered into a period known as **Archaic Greece,** with the word Greek *archaic* derived from the Greek word for "old". Historians generally date the beginning of the Archaic period with the first **Olympic games**, held in 776 BC, and label the end of Archaic Greece with the Persian Wars that lasted from 499 to 449 BC. The Olympics were athletic competitions held in honor of Zeus and named for Olympia, the city in which the games were hosted.

Historians use the first Olympics to mark the beginning of the Archaic period because the Olympics seem to represent a shift in Greek culture. The Greek settlements were now large enough and sophisticated enough to organize games on a large scale. The Greek world must have been wealthy enough to afford games on this scale but also united enough by a common culture, language, and religious system that it made sense for them to gather together in the shadow of Mount Olympus. Often, this kind of movement is called *panhellenism*. **Panhellenism** is the notion that the things uniting the Greeks—language, religion, and customs—were more important than what separates them. But what enabled the Greeks to reach this level of culture and political

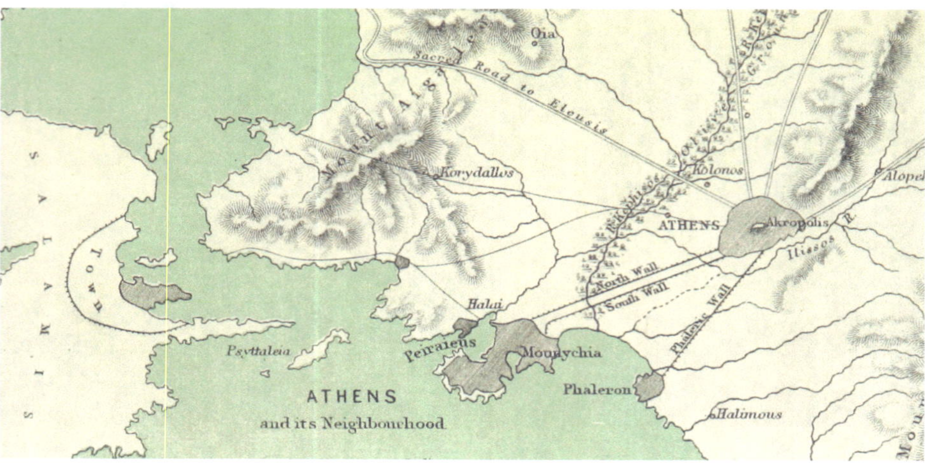

‖ ANCIENT ATHENS & SURROUNDING AREAS

sophistication? How was Greek society organized in the ninth and eighth centuries BC that it could do such things? The answer lies in a unique kind of community, one that arose naturally in ancient Greece and which we have seen before in the ancient world: the city-state.

The Rise (or Return) of the City-State

During the Archaic period, we see the return of the city-state, something we have not seen since the days of ancient Sumer. A **city-state** is, at its heart, a city, but a city operating independently of any other city. Such a city was a large commercial and political center, often surrounded by walls and filled with thousands of people living and working at its center. Today, most cities are a small part of a much larger entity like a state or a country. In the United States, a city like Raleigh might be large and influential, but it is only one city in the state of North Carolina and, even then, Raleigh is not the biggest city in the state (yet).

Many cities are not responsible for large-scale infrastructure projects, nor do they provide for their own defense apart from police officers and firefighters. They certainly do not make alliances with foreign countries. In America, the federal government in Washington, D.C. and the state government handle those sorts of functions.

In contrast, a city-state provided many of the services we might expect of modern-day states. A city-state was centered on a site well suited for trade and commerce, one capable of supporting large numbers of people. In Greece, city-states arose at places convenient for both trade and defense. As with Mycenaean Greece, the city-states of the Archaic and the later Classical period had an **acropolis** at their center, literally the "highest" part of the city.

There, on a towering rock, the citizens of Corinth or Thebes or Athens built not only forts from which to organize a defense of their city but also temples

Vocabulary

Panhellenism
Derived from the words *pan*, meaning "all", and *Hellenes*, the word the Greeks used to refer to themselves, this word refers to *all* the Greeks and the common culture, language, and customs they all share.

City-State
A city-state is an independent commercial center responsible for drafting and maintaining its own laws, infrastructure, military, and other services we might expect of modern-day states.

Acropolis
The highest part of a Greek city that contained that city's citadel.

Division of Labor / Job Specialization
As communities grow in population, less people need to be directly engaged in farming and agriculture. More food means more people, and more people means more "activities" can be done that are directly related to farming.

Synoecism
Made of the Greek preposition *syn* for "with" and *oikos* for "household", this term refers to the process of the Greek countryside identifying with a Greek city-state.

Demes
The Greek word for political units in Attica, the region of which Athens is the largest city.

Polis
The Greek word for *city-state*.

and other public buildings. The acropolis was not only the highest point of their city but also its heart, containing the civic buildings that hosted festivals that brought that city together and gave them a common culture.

Then the inhabitants of the countryside around the city would bring their goods to that city to barter and trade and obtain all the goods they were not able to produce on their own. A city-state was independent of other cities and also controlled much of the territory surrounding the city itself. From the countryside, a city-state like Athens or Sparta obtained the resources the people of that city-state needed to survive. Since the farmers brought wheat, barley, or sheep to the city, the people in that city focused on making clothing, pottery, or other goods with which they can trade for foodstuffs. In this way, cities fostered the kind of **division of labor** or **job specialization** crucial to the growth of large cities.

People living in the countryside identified with a much larger city center, like that of Athens or Sparta. This kind of identification was called **synoecism**, a word that means *living together*, derived from the Greek preposition *syn* for "with" and the Greek word *oikos* for "household." The farmers and herders living in the countryside thought of themselves of Athenians or Thebans before they thought of themselves as Hellenes. Some cities had mythological stories that explained how this coming together took place, as with Athens and the Greek hero Theseus. It is Theseus who organized the **demes**—political units in the region of Attica—into a single unit, with Athens as the region's principal city.

The Greeks thought highly of their cities and the kind of dynamic urban culture they produced. We often use the word **polis** to refer to this type of political community, given that we received the idea of the city-state from the Greeks and not the Sumerians. The Romans used the word *civitas* for *city* or *community*, as well as the word *urbs*, from which we get the words *urban* and

THE ACROPOLIS / ATHENS

Important civic buildings occupied high, rocky outcrops in the center of Athens; the buildings there today were built during the time of Pericles.

urbane. The word *polis*, meanwhile, provides us with our English words *political* and *politics*, words that refer to the study of how we conduct ourselves in a community called a *polis*. The Greek philosopher Aristotle said that the highest end of human beings was to live in a *polis*, for it is in such a community that each individual can best pursue the good life:

> *Every state is a community of some kind, and every community is established with a view to some good; for mankind always acts in order to obtain that which they think good. But if all communities aim at some good, the state or political community, which is the highest of all, and which embraces all the rest, aims at good in a greater degree than any other, and at the highest good* (Book 1, *Politics*).

Reading Comprehension Questions

Why were the *Greek Dark Ages* so dark?

What event marks the beginning of the Archaic period? Why was that date chosen?

What is a city-state? What other civilizations produced city-states?

Where did Greek city-states tend to form? (please use the word *acropolis* in your answer)

The Greek Polis / Innovations among Greek City-States

THE REGIONS THAT PRODUCE a large number of city-states is unique in its own right. Such a region tends to produce an array of sophisticated inventions, new ideas, wonderful literature, and beautiful works of art. These innovations occur because city-states can support a large number of people, each of whom can specialize in a particular task apart from farming. Thus, individuals can afford to focus on making goods or creating works of art instead of worrying about growing their own food.

More importantly, these innovations tend to happen because these city-states are all competing with each other. In Greece, as in ancient Sumer and later in Renaissance Italy, these city-states may operate independently of one another. But they are not so far away they could not interact with and trade with nearby cities. After all, the city-states of ancient Greece shared a common language and common customs, so that even if dialects differed in the Peloponnese from those in **Ionia**, they could still talk to each other. And they worshiped the same gods and followed many of the same customs.

Since they traded with each other, merchants could bring news of a neat invention from Athens or new weapons from Sparta. City-states *wanted* to keep up with such innovations because, if they did not, they could be destroyed by a neighboring city-state in a fight over land and resources. City-states typically fought with each other over a productive field or access to a river, since control of such resources might mean survival for one city and destruction for another. Thus, if Sparta, famous for its warriors, used armor that gave them an edge over their rivals, other city-states wanted to copy, make, and use that weapon as quickly as they could.

Lastly, city-states tend to produce new innovations and ideas because of what can most easily be termed *bragging rights*. The city-state with the largest and most beautiful temple could lay claim to being the best city in all of Greece. That gave each city the incentive to beautify their public buildings with massive columns, intricate relief carvings, and detailed scenes of Greek heroes and gods.

Such was the case with Athens, who had the most beautiful acropolis, so beautiful that it is known simply as the Acropolis. A similar phenomenon happened in Renaissance Italy, with Italian city-states like Florence and Milan competing on both the battlefield and in the

Civilizations like ancient Sumer, classical Greece, and Renaissance Italy were composed of a network of city-states, independent and dynamic urban centers that produced beautiful works of art and architecture and grew rich off of trade with each other and the wider world. But there is a downside to city-state culture, as these civilizations tend to fight with each other for valuable resources like fields, waterways, and trading rights.

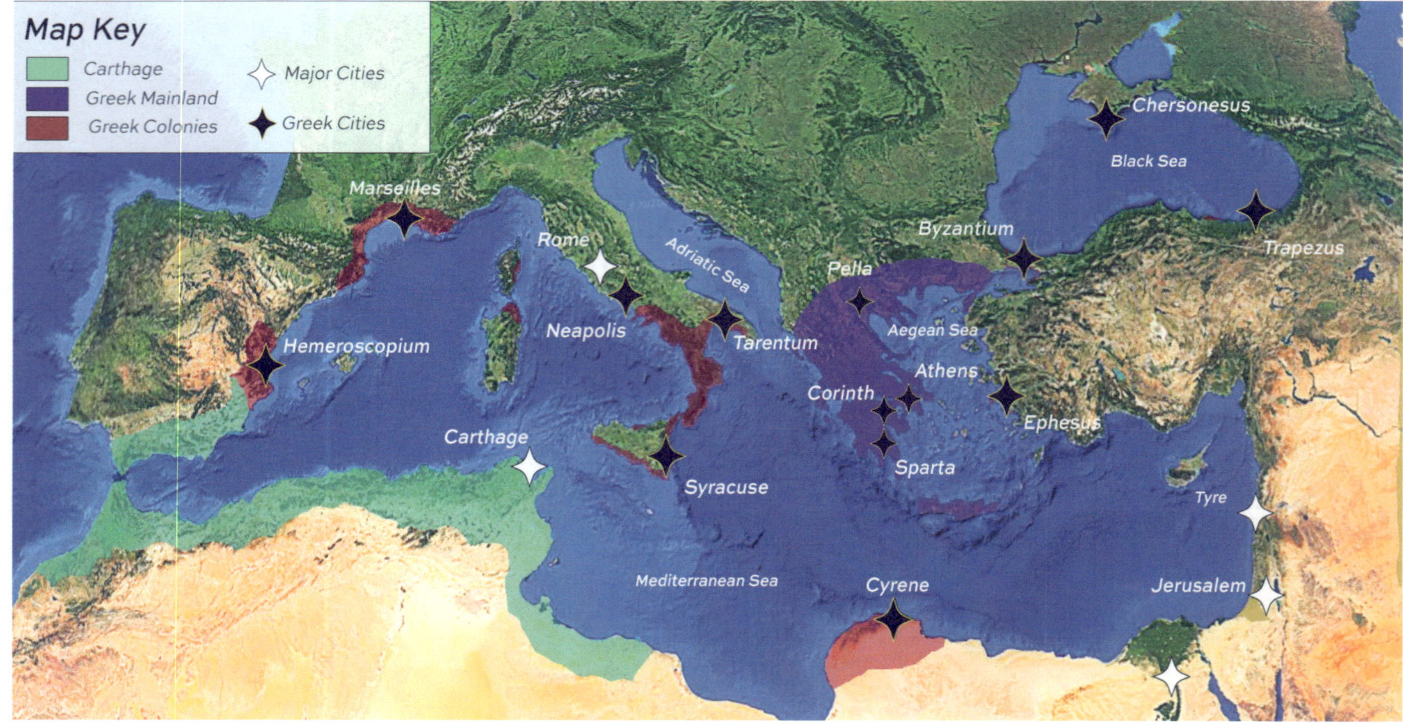

THE MEDITERRANEAN WORLD / 550 BC

Greek city-states from the mainland of Greece established colonies throughout the Mediterranean world; the map includes the Mediterranean world's other major cities such as Memphis, Carthage, and Rome.

city square to determine which was the best city-state on the Italian peninsula.

Now, with all of the opportunities offered by trade, the Greeks did not stay in their own city-states on the Greek mainland. The Greeks were capable sailors and traders, and during the Dark Ages and into the Archaic period, they established colonies throughout the Mediterranean world.

A **colony** is an outpost or settlement inhabited by residents who originally came a distant country or region. In founding a colony, a larger city—the **metropolis**, or the *mother city*—would send large groups of its own citizens to a distant region to establish a new settlement there. The reasons for establishing a colony were manifold. Land and resources were scarce, so if the population grew so large the land could no longer support its inhabitants, a city like Athens might send a group abroad to establish a colony. Or, perhapsthe mother city was so focused on commerce and trade they wanted a select, dedicated group of its citizens operating a trading post in that region.

These colonies helped to export Greek culture outside the traditional boundaries of Greece. Greek-speaking tribes such as the Aeolians, Dorians, and the largest such group, the Ionians, many of whom came from Athens, sailed across the Aegean Sea to establish colonies on the west coast of Asia Minor, a region they named **Ionia**. Citizens from Corinth could easily trade with cities in Sicily, since residents from Corinth had actually founded the city of Syracuse, one of the largest and wealthiest cities in the Greek world. And the Greeks colonized so much of southern Italy the later Romans called the region **Magna Graecia**.

Most interestingly, the experience of these Greek colonies back to the Greek mainland via the mythology of great heroes like Odysseus and Heracles. Odysseus was a hero of the Trojan War who spent ten long, miserable years trying to sail home to Ithaca. Along the way, Odysseus visits many of the far-off locations where the Greeks had planted colonies. Famous episodes in Homer's *Odyssey*, like Scylla and Charybis, the Cyclopses, and the Lotus-Eaters were set near Greek colonies like southern Italy or northern Africa. Jason and the Argonauts travel to the shores of the Black Sea and the

Vocabulary

Ionia
The west coast of Asia Minor that had been colonized by Greek city-states.

Colony
A colony is an outpost or settlement inhabited by residents who originally came from a distant country or region.

Metropolis
From the Greek for *mother city*, a *metropolis* is city that founds a colony or settlement in a distant place.

Magna Graecia
Located in southern Italy, Magna Graecia is the name given to the cities founded by Greek city-states.

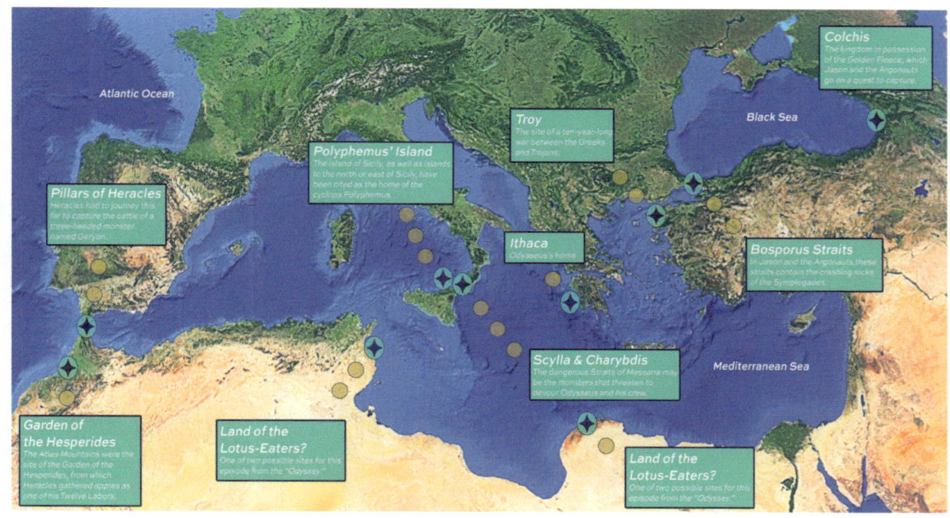

GREEK MYTHOLOGY & GREEK COLONIZATION

As the Greeks established colonies throughout the Mediterranean, those colonies became part of Greek mythology.

kingdom of Colchis, another site of Greek colonization. Through this kind of epic storytelling, the two worlds of mainland Greece and their colonies were brought closer together.

Let's summarize the rise of Archaic Greece. Remember that the Greek world fell into a kind of *dark age* following the collapse of the Bronze Age. Trade routes and the considerable wealth trade generates disappeared, leaving ancient Greeks without the means to support a class of scribes dedicated to reading, writing, and recording events—leaving them and anyone who tries to study this period very much in the dark.

The Dark Ages ended at approximately 776 BC with the first Olympic Games, beginning what historians call the Archaic period. The Archaic period was characterized most by the city-state, an urban center that maintained its own military, built its own roads and other infrastructure, and controlled the surrounding countryside to obtain food and other vital resources the residents of that city needed to survive.

Accompanying the rise of the city-state was a kind of dynamism evidenced by beautiful civic buildings, new innovations, and high literary culture. These Greek city-states also exported their culture abroad through trade and colonization. When a group of city-states, like that of ancient Sumer, ancient Greece, or Renaissance Italy, develop in a region, those city-states typically produce beautiful civic buildings, new innovations, and other elements of high literary culture.

In addition to such innovations, the Greek city-states also exported their culture abroad through trade and colonization. Such was the case with ancient Greece and its network of dynamic, powerful city-states—principally the city-states of Corinth, Athens, and Sparta—to which we will turn now.

Reading Comprehension Questions

1. Why were city-states in competition with each other? What were they going after?

2. What is a *colony*? Why did the Greeks begin settling in regions outside the Aegean Sea?

3. What kind of innovations did Greek city-states produce?

Corinth, Athens, & Sparta / ~750 BC

THREE CITY-STATES cast a long shadow over Greek history: Corinth, Athens, and Sparta. These three *poleis* were powerful in their own right, but they were different enough that by examining them, we can obtain profound insights about ancient Greece, political theory and ideas of government, and human nature itself. With that in mind, let's turn to the city-state of Corinth first.

Corinth & Commerce

Corinth was one of the wealthiest cities in ancient Greece. Their wealth came from its unique position on the Peloponnese, located as they were on the Gulf of Corinth, a long narrow waterway separating the Peloponnese from the Greek mainland.

Sailing ships and merchant vessels preferred to take the longer but safer route through the Gulf of Corinth instead of going around the Peloponnese—even though it meant that their ship had to be dragged over the isthmus by Corinthian laborers. South of the Peloponnese, seas were rougher and the weather more erratic. The longer and more expensive route through the Gulf of Corinth made financial sense, since it would be cheaper than losing a ship in a storm. Those Corinthian laborers heaved up huge seagoing vessels onto logs, then rolled the ships across the **Isthmus of Corinth** until the ships reached the other side. The kings of Corinth, subsequently, became fabulously wealthy, charging seagoing vessels handsomely for safely delivering their ship from the Gulf of Corinth to the Saronic Gulf.

In mythology, Corinth was founded by none other than **Sisyphus**, a figure famous in Greek mythology for his attempts to fool the gods. Sisyphus was a cruel leader, one who murdered guests to his palace in cold blood, and Zeus demanded that Thanatos, the Greek god of death, take Sisyphus to the Underworld himself. Sisyphus cleverly asked Thanatos how his chains worked, then bound Thanatos, preventing anyone from dying. When Sisyphus was finally captured, he was forced to push a boulder up a hill where, upon reaching the top, the boulder would roll back down again. Still, Sisyphus founded a dynasty that ruled Corinth, and Corinth's early kings considered themselves descendants of the infamous Sisyphus.

That is, of course, Greek mythology. In history, Corinth had the same, albeit much smaller, palace culture as other cities in Mycenaean Greece during the Late Bronze Age. Their society radically decreased in size

Athens, Sparta, and Corinth were three of Greece's largest and most powerful city-states, each of which contributed significantly to Greek culture and to the history we are studying today.

CORINTH'S RUINS
Photo by Chris Oxford

and stature during the Greek Dark Ages but experienced a return as the Dark Ages came to a close. In 747 BC, a group known as the **Bacchiadae** became rulers of Corinth and helped transform the city into one of the wealthiest city-states in Greece. The Bacchiadae were a clan, a large group held together either because they were family or extended family, or they were useful and trustworthy to the more prominent members of the clan.

The Bacciadae clan ruled Corinth as a group, electing one of its own members to serve as king and serving as advisers to that king. These rulers are known as tyrants, a word that has a rather different meaning from how we use it today. In the ancient world, a **tyrant** was a king who wielded great authority and power, but they were not necessarily cruel and oppressive. Instead, tyrants were leaders who did not receive their power from ancient, traditional heredity and were not bound by a constitution, but some could solve the kinds of practical problems facing their polis.

Often, these tyrants became cruel and used violent means to control their states, but initially, tyrants were elected by the people to rule. This election by the people occurred because the people recognized that such an individual was a skilled, capable administrator who could get things done. And what did the various rulers elected from among the Bacchiadae do?

First, they constructed huge temples and other civic buildings. They oversaw efforts to plant colonies abroad at places like Syracuse in Sicily and Corcyra on the Adriatic Sea, both of which became prosperous cities in their own right. These colonies helped ease population pressures in Corinth, so the Corinthian government could financially support a colony in the short term, and in the long term enjoy a close relationship with a new settlement that looked to Corinth as its metropolis, or *mother city*. Corinth would remain one of the wealthier and more significant cities in Greece through the Classical Period. But Corinth's example still pales in comparison to that of our next two city-states: Athens and Sparta.

Vocabulary

Corinth
A Greek city-state whose location on the Peloponnese, near the Isthmus of Corinth, which made it especially wealthy through commerce and trade, as well as their job in dragging ships overland to the Saronic Gulf.

The Isthmus of Corinth
The Isthmus of Corinth connects the Peloponnesian peninsula to the regions of Attica and Boeotia.

Sisyphus
In Greek mythology, Sisyphus founded the city of Corinth. He was also famous for cheating death; in Tartarus, Sisyphus was condemned to push a boulder up a hill, and when the boulder reached the top, it would fall back down.

Bacchiadae
The Bacchiadae were the rulers of Corinth.

Tyrant
In ancient Greece, a tyrant was not necessarily a cruel leader, but a leader who did not receive his power from ancient, traditional heredity and was not bound by a constitution.

Laconia
A region in the southern Peloponnese, of which Sparta was the dominant city.

Reading Comprehension Questions

1. How did Corinth's position on the Peloponnese help them grow wealthy and prosperous?

2. According to Greek mythology, who founded the city of Corinth? What did this mythical figure do, and what was his punishment?

3. What is a tyrant, and how was a tyrant in the ancient world different from a tyrant in the modern world?

A Spartan Existence / ~800s BC

SPARTA HAD MANY OF THE SAME problems as other Greek city-states: too many citizens and not enough land to support them. The similarities tend to end there, as Sparta stands in many ways in stark contrast to the rest of Greece. While many Greek cities sit on rocky plains with poor farmland, Sparta sits on the Eurotas River in a relatively fertile valley. Sparta sits at the southern tip of the Peloponnese in a region known as **Laconia**. In the ancient world, Sparta was known as **Lacedaemon**, for which Spartans painted the Greek letter *lambda* on their shields for the name of their city.

Whereas Corinth supported colonies abroad, and as we will soon learn, Athens pursued overseas trade, Sparta had a very different solution. They organized their entire society to support and train an elite group of soldiers, whom Sparta used to force their neighbors to grow their food for them. Let's look at the Spartan system in closer detail, beginning with its legendary founder, **Lycurgus**, even though his life is shrouded in mystery. We know precious few details about him beyond giving Sparta its constitution, laws, and unique way of life. The Greek biographer Plutarch writes,

> *The city of Sparta was in chaos and confusion. Lycurgus was asked by the citizens to help them. Like a doctor who has a very sick patient, he realized that small changes and a few new laws would not help. He decided to change everything, every law, and every way in which the people lived their lives* (Comber, et. al, 7-8).

LYCURGUS / 800s BC

Lycurgus also did not write down his constitution. He believed if his ideas and reforms were written down, they might be misinterpreted or changed by later generations of Spartans.

On the other hand, if Lycurgus founded institutions that instilled habits, the Spartans might willingly followed all of his ideas to reach the same goals. So, he changed almost every institution in Sparta to encourage each Spartan to think of Sparta first and himself second.

To accomplish this, Lycurgus first seized all private property from individual Spartans. He then distributed equal portions to each of them. To discourage greed, Lycurgus introduced iron coinage. These coins were basically blocks of iron, and large, unshaped hunks of iron are practically worthless. He then forced all citizens, rich and poor alike, to eat the same food and always in common, so Spartans became friends with their fellow Spartans across social classes. In every way, Lycurgus discouraged the men of Sparta to care about their own affairs or their own families and instead think only of Sparta as a whole.

Once these reforms were initiated, Lycurgus asked that the Spartans refrain from making any changes to them. He wanted to journey to Delphi and consult the oracle about his ideas and receive the gods' blessing for them. Until he returned, he asked the Spartans to follow his new policies faithfully. The Spartans agreed, but Lycurgus never returned. Instead, after visiting Delphi, he starved himself to death, recognizing the Spartans would be bound by their oath and never make any changes since he never actually returned home.

This is the story of Sparta's transformation into a highly militarized society according to the historian and biographer Plutarch. Based on other sources, the transformation was most likely longer and more gradual, with smaller changes taking place in response to problems that arose in Sparta. Those problems centered on obtaining resources for Sparta's growing population. Sparta solved those problems by conquering its neighbors. They reduced the peoples they conquered into two categories: **helots**, hereditary slaves owned by the Spartan state, and **perioikoi**, free men who made manufactured goods or acted as merchants who traveled between Greek cities. The problem, however, was that these regions would not stay conquered—not unless Sparta made drastic changes to keep them in line. And the state that caused the most trouble, and that Sparta went to the greatest lengths to subjugate, was the neighboring state of Messenia.

Messenia was located in the southwestern corner of the Peloponnese, and Sparta spent twenty years trying to subjugate the Messenians. The few accounts of the war that survive describe a decade-long siege around the citadel on Mount Ithome in northern Messenia. The war ended with Sparta conquering Messenia and Messenia disappearing from the list of participants and victors in

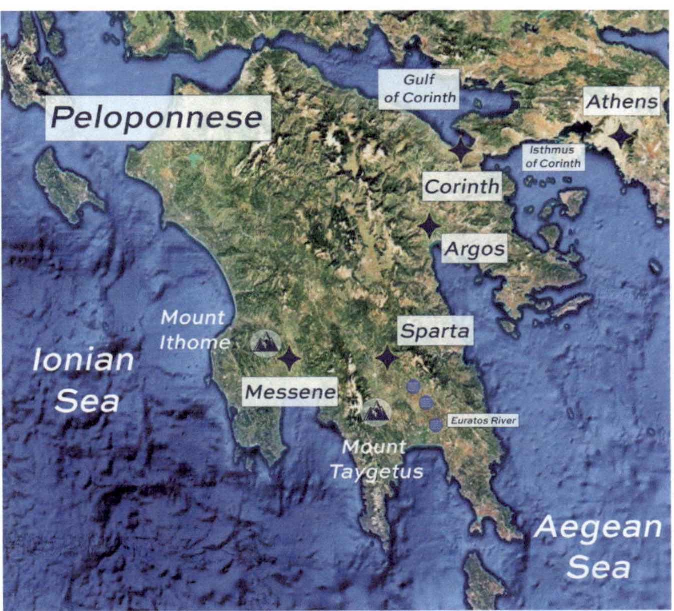

SPARTA AND THE PELOPONNESE / 800S BC

Sparta's highly-militarized society was all about raising soldiers to keep the helots *living in Messene under control.*

the Olympic Games, as if Sparta had erased the smaller city from the face of the Greek world.

At this point, Sparta controlled a state of 3,000 miles, territory that would be hard enough to monitor on its own. But a generation or so after the conquest, the Spartans grew lazy and gave themselves over to luxuries, and in the sixth century, the Messenians rebelled and almost regained their freedom.

The Spartans put down the rebellion at great cost to themselves, but now faced a choice as to how to govern their territory. Would they integrate the Messenians in a meaningful way, allowing them to retain some freedoms and some aspects of their former way of life? Or would the Spartans try even harder to control the Messenians and keep them from ever regaining their freedom? In short, they chose the latter; they reorganized Spartan society to produce all the soldiers they needed to keep the Messenians and their other territories down and maintain their control in the Peloponnese.

So what did the Spartans do to maintain this kind of control? Let's start with the king first and work our way through the layers of Spartan society.

THE EUROTAS RIVER

While most of Greece is rocky and mountainous, Sparta sits in a relatively fertile valley on the Eurotas River, pictured above.

The Spartan Way of Life

During the Archaic period, Sparta was ruled by not one but two kings. These kings inherited their power, but they alternated command of the Spartan army in times of war. Then, assisting the king was a council of elders called the **ephors**. Since Sparta was ruled by a mixture of kings and a select, relatively small group of advisers, we would call Sparta an **oligarchy**—that is, the rule by the few. Even so, Spartan kings and ephors were known for their sense of justice and fair play, and they were often called in to help mediate disputes between other *poleis*. The *ephors* were Spartan men who had survived their decades of service in the Spartan army. Their primary job was to make sure that Spartan traditions were followed and that the king did nothing to undo Spartan traditions. To produce a class of professional soldiers, the Spartan system had to reign supreme in all aspects of life. Such supremacy came at the expense of the individual, as no individual Spartan could have an opinion that ran against the Spartan system.

In Sparta, training for the military began practically at birth. Sparta's priests inspected each male child to make sure the infant was strong and healthy enough. Tragically, if the priests considered an infant to be unfit—that is, the baby was not worth raising—that baby was abandoned in the woods or exposed on a mountainside. From birth to age seven, Spartan boys received an education under close supervision of the *ephors*. At age seven, the boys were taken from home to live with other Spartan youths. Their education focused on enduring the kind of hardships one finds in war, so they went barefoot and they were given one cloak per year.

Spartan youths were not given beds or private bedrooms, and they ate together in large mess halls with older soldiers. They were given meager food rations and were actually encouraged to steal to make up the difference. After all, a soldier may have to resort to such measures on campaign. Spartan boys

Vocabulary

Sparta
One of the three most important cities in ancient Greece. The city of Sparta was famous for its strict, highly regimented society and its highly disciplined soldiers.

Lacedaemon
An alternate name for Sparta used in ancient Greece.

Lycurgus
Lycurgus is the legendary founder of Sparta, credited with writing the city's laws and constitution to produce a class of highly disciplined soldiers.

Helots
The *helots* were the class of slaves in ancient Sparta.

Perioikoi
The *perioikoi* were the craftsmen and merchants of ancient Sparta.

Messenia
A Greek city-state that Sparta conquered in the eighth century BC. Sparta then forced much of its population to live as *helots*.

Ephors
The elders in ancient Sparta, who met together as a council, advised the Spartan king on important issues, and made sure that Spartan traditions were followed.

Oligarchy
A form of government in which political power is placed in the hands of a relatively small number of people.

continued in this kind of education from age seven until sixty, when they could join the council of ephors.

As a rite of passage, Spartan youths participated in a festival at the Sanctuary of Artemis Orthia. There, on a large, raised altar, Spartan priests placed blocks of cheese, and they tasked older Spartans to guard the cheese with whips. Spartan youths would brave the whips to steal the cheese from the altar as a way of preparing them mentally and physically for the brutal nature of military campaigns.

The population of *helots*—the slaves forced to grow food for the Spartans—outnumbered Spartan soldiers perhaps as much as seven to one. The Spartans recognized slave rebellions were a constant threat, and the Spartans were always at the ready in case of a rebellion of the *helots*. At times, older Spartans would get the *helots* drunk and parade them around in front of groups of younger Spartans. That way, the Spartans would learn not to drink to excess and to think of the *helots* as subhuman and inferior to the Spartans. And as one last way of instilling fear in the *helots*, elite Spartan soldiers were encouraged on an annual basis to go out into Messenia, live off of the land, and attack *helots* at random so that they would live in constant fear that a Spartan may be lurking in the shadows, waiting for them. This practice was part of the initiation rites into the Crypteia, a secret society for future leaders, the very best of the very best of Spartan soldiers.

In this way and over a period of centuries, the Spartans created a system that produced the finest and most highly disciplined soldiers in all of ancient Greece. The Greek historian Xenophon said of the Spartan system *that all men praise [their] institutions, but no state chooses to imitate them.* Greek writers recognized the Spartan system was incredibly stable and secure, its kings shielded from coups and revolutions that rulers in other Greek city-states feared. But that stability came at a remarkable cost: individual Spartans had no real freedom at all, no meaningful choices to make, and no occupations for themselves apart from serving in the military.

If Spartan priests decided a Spartan infant was worth raising, that Spartan infant would grow up to serve in the army until either death or age sixty. Ironically, Spartan women received more education and enjoyed more freedoms than other women throughout Greece, but these freedoms may have been a trade-off for living without their husbands and giving up their children to the state at age seven. Lastly, these reforms and initiatives came about to subjugate Messenia and the rest of Laconia and keep them in a state of constant fear because Spartan soldiers might always be lurking in a corner, waiting to harm them. Such initiatives devalued human life, reducing their neighbors to a position not unlike that of an animal. Indeed, the rest of the ancient world may have envied Sparta for their strength and their discipline, but few other states imitated them because of the sacrifices needed to do so.

As a result, Sparta leaves us little even to study. They did not produce beautiful temples, civic buildings, or even walls. Ancient writers quipped the Spartans had no walls because they did not know how to build them. The Greek historian Thucydides described Sparta and her accomplishments in the same way: ***For I suppose if [Sparta] were to become desolate, and the temples and the foundations of the public buildings were left, that as time went on there would be a strong disposition with posterity to refuse to accept her fame as a true exponent of her power*** (Book I, Chapter 1). In contrast, Spartan strength and stability met its match in its most powerful and formidable rival, a state that contrasted with Spartan austerity in almost every conceivable way: Athens.

Reading Comprehension Questions

1. How did Sparta respond to its problems of overpopulation and land shortages?

2. What was the Spartan system like? What was its goal, and what was the most extreme thing that the Spartans did to achieve that goal?

3. How was the Spartan system stable? What did the Spartans have to give up in order to achieve that stability?

ACTIVITY

Map Practice: The Greek World

Instructions: Carefully look over the map below, which are identical to maps provided in the rest of this chapter. However, there is one crucial difference: these maps have blanks in the place of the name of a sea, a region, or a site. Fill in the appropriate blank with the term list provided above each map.

Greek Colonies & the Mediterranean: Greek cities such as Corinth, Sparta, Athens, Ephesus, Neapolis, Cyrene, Trapezus, Hemeroscopium, Marseilles, Syracuse, Byzantium, and Chersonesus; and other major cities such as Tyre, Carthage, Rome, Jerusalem, and Memphis.

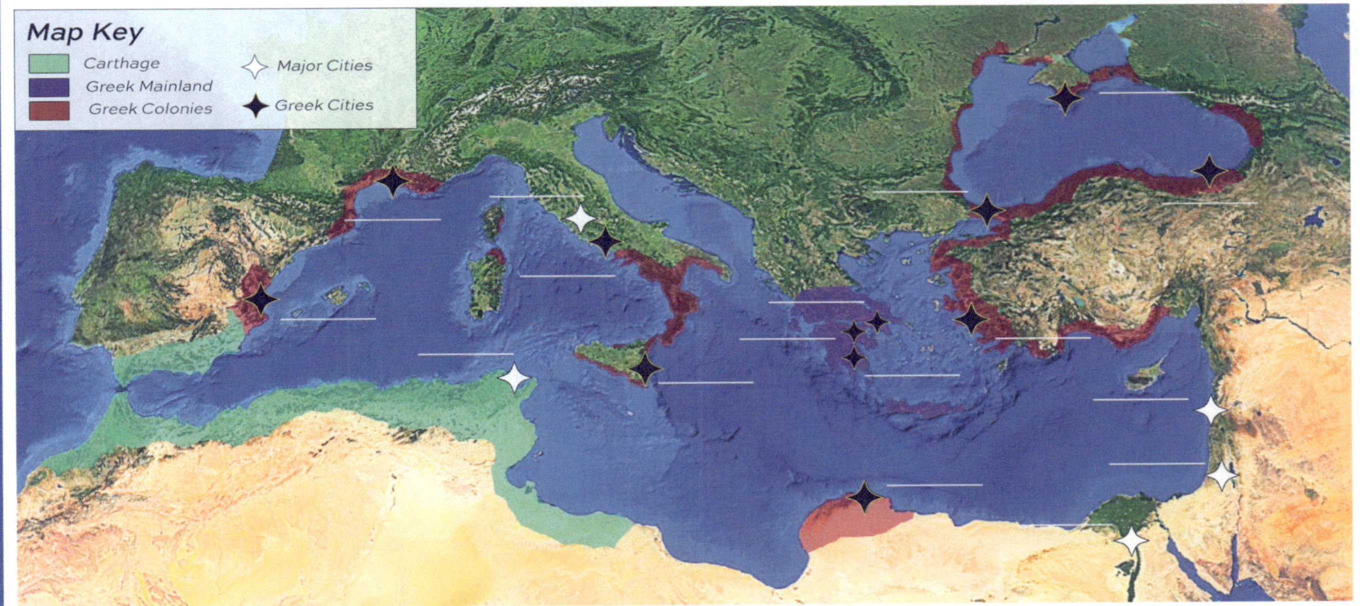

Want to study this map online? Type in the link below or scan the QR code to access an interactive diagram: **https://bit.ly/3okSogF**

A Closer Look at Greek Warfare

HOPLITE SOLDIERS / 550 BC VASE

SOLDIERS FIGHTING IN PHALANX FORMATION

1. Greek soldiers, called *hoplites*, fought in a formation known as the *phalanx*. Looking at the photos above and on the next page, how the phalanx might have operated. Did the Greeks fight in duels as in the *Iliad*, or something more organized and cohesive?

This exercise presents the idea of the Greek phalanx and Greek hoplites before students have really read and studied these concepts. They are treated on the following page, and teachers and teaching-parents can use their best judgment what exercise to do first and why.

‖ GREEK HOPLITES

‖ SPARTAN HOPLITES IN ARMOR

‖ GREEK ARMOR

‖ GREEK HOPLITES IN ARMOR

‖ GREEK HOPLITES FIGHTING

‖ ATHENIAN HOPLITES (ABOVE RIGHT)

Greek Warfare Explained

WHILE THE PICTURES above featured individual hoplites, the secret of the hoplites' success in battle lay in their organization, that is, in their ability to fight in a well-organized group of soldiers working together. Greek city-states fought in a unit known as the **phalanx**, which is, in effect, a tank composed of people. The most important piece of armor carried by a Greek soldier was a shield called an **aspis**, From the term *hoplon*, used to refer to all of a Greek soldier's armor, comes the name of the Greek soldier: *hoplite*.

The *aspis* was the most important piece of equipment because it encouraged the kind of close-knit that made the *phalanx* so effective. The phalanx is a formation wherein soldiers fought in a close, well-organized formation. Numbers vary, but most sources indicate that the Greek phalanx had eight rows of soldiers. Each soldier carried an *aspis* shield, which covered half of their body and half of the body of the soldier to their right. As a result, each soldier depended on the soldier next to him for survival, a fact that encouraged each soldier to maintain ranks and not throw down their shields. Spartan mothers, in fact, told their sons to come home either with their shields or on their shields (dead), for if they came without their shields, they must have retreated.

The *phalanx* won its battles on account of the cohesion and the organization of its troops fighting together. The individual strength or valor of a soldier did not matter so much as how well the soldiers fought as a group. In battle, soldiers would form into ranks, with a shield wall in front and soldiers holding spears in the rows behind the shields. Then the army in *phalanx*-formation advanced towards the enemy at a slow march. A musician playing the flute would play to help the hoplite soldiers maintain a steady pace. Soon, the soldiers broke into a run until they crashed into the enemy, followed by a melee of pushing, shoving, and stabbing with spears until one side or the other lost their nerve and broke ranks. A Greek poet named Archilochus described the ideal hoplite soldier in this way: ***a short man firmly placed upon his legs, with a courageous heart, not to be uprooted from the spot where he plants his feet*** (Martin x).

Historians speak of the transition from less organized styles of fighting to the Greek *phalanx* as the **Hoplite Revolution**. Often, they speak of this transition not only in military terms, as Greek city-states developed more efficient ways of fighting but also in political ones. If a Corinthian or an Athenian soldier could afford the *hoplon* kit and fought in the *phalanx*, that soldier had cause to demand more of a say in the workings of their government. He could, indeed, refuse to fight and thereby leave his polis at the mercy of an invading army. Moreover, the *phalanx* was something of an equalizer in ancient Greece. Courage in battle mattered more than one's lineage, and those who fought as hoplites could claim the right to greater political participation within the state.

The Greek *phalanx* did have its weaknesses. Eight rows of soldiers clad in heavy armor cannot maneuver very well. It is practically impossible for them to turn, and they had great difficulty holding rank on uneven terrain. They were also extremely vulnerable to attacks from the side or from behind, as their shields only protected them from the spears of an army in front of them.

Vocabulary

Phalanx
The phalanx was a military formation used in ancient Greek warfare. Soldiers would fight in organized, close-knit ranks, forming a shield wall and stabbing at the enemy with spears.

Aspis
A large shield used in Greek *phalanxes* that covered half of the bearer's bpdy and half of the body of his neighbor on his right.

Hoplite
The word *hoplite* refers to a soldier in ancient Greece who fought with a hoplon shield.

Hoplite Revolution
The term *Hoplite Revolution* refers to the greater political and civic privileges that hoplite soldiers could demand of their city-state. If a soldier risked his life for his polis, then that soldier should have a say in the political affairs of that polis.

THE MACEDONIAN PHALANX
Notice the shield wall in front, with soldiers carrying twenty-foot spears in the rows behind them.

Later, the Macedonian king Philip II, who lived from 382 to 336 BC, would reform the phalanx and equip its soldiers with twenty-foot spears called *sarissas* (see illustration above).

The Romans fought in the *phalanx* initially, but they adapted the formation for use on the rough, hilly terrain of southern Italy. The Roman way of fighting was called the maniple system, which was, in effect, a *phalanx* with joints. These joints allowed each *phalanx*-like unit to maneuver over uneven terrain and respond to threats much more quickly than the Greek *phalanx* could. The Roman victory over Macedon at the Battle of Cynoscephalae in 197 BC demonstrated the superiority of the Roman maniple over the Macedonian *phalanx* once and for all.

Still, the *phalanx* remained the most formidable fighting formation throughout the Greek world. The organized, close-knit formation allowed the Greeks to defeat the army of an empire considerably larger in size than any of the armies fielded by the ancient Greek city-states. And indeed, such an empire was coming. At the close of the fifth century BC, a new and terrifying power was preparing to invade Greece: the Empire of Persia.

Reading Comprehension Questions

1. How did the phalanx operate, and what was the source of its strength?

2. Why did the soldiers serving in the phalanx carry a shield that covered only *half* of their body?

3. What were the weaknesses of the phalanx?

4. What was the so-called Hoplite Revolution?

The School of Hellas / Athens & Athenian Democracy

ATHENS WAS NOT MUCH during the Greek Dark Ages. Indeed, Athens was little more than a cluster of villages centered around the towering outcrop that would one day boast Athens' grand civic buildings. At the end of the Archaic period, circa 510 BC, Athens was the most powerful city-state in Greece. It possessed Greece's largest navy and most prosperous economy and controlled territory across the Aegean world.

More importantly for students, Athens passed on an intellectual tradition almost unrivaled in the history of the ancient world. Amongst the intellectual treasures the Athenians gave to Western civilization were democratic institutions, whereby ordinary citizens had a meaningful say in their government. Athens' civic culture helped educate the likes of Plato, Aristotle, and Xenophon, who wrote books addressing the kinds of questions we ask about the nature of the good life. Such books we still read thanks to the quality of their insights.

Lastly, Athens helped produce playwrights and the concept of the theatre as we know it: tragedians like Sophocles and Aeschylus and comedians like Aristophanes penned works that still stir the heart and inspire the soul two thousand years after being written.Thus, we may agree with the praise of Pericles, leader of Athens during the Peloponnesian War, that Athens was, indeed, the **School of Hellas**.

Still, the Founding Fathers were somewhat wary of the legacy of ancient Athens. Individuals like James Madison and John Adams who wrote the Founding Documents, valued Athens' contributions to Western history. But they did not want to model everything in the United States after Athens and other Greek city-states because Athens did not endure—indeed, Athenian democracy tore itself apart as ambitious politicians made wild and outlandish promises to ordinary Athenian voters. Madison and the Founding Fathers did what they could to temper the "excesses" of democracy they saw in Athens' history.

Such men were called **demagogues**, a Greek word that means "drivers of the people," for the way they excited the passions and emotions of the men in the Assembly. Even the very best of the Athenian leaders, men like Pericles (495 to 429 BC), gained power and influence by dispensing huge sums of money from the public treasury. For these and other reasons, the Founding Fathers of the United States looked at the city-states of Greece, and of Athens in particular, as a warning to them about

The Greek statesman Pericles called Athens the School of Hellas *for good reason, for Athens showed what a city might accomplish if it gave its citizens more freedom. But Athens also did things we would consider unworthy of imitation. Thus, we may learn from Athens, the* School of Hellas, *what does and does not constitute human flourishing.*

the dangers of demagoguery and faction and what could happen if that democratic impulse went unchecked.

Athens sits within the region of Attica, surrounded by the mountains Cithaeron and Parnes and the Gulf of Salamis to the south. Those mountains shielded Athens from the mayhem that characterized the collapse of the Bronze Age. When Mycenaean Greece collapsed, Attica actually increased in population from groups of Greek speakers called Ionians fleeing the Peloponnese.

During the Dark Ages and into the Archaic period, Athens sponsored colonization efforts to help solve some of the problems caused by overpopulation. Attic Greeks and Ionian Greeks colonized the western coast of Anatolia during the Greek Dark Ages, founding cities like Ephesus and Miletus. These colonies are especially important since they served as a kind of middleman between the Greek world and the ancient Near East, particularly the Persian Empire.

ATHENS & THE GREEK WORLD
Athens famously sent its citizens across the Aegean to start new cities and settlements.

To help alleviate some of the problems caused by overpopulation, Athens focused on overseas trade and commerce. The soil in Attica is relatively poor and rocky, its mountain ranges preventing its residents from planting and harvesting crops. Still, olive trees grow there in abundance, and olives are useful not only for food but also used for cooking and cleaning.

Much of the ancient world used olive oil as a kind of soap: they would pour it on their bodies, let it dry, and then scrape it off, which removed dirt and debris from the skin. Growing olives gave Athens something they could use to trade for goods not readily found in Attica. They traded olives and olive oil for grain and other goods in areas with better farmland like Macedon and Thrace.

Vocabulary

Athens
One of the three most important cities in ancient Greece, famous for its civic and political freedoms, its wealth, and its navy.

Demagogues
A "driver of the people," a *demagogue* is a politician who lacks scruples, makes wild promises, and cares only for his own power and influence.

Olive Trees
The soil of Attica is particularly good for growing olives, which are used for food and for making oil.

Theseus
An Athenian hero who brought the *demes* under the authority of Athens. He also slew the Minotaur, a monstrous half-man, half-bull creature who lived on the island of Crete.

Democracy
A form of government where the people rule. The word democracy comes from the Greek word *demos* for "people" and *kratos* for "rule."

Aristocracy
A form of government in which the very best individuals rule. Presumably, the best individuals are those who are the best fighters or those capable of giving the best advice on political issues.

Areopagus
Greek for the "Hill of Ares," this place was the heart of Athenian civic government and sat atop the Athenian Acropolis.

Olives also play a prominent place in Athens' foundation myth. In Greek mythology, Athena and Poseidon competed to be the patron of ancient Athens, and Athena, goddess of wisdom, gave Athens the olive tree. Poseidon, god of the sea, gave Athens a saltwater spring. The Athenian king Cecrops recognized Athena's gift produced far more value for Athens and gave the contest to her, naming the city for her and building temples to honor the goddess of wisdom and the household arts.

Cecrops was Athens' mythical founder. The Athenians also believed Cecrops helped organize Attica's twelve *demes*, the political divisions (kind of like a county in the United States) surrounding Athens. Those *demes* remained somewhat independent until the reign of another Athenian king and Greek hero, **Theseus**. Theseus is more famous in mythology as the hero who slew the Minotaur, a monstrous half-man, half-bull who lived beneath Minos' palace at Knossos. The Athenians attributed the unification of the demes to Theseus, who traveled around the demes, banished the local kings, and proclaimed Athens with its superior location and resources to be the head of the region.

Herein, the history of Athens blurs with its mythological heroes, who may or may not have existed. They explained the origin of important Athenian institutions and values Athenians held dear. Over time, members of the *demes* around Attica considered themselves to be Athenians, regardless of how far their village was from the big city of Athens. So how exactly did the city and government in Athens function, to help bring together so many residents from such a relatively large area?

Athens & Democratic Institutions

Today, we celebrate ancient Athens as the birthplace of democracy. The term **democracy** refers to a form of government wherein real political power ultimately derives from, and is accountable to, the people. The word *democracy* comes from the Greek word *demos* for

PARTHENON & THE ATHENIAN SKYLINE

The Parthenon dominating the skyline was built in the fifth century BC.

"people" and *kratos* meaning "rule". Today, democratic societies—like those of the United States, Great Britain, and other like-minded nations—emphasize the rights and freedoms of individuals and provide them with meaningful opportunities to exercise their political power through voting or running for public office. In ancient Athens, this process took centuries to develop. Like Sparta, Athens developed its unique constitution over a long Initially, Athens had a basileus—a king—like other city-states in Archaic-era Greece.

That single basileus gave way to a group of leaders drawn from the best fighters or the wisest counselors, a class often referred to as an **aristocracy**, a name that means "rule by the best". The role of that original basileus changed into that of a chief priest, responsible for conducting sacrifices and judging religious disputes. A figure called the polemarchos was the head of Athens' armies. Lastly, there was an archon, who presided over the Athenian assembly and served as a judge in non-religious cases. The Athenian assembly was a council originally composed of former archons.

They met on the **Areopagus** (or "Hill of Ares"). Sometime early in the seventh century, a council of nine archons was formed, with candidates being chosen from the leading families of Attica. This small council of former archons held considerable power over the current archon. After all, no archon would want to flout the demands of the council if they were going to join that group for the rest of their lives.

Reading Comprehension Questions

1. What does the phrase *School of Hellas* mean? What can we learn from Athens, both good and bad?

2. How did Athens respond to problems of land shortages and overpopulation?

3. What is a democracy, and what sort of democratic institutions did Athens help to establish?

4. Who was Theseus? What do the Athenian people credit him with doing?

Athenian Democracy / Draco, Solon, and Athenian Tyrants

ATHENIAN POLITICS CHANGED in the middle of the seventh century. In 632, a figure named Cylon, a former champion at the Olympics, attempted to seize power in Athens. He married the daughter of the tyrant of the nearby city of Megara, a move Cylon hoped would help him become the tyrant of Athens. He then tried to seize the Areopagus, but the move failed. Cylon and his supporters hid in the temple of Athena, hoping to avoid execution. The nine *archons* cornered Cylon and his brothers and convinced them to stand trial. According to tradition, Cylon left the temple holding a string to Athena's massive statue located inside the temple so as to enjoy Athena's protection for as long as he continued to touch her statue. But the thread snapped, and the *archons* stoned Cylon and things returned to normal—for a while.

Other problems soon arose. Wealthier Athenians had taken advantage of their knowledge of the legal process to benefit themselves. Laws were not written down, and the poorer classes did not have the connections or the education that Athenian aristocrats possessed. If Athens' poorer citizens went to court against an aristocrat, they almost always lost. When the poorer residents lost, they often turned to violence and bloodshed and started feuds that lasted for decades. To alleviate this problem, the wealthier Athenians turned to one aristocrat who at least had a reputation for wisdom: Draco. They asked Draco to write down Athenian laws and the penalties for breaking them, which would be inscribed and displayed in public spaces. That way, no one would be ignorant of the law and the penalties for lawbreakers.

In 621 BC, Draco wrote such a constitution, about which there were many good things. He appointed a much larger assembly to help administer day-to-day affairs in Athens. He promulgated his laws in public so no one would be ignorant of them. But Draco's penalties were so strict that the new system was unworkable. Draco imposed the death penalty for almost every infraction an Athenian could commit, even ones as insignificant as stealing apples or cabbage.

THE AREOPAGUS / HILL OF MARS

Today, we call laws that issue such severe punishments *draconian*, so named for the Athenian lawgiver. According to legend, the laws were written in blood instead of ink. Thankfully, these laws were repealed relatively soon after his death, and the next lawgiver—Solon—exercised far more restraint in his reforms than did Draco.

The Reforms of Solon

Solon may be the most famous Athenian who lived during the Archaic period. Little is known of Solon outside of his accomplishments as an *archon*, even though he stands among the Seven Sages of Greece, a group that includes Thales of Miletus and other individuals renowned for their role in giving laws and building states. Solon first came to prominence for his support for war with Athens' longtime rival Megara. The Areopagus had opted to stop its war with Megara and give the valuable island of Salamis to the Megarans, in response to which Solon composed a poem celebrating Athenian bravery. In this poem, he urged his citizens to continue the war until its conclusion.

With support for the war renewed Solon tricked the Megarans into an ambush. He sent an Athenian soldier pretending to be a deserter to a group of Megarans. The deserter told them that a group of Athenian women had been left unguarded on the island of Salamis and that the Megarans could kidnap them if they acted quickly. The Megarans took the bait and hurried off to ambush a group of what they thought were unsuspecting Athenian maidens but were instead a group of Athenian soldiers armed and ready to fight, albeit dressed like the maidens the Megarans expected to find. Athens defeated its longtime rival Megara and gained possession of the valuable island of Salamis that lay between them.

Solon repealed the laws and punishments that prescribed the death penalty where it was unwarranted. He had a reputation for being wise, and in 594, the Athenian aristocrats turned to him for solutions to the problems facing their city.

Chief among these problems was the amount of food Athenian farmers could grow. The poor, rocky soil of Attica could not grow enough wheat and foodstuffs to support Athens' growing population. The wealthier Athenians owned the best land and even then, they typically raised goods on it apart from foodstuffs like wheat. Instead, they raised cattle, made dairy products, and grew figs, grapes, and olives. They then made olive oil from the olives, which they exported around the Mediterranean in beautifully decorated vases and pottery. Athenian merchants traded olive oil for wheat, grown in Macedon and other regions in northern Greece.

Such an arrangement benefited the olive growers and merchants, both of whom grew wealthy but were still excluded from government offices. The poorer residents,

SOLON / 630 TO 560 BC

who often received a small daily wage for working in the fields, fell into debt to wealthier Athenians. At times, they were sold into slavery.

The Athenian aristocrats asked Solon for a solution to these problems. The wealthier Athenians may have initially wanted to protect their privileges while the poorer Athenians wanted their hardships eased, perhaps by receiving some of the land owned by the aristocrats. Athenian merchants and craftsmen wanted more of a formal role in the political affairs of Athens since the best jobs were taken up by the wealthier, better-connected Athenians. Solon's reforms gave each group something they wanted that, in turn, benefited the city-state of Athens and its surrounding areas as a whole.

For instance, Solon canceled debts and freed anyone held in debt slavery. He even tracked down numerous individuals sold into slavery, bought them out of slavery, and resettled them back home in Athens. But Solon did not go as far as Athens' poorer citizens wanted. He did not redistribute the land of the aristocrats to the poor, an action the poor demanded. Solon believed in moderation and restraint, and he saw that the act of redistributing the land would set a poor precedent for the future.

If Solon took some land from wealthier Athenians and gave it to poorer ones, he would, in practice, be stealing from one group and giving it to another. Such actions

Vocabulary

Draco
An Athenian aristocrat who wrote down the first set of laws for ancient Athens. The laws were so strict and severe, however, they were quickly repealed.

Solon
Solon was an Athenian *archon* and poet. He stands among the Seven Sages of Greece on account of the wise and moderate reforms he gave to Athens in the sixth century BC. These reforms helped alleviate much of the tension between social classes in Athens. He lived from 630 to 560 BC.

ATHENS & ATTICA
Pictured above are Megara, the island of Salamis, and Piraeus, Athens' longtime port.

often make the problems worse, since one act of injustice—taking someone else's property—does not make up for or make better other acts of injustice. Indeed, they tend to contribute to greater losses in food production, since the incentive to work hard has been taken away. So Solon canceled the debts of the poor but refrained from redistributing the property of wealthier Athenians.

To ease more of the problems posed by poverty and food shortages, Solon encouraged trade and industry. He even made it illegal for fathers *not* to teach their children how to make something of value such as shoes, pottery, or other valuable goods that people can't make on their own. That way, most Athenian citizens could take care of themselves by some means other than farming.

Solon also made it illegal to export anything other than olive oil, since Athenian merchants had exported foodstuffs in such large quantities there was hardly enough food at home to feed Athens' growing population (Cadoux). Solon's economic reforms seemingly worked, as the problems at home in Athens leveled off and food security increased. Moreover, the presence of Athenian pottery and trade goods increased across the Aegean world, which usually indicates that conditions at home are thriving.

Politically, Solon made changes to bring more people into the civil and political life of Athens. Previously, the Athenian nobility handled all the important jobs and responsibilities in the Athenian government. The rising class of merchants and craftsmen, individuals who had become wealthy over time through trade and related fields, lacked the political privileges they felt were their due. To calm down this tension, Solon proposed an annual census—that is, an annual survey of the Athenian population, its property, and its wealth.

From this census, Athenian society was divided into different classes, and each class had certain responsibilities or government offices particular to it.

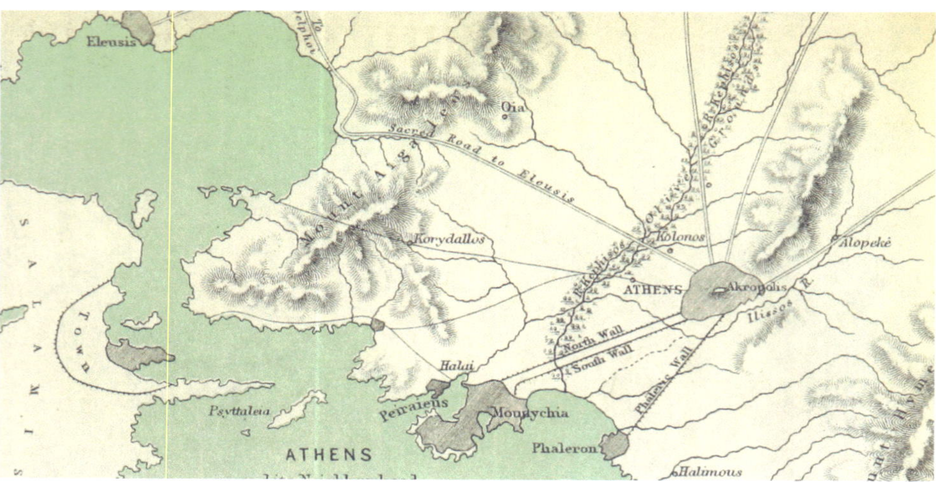

ATHENS & ATTICA

For instance, Solon's census divided people into those who could produce 500 measures of olives, grain, or wine; or could keep a horse; or could purchase hoplite armor. As a reminder, the word *hoplite* comes from the Greek word *hoplon*, meaning shield, and the Greek shield was the most important piece of equipment a soldier needed to serve in the military and defend his *polis*. One man's ability to buy the equipment to serve in the military indicated how he might serve the good of the whole *polis*, and anyone serving in the Athenian military should have some say in the affairs of Athens.

In short, Solon made it possible for every Athenian, regardless of their wealth or status, to have some say in the affairs of state. Every Athenian citizen could serve in the Assembly, known by its Greek name **Ekklesia**, or "the called-out ones", who helped pass laws and vote on different office holders in Athens. Most importantly, they could address the assembly and have some in the affairs of their government—indeed, the Assembly opened with an invitation, "Who wishes to address the assembly?" Four hundred individuals served in the aptly named **Council of Four Hundred**, a group that set the agenda for the Ekklesia. The most important positions of government were still reserved for the wealthiest residents of Athens, but not because they still monopolized—controlling for their own benefit—the best jobs.

It is exceedingly expensive to obtain an education and to learn how to read, so presumably Athens' wealthier citizens would have the best preparation for their time serving the needs of the Athenian *polis*. Solon had his reforms inscribeds on tablets and displayed in public areas. That way, no one could claim they did not know of Solon's laws and reforms. Solon asked the Assembly to agree to follow his reforms unchanged for a hundred years.

Then Solon decided to leave Athens and travel the ancient world. According to legend, he traveled to Egypt, to Miletus (where he met Thales), and Sardis, the capital of Lydia. There he may have met with the Lydian king Croesus, who ruled from 585 to 546 BC. The dates do not exactly correlate with other historical sources with Solon's life, so the following story may not

Vocabulary

Ekklesia
From the Greek words for *called out ones*, the Ekklesia was the Athenian assembly.

The Council of Four Hundred
A subset of the Athenian Assembly that set the legislative agenda for the Assembly. Everyone in Athens could serve in the Council of Four Hundred except for the poorest residents in Athens.

Peisistratus
Peisistratus seized power in a coup and ruled Athens off and on until his death in 527 BC. Peisistratus was technically a tyrant, and he did build large public buildings and expand Athenian trade across the Mediterranean world.

City Dionysia
The City Dionysia was a religious festival held each year in Athens to honor the god Dionysus. Since Dionysus was the god of wine, comedy, revelry, and the theater, the City Dionysia featured plays written by Athenian playwrights.

be historical fact. But it is worth quoting here because of the valuable advice Solon gave to Croesus. As king of wealthy Lydia, Croesus possessed unimaginable wealth and power, and he expected Solon to praise him as being the happiest and most fortunate man alive on account of his wealth.

Solon refused to do so, and he explained to Croesus why: Solon would wait until a man died before he would say he was happy and fortunate, for a man's fortunes may change in an instant and leave him more miserable and wretched than ever before. Croesus dismissed Solon, and Croesus only remembered Solon's wise advice only after he had lost his kingdom and his wealth in such an instant, when he had picked a fight with Cyrus the Great and been defeated in the ensuing battle.

When Solon died at the age of 80, he asked that his ashes be scattered on the island of Salamis, the place of his birth. Solon described his accomplishments in the following way, quoted in Aristotle's *Athenian Constitution*, translated by Sir Frederick Kenyon:

> *I gave to the mass of the people a rank appropriate to their need. In so doing, I did not take away their honor, nor did I give into their greed;*
>
> *While those who were rich in power, whose wealth was already great and glorious, I acted so that nothing should happen to them unworthy of their station and splendor.*
>
> *In this way, I stood with an outstretched shield, and both were safe in its sight, willing that neither side would triumph over the other if such a triumph was not right and just and good.*

THE RETURN OF PEISISTRATUS

Solon's reforms laid the foundation for even greater democratic reforms in later generations. Indeed, Solon's reforms withstood challenges from ambitious individuals hoping to seize power for themselves. One such man was a relative of Solon named **Peisistratus**, who had support largely from the poor but also from some of the wealthy landowners. With their help, Peisistratus seized power in a coup.

First, Peisistratus told a story to the Assembly he was under threat. He then asked the Assembly for soldiers to guard and protect him. Once the Athenian Assembly grew used to him walking around with armed bodyguards, he increased their number beyond what they had allowed him to have guarding them. Then Peisistratus used these guards to seize the Acropolis and take over Athens.

Peisastratus fell from power relatively quickly, but he staged a second coup. This time, Peisistratus had help from the goddess Athena—or at least, a tall, beautiful teenage girl dressed up like the goddess (*see illustration above*). The maiden proclaimed that Peisistratus should be reinstated as the ruler of Athens. And who would *dare* argue with the goddess herself?

A tyrant may initially use violence to obtain power—as in the case of Peisistratus and his army of bodyguards—but he also used his power to accomplish some things we would consider good and beneficial. As the tyrant of Athens, Peisistratus encouraged exports of olive oil to the Black Sea, Italy, and the coast of modern-day France.

He also spent public money on temples and other projects that helped to beautify Athens. He also expanded the **City Dionysia**, a festival held each year where plays were performed in honor of the god Dionysus. In later ages in Greek history, the City Dionysia produced such seminal playwrights as Sophocles, Euripides, Aeschylus, and Aristophanes, each of whom produced works of great value to Western literature. The first such plays were performed in 534 BC. While Peisistratus was removed from power no less than three times, his last and final coup was successful enough that he remained in power until his death in 527 BC.

Athens deserves the title *School of Hellas* for her history and contributions to Greek culture. Yet we should point out that Athens was not an idealized state with the kind of social mobility we might find today. It may have been illegal to bring an Athenian into debt slavery, but it was also easy to enslave foreigners who came from outside of Athens. When Athens became a major military power in its own right, it did many things that stand in stark contrast to its reputation as the *School of Hellas*.

Still, the next episode in our story of ancient Greece and its city-states may be the high point of Greek culture and of Greek civilization: Persia's invasion of and subsequent shocking defeat at the hands of the Greek city-states. For at the close of the Archaic Period, Darius the Great, king of Persia and the thousand nations under his command, set his sights on the Greek mainland, determined to add its proud city-states to his domain.

PARTHENON / ATHENS, 432 BC

The iconic temple to Athena dominates the skyline of Athens.

ATHENA PARTHENOS / 300S AD

A Roman copy of an original Greek statue of Athena Parthenos *(Parthenos means* maiden *in Greek).*

ODEON OF HERODES ATTICUS

A Roman-era theatre built on the Athenian Acropolis; photo by Salvador Calyso

Reading Comprehension Questions

1. Who was Draco, and what did he do for the city of Athens?

2. Who was Solon, and what did he do for the city of Athens?

3. How did Solon's reforms help to bring about more democratic freedoms to ancient Athens?

Reading Comprehension Questions

1. Who was Peisastratus, and what did he do for the city of Athens? How did he seize power?

2. How was an ancient Greek tyrant different from our modern conception of a tyrant? Were they always such cruel rulers, as are tyrants in the modern sense of the word?

3. What was the City Dionysia? How did it bring together people from ancient Attica and help unify Athenian culture?

A Closer Look at Greek Pottery

RECALL THAT ARCHAEOLOGY is the study of ancient objects, which an archaeologist often finds buried in the earth. We think of archaeology as an exciting subdivision of history in which historians hunt down ancient relics and long-lost treasures. Such may have been more typically of archaeology in the early days of the field, when large tombs lay undiscovered and the field was not so well regulated. Today, the field of archaeology is certainly still a dynamic and exciting field, even if the objects it studies do not seem all that exciting —at first. One class of objects that excites archaeologists working in Greece and the wider Mediterranean world is pottery.

The term **pottery** refers to earthenware vessels used for eating and drinking, or for storing and transporting food, oils, and wine. Pottery is made from clay that, once it is shaped into a bowl or a jar, is then baked in a special kind of oven called a **kiln**. Because clay is effectively mud, and mud is found practically everywhere, peoples in the ancient world used clay pots for all sorts of storage needs. Large jars used for transporting grain or wine were called **amphorae**, and the discovery of such a pot can tell us a lot about ancient trade routes. For instance, if an archaeologist finds pottery from ancient Athens somewhere along the Nile River, it meant that there must have been some sort of trade and commerce going on between ancient Athens and ancient Egypt for a pot to turn up so far from its country of origin. The Greeks also made especially large drinking jars called **kraters**.

Moreover, we know many things about the style and the production of Greek pottery. Upon seeing a Greek pot, we can estimate when it was made based on the kind of decorations used on the pottery. Let's look at the different types of Greek pottery now and then some examples of Greek pottery to see if we can correctly identify when those pots were made.

Geometric Pottery: 1000 to 700 BC

The earliest known style of Greek pottery is **Geometric**. This style of pottery was popular during the centuries 1000 to 700 BC. After 700 BC, Greek pottery shows more foreign influences and styles, a trend that makes sense in light of Greece's contact with the Persian Empire and various civilizations around the Mediterranean world. Pottery in the Geometric style typically features horizontal bands with patterns like squares and other shapes filling in the spaces between them. In time, Geometric pottery would include not only geometric shapes but also figures of animals and humans. Such figures were often less realistic and more like geometric shapes—hence the name. Greek potters still painted these figures and shapes in a balanced, unified way around the pot. In time, such scenes were replaced by figures from Greek mythology.

Corinthian Pottery: 725 to 600 BC

Corinthian pottery was produced from 725 to 600 BC and was a popular style in the city of Corinth, as well as Corinth's trading partners. Recall that the city of Corinth was long one of the wealthiest and most powerful cities in Greece thanks to its position on the Gulf of Corinth and the Isthmus of Corinth. Corinth's status as a wealthy trading center helped them become a leading producer and exporter of pottery and other valuable trade goods.

Corinthian pottery was much more visual and decorative than Geometric pottery, often showing influence from Near Eastern artistic styles. Instead of geometric features, Corinthian pottery had flowers, trees, and other examples of plant life.

Athenian Black-Figure Pottery: 700 to 500 BC

The name **Athenian Black-Figure Pottery** derives from the color of the scenes painted on the vessels, as well as the city (Athens) where this pottery was largely produced. Ironically, this style originated in Corinth circa 700 BC. The style and subject matter differed from pottery produced in Corinth versus that made in Athens. Corinthian potters preferred animals and animal scenes, whereas Athenian painters and potters preferred human beings and gods and goddesses for their pottery. In both Corinth and Athens, the artists aspired to a high level of realistic detail and rendered their figures with as much detail as possible.

Pottery produced in Attica looks remarkably different from that produced elsewhere. The soil in Attica contains a high amount of iron which, when fired in a kiln, helps produce the vivid orange color characteristic of Athenian Black-Figure pottery. In the production process, potters added other ingredients such as potash, more iron, and vinegar to change the color of the clay to the brilliant orange color that characterizes this type of pottery. These ingredients could also be mixed into a kind of black gloss used to make these shimmering black figures.

When potters applied this gloss to either the vase as a whole or simply part of the pot, they added a kind of **relief effect** to the pottery. A relief is a kind of artwork where material is removed from a flat surface so that all remains is the person or animal being depicted. The artists would also add realistic features to each figure, including hair and muscle tone, by cutting into the black gloss with a knife.

Athenian Red-Figure Pottery: 530 BC

Eventually, the Black-Figure style was replaced by the **Athenian Red-Figure Style**, circa 530 BC. This type of pottery was popular from the sixth to the fourth century BC and remained in production until the third century. As a helpful explanation, Red-Figure pottery is the opposite of Black-Figure. The background is covered with a gloss of potash and vinegar, and the artist removes that gloss to reveal the red figures for whom this style of pottery is named. Artists used a brush instead of a knife, which permitted greater and more naturalistic details on their figures including muscles, expressions, movement, and even elements of shading.

Vocabulary

Pottery
A vessel used for drinking and eating or storing for food made from clay that is fired in a kiln until it hardens.

Kiln
An oven used to make pottery.

Amphora
A large jar used for transporting commodities in the ancient world.

Kraters
A huge drinking vessel.

Geometric Pottery
In use from 1000 to 700 BC, this style of pottery used geometric designs and shapes for decoration.

Corinthian Pottery
In use from 725 to 600 BC, this style of pottery used flowers, animals, trees, etc. for decoration.

Athenian Black-Figure
In use from 700 to 500 BC, this style of pottery is known for its bright orange background and the realistic black figures decorating these pots.

Relief Effect
A relief carving is done on a flat surface, where unwanted material is removed to leave only the person or thing being depicted.

Athenian Red-Figure
In use from 530 BC onwards, this style of pottery is known for its dark black background and the realistic red figures decorating these pots.

ACTIVITY

Greek Pottery Identification

Instructions: Each row contains a photograph of a particular piece of Greek pottery. Each piece could be *Geometric, Corinthian, Black-Figure, or Red-Figure pottery*, which would also help you identify the *time* it was made. In the space provided, explain what type of pottery each figure is and when it was made based on the explanation of each style of pottery on the previous pages.

Example	***Photo***	***Explanation & Response***
Example #1	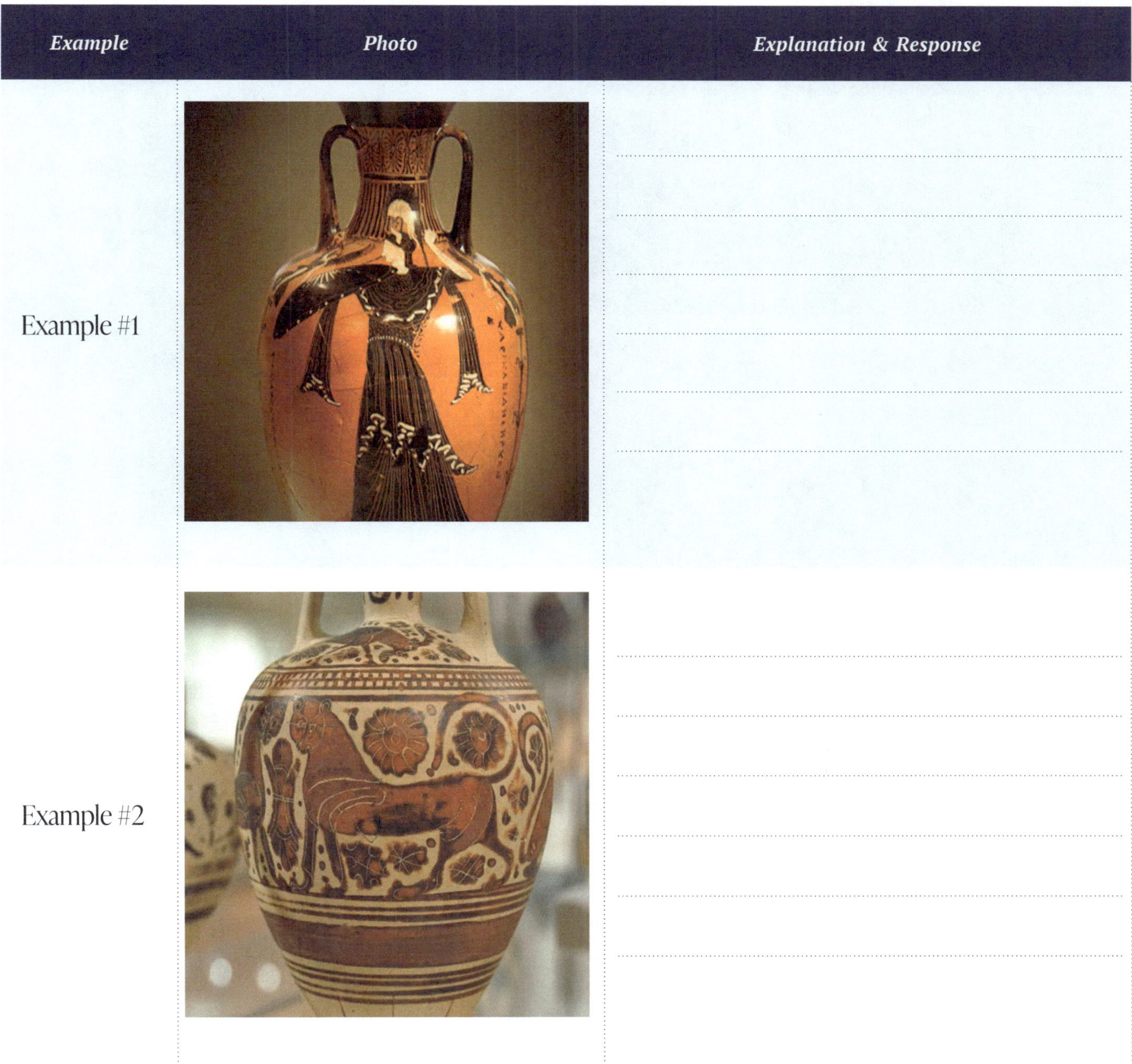	
Example #2		

Greek Pottery Identification (Continued)

Example	*Photo*	*Explanation & Response*
Example #4		
Example #5		
Example #6		

Greek Pottery Identification (Continued)

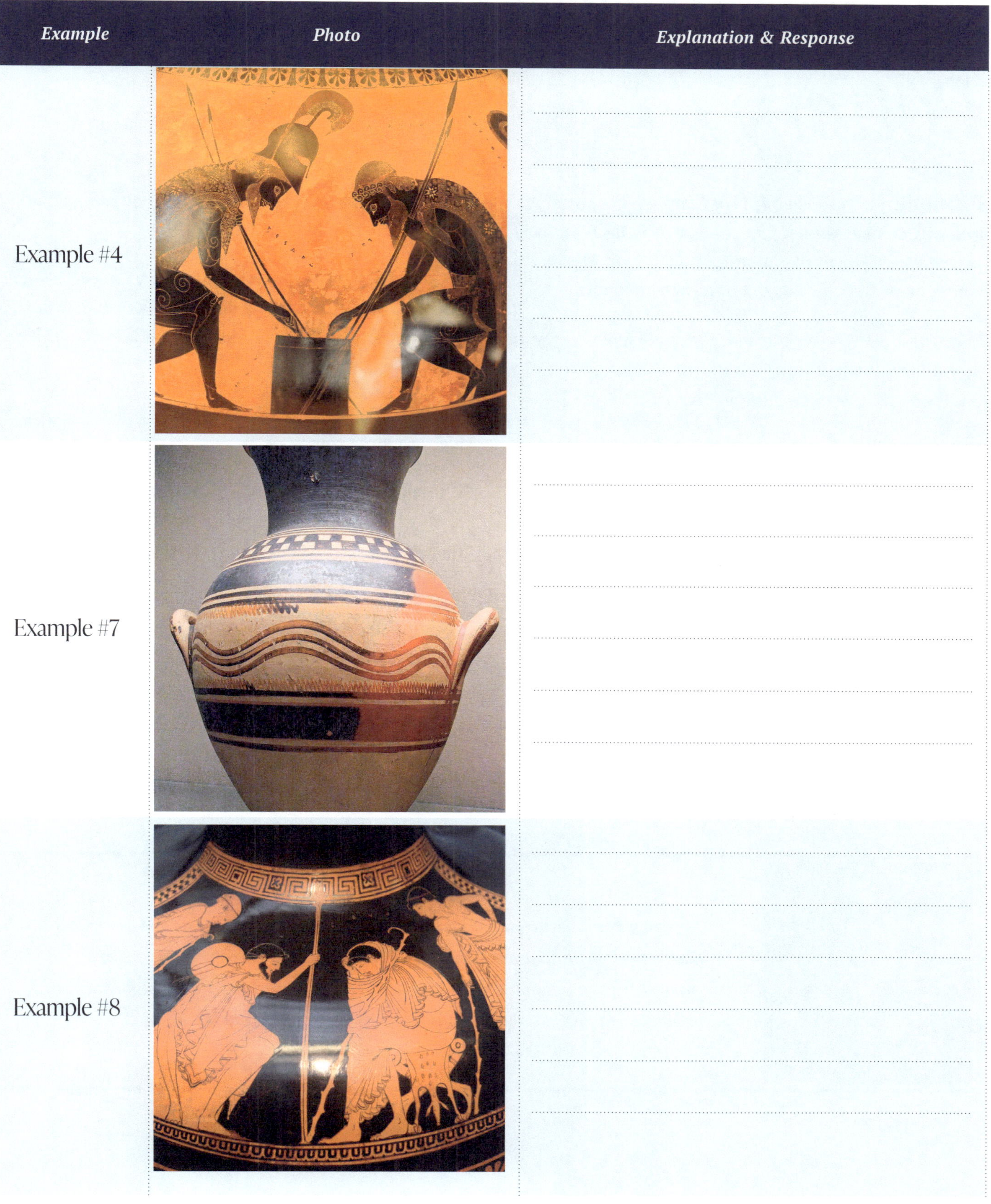

Example	*Photo*	*Explanation & Response*
Example #4		
Example #7		
Example #8		

A Closer Look at Greek Pottery / Answer Key

Example #1: *The example is of Black-Figure pottery and was made in mid-eighth century BC. The work itself was made in Athens by the so-called* Diplyon Master, *whose name and identity are otherwise unknown.*

Example #2: *The example is of a small-scale amphora jar and was made sometime between 575 to 550 BC. The pot is an example of Corinthian pottery.*

Example #3: *The example is of Geometric pottery and was made in 575 to 550 BC. More specifically, this particular pot is known as a* krater, *a massive drinking vessel.*

Example #4: *The example is of a miniature amphora and was made sometime between 575 to 550 BC. The pot is an example of Corinthian pottery.*

Example #5: *The photo is of a amphora featuring Greek warriors, Athena, and Hermes. The amphora was made sometime around 530 BC and is an example of Athenian Red-Figure pottery.*

Example #6: *The photo is of an Athenian Black-Figure pot featuring Ajax and Achilles playing dice. The pot was produced sometime around 530 BC.*

Example #6: *The photo is of an Athenian Black-Figure pot featuring Ajax and Achilles playing dice. The pot was produced sometime around 530 BC.*

Example #7: *The photo is of an amphora that is technically* Protogeometric, *but the answer* Geometric *is correct as well. The pot was produced sometime around 950 BC.*

Example #8: *The photo features a scene from the* Iliad *wherein the Greek warriors try to reason with Achilles. The pottery is an example of Red-Figure pottery and was produced sometime around 480 BC.*

The designs and the decorations on each piece of pottery are so intricate and well-made that historians can accurately estimate the period in which the pottery was made, as well as serve as an encouragement that objects of great value and craftsmanship may inspire generations to come and serves to deepen our appreciation for life itself.

A Closer Look at Constitutions

THROUGHOUT THIS BOOK, we have used words like *politics, governments, states* and other related, almost interchangeable synonyms. Given we have focused so much on the polis, the Greek word for *city-state* that gives us the words *politics* and *political*, among others, let us examine the different types of governments that exist. Herein, the word **constitution**, given above, refers to the ordering or the composition of a particular city-state or government. That constitution lays out what groups of people can vote, what kinds of offices there are, and the responsibilities given to each decision-making body. For example, the United States Constitution grants certain powers to the President, other powers to Congress, and still other powers to the courts.

By government, we mean an institution that is responsible for maintaining some semblance of order among a relatively large population of people. Such forms of government are, in fact, the rulers of that particular area. Accordingly, we will find the suffix - *archy* in the name for each form of government from *monarchy* to *democracy.* As a reference point, remember it was the *archons* who were the rulers in ancient Athens. These kinds of institutions are especially needed when the members of a given society—whether that is a village, a city-state, or a sprawling kingdom—do not know each other, and the bonds of family and kinship no longer tie those individuals together.

Moreover, these groups are not only responsible for making decisions, but they also have a *monopoly* on enforcing them. If the king (or whoever happens to be in charge) says that murder is not a good thing, and that the penalty for murder is death, then it is the king or his attendants who carry out that sentence—no one else. The use of the word "monopoly" means that the duty of maintaining and enforcing justice is the special duty of the king and the king alone.

As far as the different forms of government, we will look at the models proposed by the Greek philosopher Aristotle. Aristotle lived from 384 to 322 BC and wrote on a staggering number of topics, whose titles refered to the subject matter upon which Aristotle wrote. The work most pertinent to our discussion is the *Politics,* Aristotle's treatise on political theory and why states do the things they do. In this work, Aristotle identified three main forms of political institutions, each of which is good when its leaders are focused on the needs of the community as a whole. But these forms of government have a dangerous flip side when its leaders become more focused on their own personal enrichment than the needs of the *polis*. Aristotle gives these matching negative types of government a different name from each of the three positive types. That is, there is a name when that kind of government is good, and a different name when it is bad.

Monarchy: The Rule by One (Good) Person

Monarchy is the rule by *one* person, and it is important to emphasize this *one person* is wholeheartedly concerned for the needs of his or her people. Monarchy is the rule of not just any king but a *good* king. As far as such a king is concerned, we might think of the Spartan king Leonidas, who died fighting the Persians at the Battle of Thermopylae in 480 BC.

Tyrants: The Rule by One (Bad) Person

Tyranny is a form of monarchy, as it is still the rule by one person. But the meaning of the word *tyranny* here

THE AMERICAN REPUBLIC

In this twentieth c. painting, George Washington presides over the Constitutional Convention and the Founding Fathers, a group of well-educated individuals often described as a "natural" aristocracy since they rose by merit and not by birth.

follows the term's modern usage—namely, a cruel and autocratic despot. Such a person is consumed with his or her own power, prestige, and personal enrichment. Tyrants are more concerned with themselves than they are with the well-being of their subjects, and they use their office to become rich as they possibly can at the public's expense. In the ancient world, the city of Syracuse, alternatively spelled Syracuse, in Sicily was often ruled by tyrants. One can also think of ancient Roman emperors like Nero and Domitian whose cruelty was only stopped with great difficulty, and of modern, twentieth-century despots like Adolf Hitler, Josef Stalin, and Mao Zedong. Often, tyrants rule by fear and intimidation.

Aristocracy: The Rule by the Best

The word **aristocracy** refers to the rule by the "best", whether that means the most virtuous, the wisest, or the strongest. Whoever the "best" happens to be, they are concerned with the needs of the community as a whole and not merely their own self-interest. One can think of the reforms of the Greek thinker Solon, who drafted new laws intended to benefit the polis of Athens as a whole. He did not seize the land of the rich and redistribute it amongst the poor, as that would be unjust, but he did not allow the rich to hold the poor in the sad state of debt slavery either.

One can also think of the only real, natural aristocracy that has arisen in the United States, that of the "Founding Fathers". Men like Benjamin Franklin, James Madison, and George Washington, and the other members of the Founding generations had as their aim the mutual well-being and flourishing of all segments of society as a whole and not just themselves.

Vocabulary

Constitution
The word *constitution* refers to the order of a state and the way in which power is distributed amongst different institutions and people.

Monarchy
A form of government wherein one person rules, and that one person cares for the needs of his or her subjects.

Tyranny
A form of government wherein one person rules, but that one cares only for him or herself.

Aristocracy
The rule by the *best*, typically a class of well-educated and virtuous individuals who care for the common good.

Oligarchy
The rule by the *few*, wherein a relatively small number of people rule. They are more concerned with themselves than with the common good.

Democracy
The rule of the *people*, wherein the people hold the ultimate political power—at least in principle, if not in practice.

Anarchy
A form of government wherein there is no government.

Republic
From the Latin *res publica*, meaning the property of the people", a *republic* is a form of government that mixes elements of a monarchy, aristocracy, and democracy.

Oligarchy: The Rule by the Few

The word **oligarchy** refers to the rule of a "few" people, and those few people are consumed with ruling so that it benefits themselves and their class, not the city as a whole. The Roman Republic, at times, operated more like an oligarchy when the Roman Senate made laws that benefited the patrician class at the expense of the plebeians. One may also think of the French aristocracy in the decades preceding the French Revolution of 1789; the French nobility inherited large estates, and often they squandered the income generated by this land on lavish parties and banquets.

Democracy: The Rule by the People

The word **democracy** means rule by the "people", so that all the citizens of a given polis have some say, stake, or responsibility in its form of government. The word derives from the Greek word *demos*, meaning "people", and *kratos*, meaning "power". In a democracy, the people rule themselves; as a result, the people must be virtuous and capable of ruling themselves. The residents of ancient Athens were paid whenever they participated in the functions of the Athenian democracy; moreover, they often decided who participated (deciding what job at random by drawing lots). After all, if everyone is equal in a democracy, then everyone should be qualified to serve the state in a variety of ways. In this way, Athens serves as the best example of a democracy.

Anarchy: No Rules, No Government

Anarchy is the absence of political order, a form of government in which there is no government. When the letter *a* is used as a prefix, meaning it comes before the word in question, it means the "not" or "without" that with which it is paired. Thus, anarchy is a form of government in which there is no government. At the outbreak of the Peloponnesian War, a civil war broke out in the city of Corcyra, located on the Adriatic Sea. The civil war grew so intense and bitter, with everyone in the city turning against each other, that a state of *anarchy* existed.

THE ROMAN REPUBLIC

In this eighteenth c. painting, the Roman senator Cicero denounces another senator named Catiline for trying to overthrow the Republic.

Republic: The Property of the People

Even the good kinds of government, whose rulers are concerned with the well-being of their people, have their strengths and weaknesses. Kingdoms tend to flourish when they have good kings, but when that monarch dies, the kingdom has no guarantee another good monarch will take his or her place. As a result, some states try to combine different elements from different systems, hoping that the good qualities from one type of qualities and balance out their bad qualities. That way, no one person has so much power that they can take away the rights, privileges, or property of ordinary people. We often use the word **republic** to refer to this type of system.

The word *republic* comes from the Latin words *res publica*, meaning "property of the people" or roughly "what the people own in common with each other". A republic is a *mixed constitution*, in that power and decision-making responsibilities are formally split up between different individuals and different groups of people. The word *republic* comes from Latin not because the Romans invented the system, but because the Romans founded the most successful and enduring republic in the ancient world. In the days of the Roman Republic, most political power was vested in the hands of the Roman Senate, a group of well-educated, wealthy men called *patricians* who could, at times, operate as an oligarchy or aristocracy. The lower classes, called the *plebeians*, could vote on certain issues, and their rights were guarded by a special officer called a *tribune*. Meanwhile, special officers called *consuls* controlled the Roman legions, Rome's fearsome, well-organized body of troops. In this way, the Roman Republic incorporated elements of an *aristocracy* with the Roman Senate, a *democracy* with the plebeians, and a *monarchy* with the Roman consuls.

The legends of the Roman Republic endured through the centuries. Roman writers such as Livy wrote about the heroes of the Roman Republic, urging their readers to imitate the self-sacrificial and courageous conduct of heroes like Cincinnatus. They were popular at the time of the American founding, with early American leaders like George Washington modeling his actions after that of Cincinnatus (both men gave up considerable power to go back to their farms). The American Founding Fathers modeled the American Constitution after that of the Roman Republic, albeit with modifications to fit the American experience and the possibilities before the American people. In both cases, the idea behind the *republican* form of government was to divide up power and responsibilities among different groups of people. In that way, no single person would have so much power they could abuse it.

To wrap up our discussion of political theory, let's examine different rulers and states from across ancient history. Read over each example and the description that follows, identify the type of government that best fits, and write a short explanation arguing for your position.

Political Theory and Identifying Different Kinds of Constitutions

Example	*Brief Description*	*Explanation & Response*
Hammurabi *King of Babylon* *Reign, 1792 to 1750 BC*	*Hammurabi made Babylon the dominant state in Lower Mesopotamia and established a law code—the famous Code of Hammurabi—to ensure his people received fair and just laws.* *Hammurabi hoped they might think of the ideal ruler, a king who, like the Sumerian gods, dispensed justice and ruled wisely.*	

Political Theory and Identifying Different Kinds of Constitutions

Example	Brief Description	Explanation & Response
Rome *A prosperous city located in central Italy* *Founded 753 BC*	*According to legend, the city of Rome was founded by two brothers, Romulus and Remus, on the hills overlooking the Tiber River. Initially, Rome was ruled by a king, but those kings mistreated the Roman people and were ousted in 509 BC.* *Rome's upper-class citizens, known as patricians, set up a republic that gave the most political power to themselves, albeit with some democratic participation from Rome's lower-class citizens, known as the plebeians.*	
Athens *The foremost among of the Greek* city-states *during the age of Classical Greece* ~ 510 to 323 BC	*During the age of Classical Greece, the city of Athens had means for every citizen in Greece to participate in Athenian government. While the most important offices, such as the generals (the* strategoi*), were reserved for the nobility, the lower classes in Athens could serve in the assembly, vote on political issues, and serve on juries.* *In Classical Greece, people also received pay for serving in local government, which encouraged poorer residents to take time to serve in government (Pomeroy 161-163).*	
Carthage *A wealthy trading port in North Africa* *Founded in the 9th century BC*	*Carthage was founded by the Phoenician city of Tyre, located at the far eastern end of the Mediterranean Sea.* *Carthage was ruled by a senate of influential and wealthy members who permitted access to their ranks based on wealth.* *At the same time, they had very little participation from the lower classes of Carthaginian society.*	

Political Theory and Identifying Different Kinds of Constitutions

Example	Brief Description	Explanation & Response
Qin Shi Huangdi *The First Emperor of China* *Reign, 221 to 210 BC*	*Qin Shi Huangdi ended the tumultuous fighting known as the Warring States Period when his state, the state of Qin (or Chin), conquered the rest of China.* *His reign was marked by efforts to consolidate power by intimidating the scholarly class, building massive fortifications and palaces that exacted a heavy toll on the people of ancient China, and trying to gain immortality.*	
Corcyra Founded 8th c. BC *This question is focused in the years just before the Peloponnesian War broke out in 431 BC.*	*Located on the Adriatic Sea, Corcyra grew from a colony to a great city in its own right. Athens and Corinth fought over the city, each hoping to control over Corcyra's trade and large fleet.* *The people of Corcyra took sides in the conflict between Athens and Corinth, and the debates grew so heated they often erupted into mob rule.* *Groups aligned with Athens or Corinth fought each other in the most brutal ways.*	

A Closer Look at Constitutions / Answer Key

Hammurabi: *Hammurabi is most likely a monarch, but if his conquests are emphasized, he may be considered a tyrant.*

Rome: *Rome is often described as an aristocracy, but one can argue that the Roman Senate were more concerned for their own privileges and was thus an oligarchy.*

Athens: *Athens is perhaps the best example of a democracy from the ancient world.*

Carthage: *Like Rome, Carthage is often described as either an aristocracy or an oligarchy.*

Qin Shi Huangdi: *It is easy to identify Shi Huangdi as a tyrant, providing we remember the sources may not have accurately depicted him.*

Corcyra: *The civil war that broke out in Corycya is best described as anarchy, the absence of meaningful political authority.*

ACTIVITY

Direct Instruction Review

The hardest part about history is memorizing all those facts, dates, and events. To make this process easier, we have included this short section called *Direct Instruction Review*. Direct Instruction (or DI) is a powerful pedagogical tool whereby teachers ask students a series of *call-and-response* questions, and students respond back with the aim of learning this material to *mastery*. Teacher's lines are in **bold**; student's lines in *italices*.

What was the Greek Dark Ages? *The Greek Dark Ages lasted around 1100 to 750 BC from the end of the Mycenaean civilization to the rise of Athens, Sparta, and the other prominent city-states of Archaic Greece.*

And why were the Dark Ages so dark? *The centuries between the Bronze Age and the Archaic period saw a notable lack of writing and literary documents, which accounts for the period's darkness.*

What period followed the Greek Dark Ages? *The Archaic period from the Greek word for* old.

When did the Archaic period begin? *Many historians use the date of the first Olympics in 776 BC as the starting point for the Archaic period.*

And what was the Archaic period like? *Greek culture as we know it today began to flourish in and around the Greek mainland, principally with the city-states of Athens, Sparta, and Corinth.*

What is a city-state? *A city-state is an independent city that drafts and maintains its own laws, infrastructure, military, and other services we might expect of modern-day states.*

What was the Greek word for city-state? *The Greek word for city-state is* polis, *from which we get the words* political *and* politics.

And what were three of the biggest and most powerful city-states? *The three largest and most powerful city-states were Athens, Sparta, and Corinth.*

How did Corinth become so powerful? *Corinth sat on the Isthmus of Corinth and grew wealthy from the trade they literally dragged over the isthmus.*

How did Sparta become so powerful? *In response to land pressures, Sparta enslaved their neighbors and forced them to grow their food while every part of Spartan society was devoted to fighting and warfare.*

How did Athens become so powerful? *In response to land pressures, Athens sent colonies abroad to Asia Minor and elsewhere, exported olives, taught their children valuable trades, and gave their citizens democratic freedoms, all of which made Athens into the School of Hellas.*

And when does the Archaic period end? *With the invasion of the Persian Empire, to which we turn next!*

ACTIVITY

Map Practice: The Greek World

Instructions: Carefully look over the map below and fill in the appropriate blank with the term list provided above each map.

Greek Colonies & the Mediterranean: Greek cities such as Corinth, Sparta, Athens, Ephesus, Neapolis, Cyrene, Trapezus, Hemeroscopium, Marseilles, Syracuse, Byzantium, and Chersonesus; and other major cities such as Tyre, Carthage, Rome, Jerusalem, and Memphis.

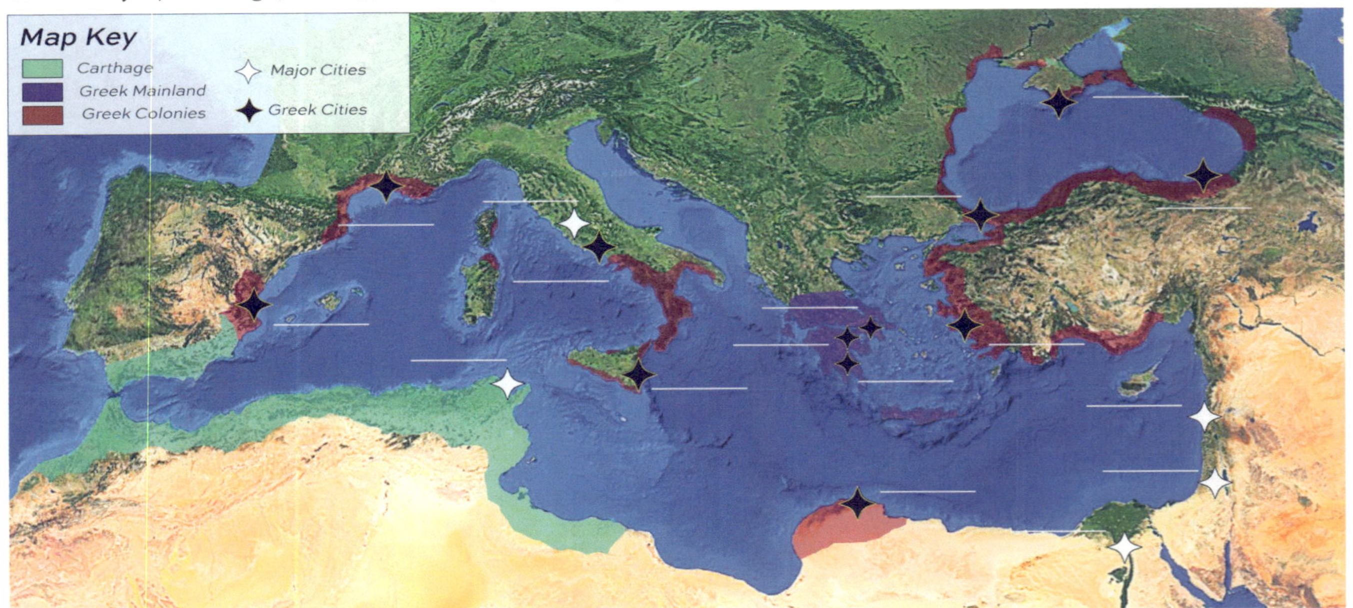

The World of Greek Myths: Sites from Greek mythology like the Pillars of Heracles, Scylla & Charybdis, the Garden of the Hesperides, Polyphemus' Island, Bosporus Straits, Troy, Ithaca, and the Land of the Lotus-Eaters.

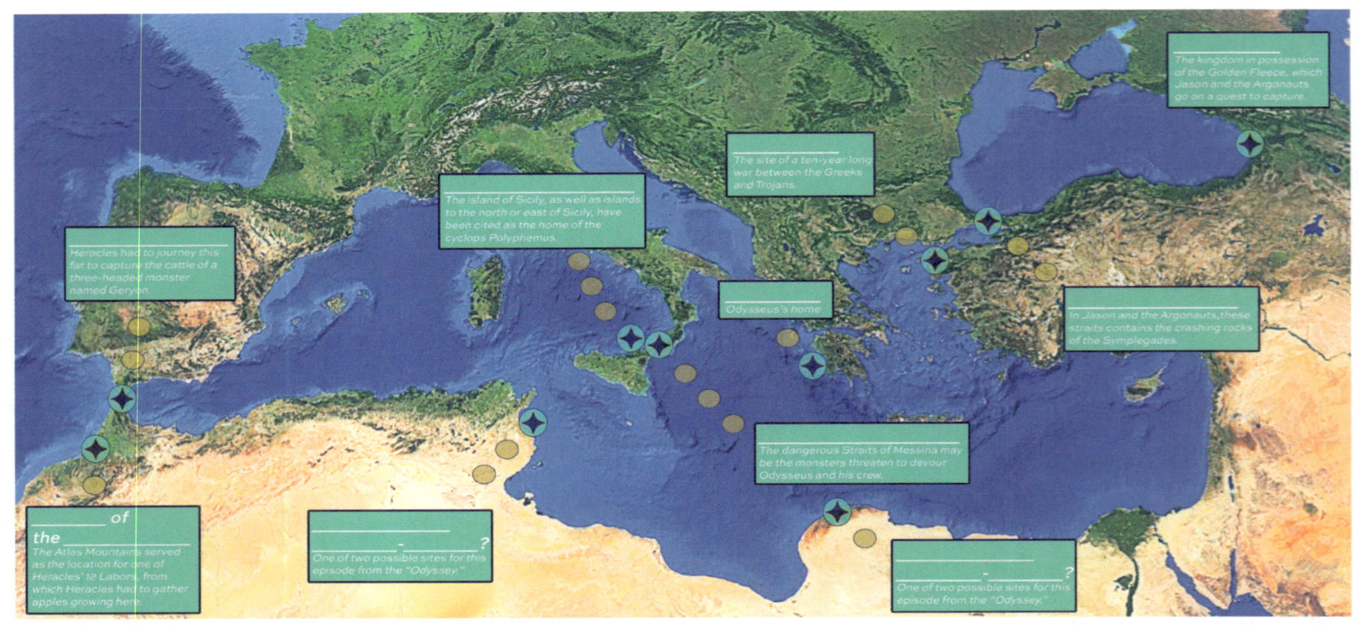

ACTIVITY

Timeline Practice / Archaic Greece

The hardest part about history is memorizing all those facts, dates, and events. To make this process easier, check out the timeline below—well, technically, there are *two* timelines. Some entries are missing dates, and others are missing the event that occurred on that date. With the information available from both timelines, fill in the missing blanks to get a better sense of the timeline for this chapter.

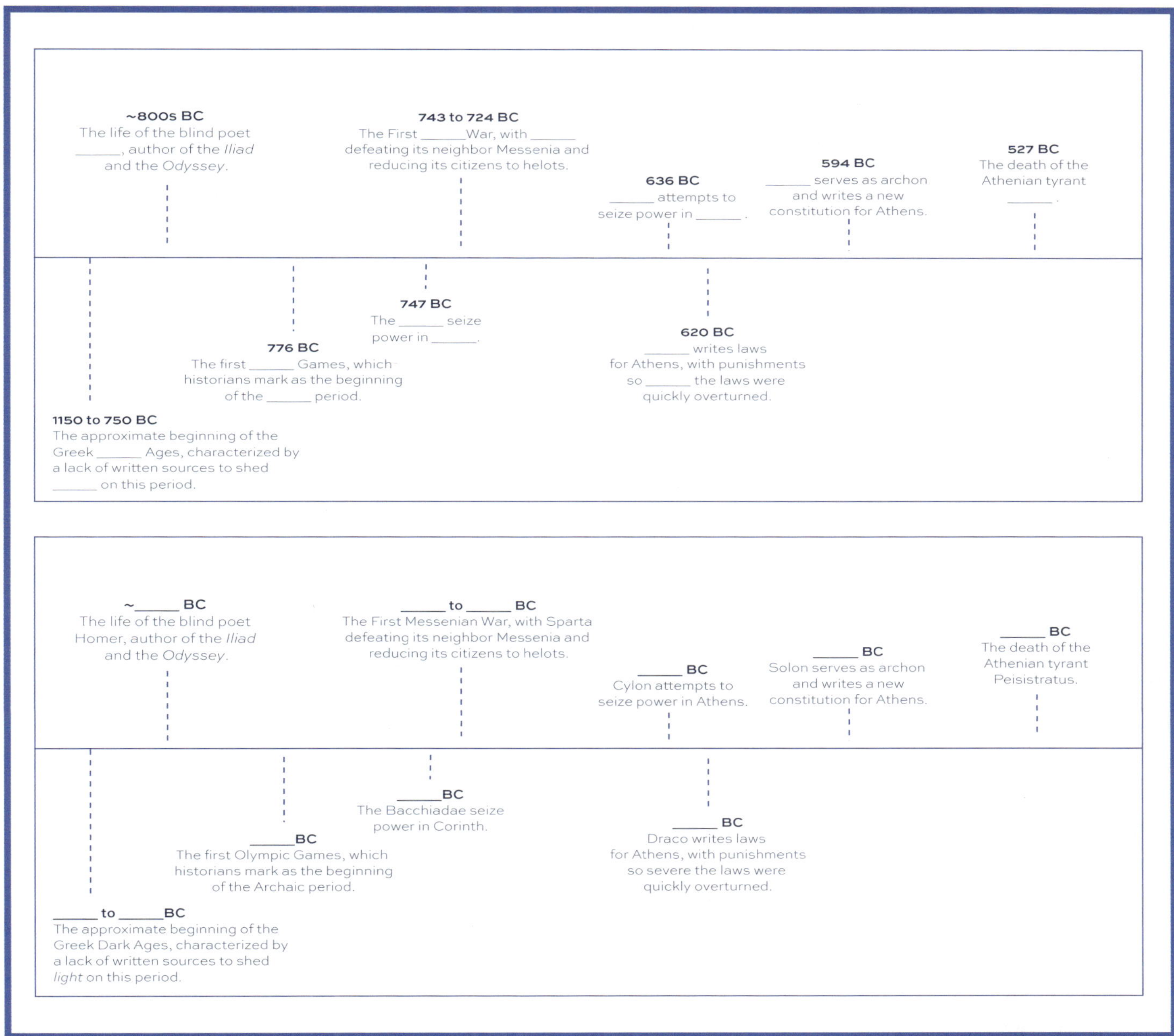

***Want to study the maps on the next page online? Type in the link below or scan the QR code to access an interactive diagram:* https://bit.ly/3okSogF**

Writing Prompt

Writing is thinking, so we will spend considerable time this year writing and thinking about history. In the space provided, write a short essay answering the question: ***How did Athens, Corinth, and Sparta respond to the same sort of problems of overpopulation and shortages in land, resources, and food? Among these city-states, which one had the* best *solution to this all-too-common problem?***

THE ACROPOLIS / ATHENS

Photo by Victor Malyushev

The Persian Wars

ROADMAP

- Read two selections from Herodotus' *Histories*: the first detailing the longstanding conflict between the Greek West and the ancient Near East, and the second about the invasion force of Xerxes and their crossing of the Hellespont.
- Take a closer look at the Battle of Thermopylae and the tactics used by the Greeks to the Persian army.
- Learn about the battles of Marathon, Thermopylae, Salamis, Plataea, and Mycale and how the city-states of Greece defeated a much larger and more powerful army of the Persian Empire.
- Learn about the significance of the Persian Wars to the Greeks and to Western culture.
- Practice our knowledge of maps and chronology, as well as our writing skills through reading comprehension questions and an essay.

THALES OUTCOME
Nº 2

A Virtuous leader with Well-Developed Judgment *generates life goals and objectives while compassionately considering individuals and the community.*

In this chapter, we turn to the Persian Wars, which lasted from 490 to 449 BC. At the time, the Persian Empire was the largest and most formidable power the world had seen up until to that point. Despite their strength, the Persians experienced one startling defeat after another at the hands of the Greeks, who may be able to attribute their success to the habits of virtuous leadership we hope all students may cultivate through their study of history.

Opening Question

What is myth, and what is history? And what is the line between them?

Feuds Between East and West / Herodotus' *Histories*

Title: Herodotus' *Histories* chronicles the Persian Wars that lasted from 499 to 449 BC. In the book, Herodotus presents an account of the history of the main combatants, namely, the Greeks and the Persians (whom Herodotus often referred to as the Medes), as well as a history of the various peoples throughout the ancient Near East that composed the Persian Empire.

Date: Herodotus wrote his *Histories* in and around 430 BC, two decades after the end of the Persian Wars. That would have been enough time for Herodotus to gather his source material and write his narrative, as well as provide some context on these seminal historical events.

Description: The *Histories* is the earliest example of what we would consider historical narrative, so much so that Herodotus has been described as the "father of history". Indeed, Herodotus opens his *Herodotus* stating his purpose in writing is so that "the deeds of men may not be forgotten by lapse of time" and "the works great and marvelous, some of which have been done by the Greeks and others by Barbarians, may never lose their renown.

In this passage, Herodotus described the origins of the ongoing feud between the Greek-speaking West and the peoples of the ancient Near East, and how it has played itself out in mythology and the Trojan War until Herodotus' own time. This text comes from Book I, Chapter 1 of Herodotus' *Histories*, translated by George Macaulay.

The Feud between East & West

01 This is the beginning of the ***Inquiry of Herodotus*** of Halicarnassus, so that neither the deeds of men may be forgotten by lapse of time, nor the works great and marvelous, which have been done—some by the Greeks and others by the **barbarians**—may lose their renown, nor especially that anyone should forget the reasons that brought them all to war.

02 Those Persians who have knowledge of history declare that the Phoenicians first began the quarrel. Such Phoenicians, they say, came from the lands surrounding called **the Erythraian Sea** to this land of ours.

03 Having settled in the land where they continue even now to dwell, they set about making long voyages by sea. They carried goods from Egypt and Assyria across

IO / PRINCESS OF ARGOS
In Greek mythology, Zeus abducted Io and transformed her into a cow to hide her from Hera (hence, the horns on Io's forehead).

the world and also at Argos. Now Argos was at that time in all points the first of the States within that land which is now called Greece. The Phoenicians arrived then at this land of Argos, and began to dispose of their ship's cargo. On the fifth or sixth day after they had arrived, when their goods had been almost all sold, there came down to the sea a great company of women, and among them the daughter of the king. Her name, as the Hellenes also agree, was **Io** the daughter of Inachos. These standing near the stern of the ship were buying such goods they found profitable, when suddenly the Phoenicians, passing the word from one to another, made a rush upon the group. The greater part of the women escaped by flight, but Io and certain others were carried off! Thus they put them on board their ship and quickly departed, sailing away to Egypt. In this manner the Persians report that Io came to Egypt, not agreeing therein with the Hellenes, and this they say was the first beginning of wrongs.

04 Then after this, they say, certain, unnamed Greek sailors put in to the city of **Tyre**. Tyre is in Phoenicia, and there they carried off the king's daughter, **Europa**. These sailors would doubtless be Cretans. And so they paid the Phoenicians back for abducting Io.

05 After this, however, other Greeks, they say, were the authors of the second wrong; for they sailed to Colchis and into the river Phasis with a warship. From there, after they had done their business at the port, they carried off the king's daughter, **Medea**. The king of Colchis sent a herald to the land of Greece and demanded his daughter back. Yet, the Greeks answered that, as the barbarians had given them no satisfaction for the abduction of Io, princess of Argos, neither would they give satisfaction to the barbarians for this.

06 In the next generation after this, they say, **Alexander** the son of Priam, having heard of these things, desired to get a wife for himself by such means. Alexander was fully assured that he would not be compelled to give any satisfaction for this wrong, since the Greeks gave none for theirs. So he carried off Helen, and the Greeks resolved to send messengers first and to demand her back with satisfaction for the wrong. But when they put forth this demand, the others alleged to them the abduction of Medea, saying that the Greeks were now desiring satisfaction to be given to them by others,

EUROPA / PRINCESS OF TYRE
In Greek mythology, Zeus abducted Europa, having transformed himself into a bull to deceive Europa and escape Hera's notice.

though they had given none themselves nor had surrendered the person when demand was made.

07 Up to this point, they say, nothing more happened than the carrying away of women on both sides. That

HELEN OF TROY & MENELAUS OF SPARTA / 550 BC

The vase above pictures Menelaus after the sack of Troy, a city he and other Greek princes besieged for ten years to bring Helen back to Sparta.

the fights between East and West only worsened, the Greeks were very much to blame. The Greeks set the first example of war, making the first expedition into Asia before the barbarians made any into Europe. Now they say that in their judgment, though it is an act of wrong to carry away women by force, it is a folly to set one's heart on taking vengeance for the wrong.

08 Yet the Greeks, on account of a Spartan princess, gathered together a great army. They came to Asia and destroyed the dominion of Priam; and that from this time forward they had always considered the Hellenic race to be their enemy. For Asia and the barbarian races which dwell there, the Persians claim as belonging to them. But Europe and the Greek race they consider to be separate from them. The Persians for their part say that things happened in the way described. They conclude that the beginning of their quarrel with the Greeks was on account of the taking of Troy.

09 But as regards Io, the Phoenicians do not agree with the Persians in telling thus the tale. Indeed, they deny they carried her off to Egypt by violent means, and that when they were in Argos, she fell in love with the master of their ship, and therefore sailed away with the Phoenicians of her own will, for fear of being found out. These are the tales told by the Persians and the Phoenicians severally. Concerning these things, I am not going to say that they happened thus or thus, but when I have pointed to the man who first within my own knowledge began to commit wrong against the Hellenes, I shall go forward with the story and give an account concerning the cities of men, small as well as great.

10 For in our days, those cities which were great have now become small, while those that were in my own time great used in former times to be small: so then, since I know that human prosperity never continues steadfast, I shall make mention of both indifferently.

Vocabulary

Barbarians
Herodotus is following Greek custom which separates the world into civilized Greeks and everyone else—the barbarians.

The Erythraian Sea
The Erythraian Sea is known as the Gulf of Aden today and is located off the coast of the Arabian Peninsula.

Io
Io was a Greek princess from Argos, located in the Peloponnese. In Greek mythology, the Greek god Zeus abducted Io, then transformed her into a cow to hide Io from his wife, Hera.

Tyre
Tyre was one of the more prominent cities in Phoenicia.

Europa
Europa was a Phoenician princess, whom Zeus abducted after he transformed himself into a bull. Tyre was one of the more significant cities among the Phoenicians.

Medea
Medea was the daughter of King Aeëtes of Colchis and, in Greek mythology, she helps Jason steal the Golden Fleece. Again, Herodotus takes a story popular in Greek myth and cites an alternative version to the story. Colchis was a kingdom located on the east coast of the Black Sea.

Reading Comprehension Questions

1. Here, Herodotus is trying to describe the conflict between the Greeks and the barbarians, between the west and the east. What event starts the fighting between the Greek west and the Persian east?

2. According to Herodotus, what had happened to Io, Europa, Medea, and Helen? Why were they abducted?

3. Based on the *Vocabulary* notes on the previous page, what does Greek mythology say happened to these princesses? Do you think they were real people? Why or why not?

4. Based on these stories, how are mythology and history intertwined?

The Persian Wars / 499 - 449 BC

IN THIS SECTION, we will look at the end of the Archaic Period and the war that ends this period, the Persian Wars. **The Persian Wars** are actually a high-point for the Greeks, as far as any war may be a high-point. The Persian Wars began in 499 and ended in 449 BC. The Persian Wars are so named because the Greeks fought the Persian Empire, which, at the time, was the most powerful empire the world had ever seen and boasted an army far larger than any city-state in Greece could match. The Persian army invaded Greece first under Darius the Great and then a second time under Darius' son, Xerxes. The army of Persia was so large it was said to drink entire rivers dry and, when Persia set its sights on a kingdom, province, or town, that kingdom ceased to exist. Persian kings could make entire regions disappear, brick by brick, if they wanted them to.

Yet, in the Persian Wars, the city-states of mainland Greece actually won. Athens, Sparta, Corinth, and other *poleis* banded together to defeat the world's most powerful empire. The first of these upsets was the Athenian victory at the Battle of Marathon (490 BC). Then, there was the legendary last stand of the Spartans at Thermopylae (480 BC), followed by the Athenian naval victory at Salamis (480 BC) and victory among a band of Greek *poleis* at Plataea (479 BC) to drive the Persians off the Greek mainland for good. Our main source of the Persian Wars is the Greek historian **Herodotus**, who lived from 484 to 425 BC and came from the city of Halicarnassus in Ionian Greece.

Indeed, we owe a great debt to the soldiers and citizens who stood against the might of the Persian Empire, for if they had lost, the influence of Greek literature, Greek philosophy, and Greek democratic institutions might never have survived. Often, the victories at Thermopylae and Salamis are described as victories for the individual rights, freedoms, and liberties we associate with the Western tradition. For if the Persian king Darius and his successor Xerxes had succeeded in their designs to conquer Greece, Western history would have taken a very different turn—in fact, it may not have taken any turns at all but instead been swallowed up by a much larger and more powerful state. In this section, we will look at the high points of the Persian Wars from the Ionian Revolt: the Battle of Marathon, the invasion of Xerxes, and then the successive battles of Thermopylae, Salamis, and Plataea.

The Beginnings of the War: The Ionian Revolt

The conflict between the Greeks and the Persians had been brewing for sometime. As related in the previous

The Persian Wars are so named because the full might and power of the Persian came against the city-states of ancient Greece. If Athens, Sparta, Corinth, and other poleis *had not stood up against the Persian Empire, we may have lost the literature, philosophy, and the understanding of individual rights and freedoms and democratic institutions we inherited from the Greeks.*

Vocabulary

Alexander

Alexander is an alternate name for Paris, the Trojan prince who abducted Helen of Sparta. These actions initiated the Trojan War.

The Persian Wars

Lasting from 499 to 449 BC, the Persian Wars are so-named because the Persian Empire invaded mainland Greece. In a series of shocking upsets, the Greek city-states defeated the Persian Empire and held onto their independence.

Herodotus

A Greek historian sometimes called the father of history, Herodotus' major work is the *Histories*, which tells the story of the Persian Wars. He lived from 484 to 425 BC.

Cyrus the Great

Cyrus the Great was the founder of the Persian Empire and one of the most successful military and political leaders of all time. He reigned from 559 to 529 BC.

Darius the Great

Under Darius' rule, the Persian Empire reached the apex of its territorial expansion, stretching from the Indus River Valley to northern Greece, and achieving its peak of commercial, political, and economic power. Darius I reigned from 522 BC to 486 BC.

THE PERSIAN WARS / 499 TO 449 BC

sections of *The Thales Canon* history series, the Persian invasion of Greece was almost inevitable from the moment that **Cyrus the Great** conquered the Greek city-states of Asia Minor. As noted in the previous pages, the Greek historian Herodotus traces the source of the conflict in the abduction of Io, an Argive princess who had been kidnapped by Phoenician sailors. The Greek abducted a Phoenician in return, with each side, east and west, returning one wrong after another until a whole civilization was burned to the ground.

War only became more likely as the Persian Empire and the Greek world came closer together. Cyrus the Great conquered the kingdom of Lydia in 547 BC, and with Lydia came Greek city-states in Asia Minor like Ephesus and Miletus. Then, in 513 BC, **Darius the Great**, king of Persia, crossed the Hellespont and invaded the Greek mainland. Darius' invasion set in motion a series of events that would see the Greek city-states in Asia Minor, a region known as **Ionia**, rebel against the Persia.

These cities had been founded by Athens at the close of the Dark Ages and enjoyed close ties with the *metropoli*, or the "mother-cities" on the other side of the Aegean. Greek-speaking tribes like the Aeolians, Dorians, and the largest such group, the Ionians, sailed across the Aegean Sea to establish new cities. Ionian Greeks, of whom many came from Athens, then made up the twelve cities of Ionia that included Ephesus, Miletus (the home of Thales), and the islands of Samos and Chios. These Greek cities still enjoyed cultural and economic ties with the Greek mainland, especially the major cities of Athens and Sparta, even after the conquests of Cyrus the Great. Cyrus the Great absorbed them into his domains following his conquest of Sardis in 547 BC.

MAP OF THE IONIAN REVOLT / 499 TO 493 BC

The spark that lit **the Ionian Revolt** began with Aristagoras, tyrant of Miletus. Aristagoras worried he may not remain in power long if he did not do something bold enough to impress the king or lucrative enough to create his own base of supporters.

Aristagoras proposed an invasion of the Greek island of Naxos to restore a group of noblemen back to their place of power. With support from no less a figure than Darius' brother Artaphernes, Aristagoras besieged the island of Naxos with a fleet of 200 Greek warships known as triremes. But the invasion failed miserably, and Aristagoras was left in a worse position than before (Cristian, Culley). What could he do now?

To protect his position, Aristagoras encouraged the other Greek city-states to revolt against Persia. As their leader, he promised them more freedom and autonomy than they enjoyed under Persian rule, and the Greek city-states pledged their support to the revolt. Aristagoras also sent emissaries across the Aegean to Athens and Sparta. Sparta declined, but Athens sent troops to aid in the revolt.

Together, the Athenians and the Ionians burned the city of **Sardis**, Persia's capital in Asia Minor, in 498 BC. The destruction of Sardis would have serious ramifications for the Greeks in general and Athens in particular, for Darius was enraged and swore he would make the Athenians pay. Rebellions in Greek cities continued to flare up until 493 BC when the Ionian Revolt ended and the Persian Empire had crushed the last of these rebellions.

Vocabulary

Ionia
The west coast of Asia Minor that had been colonized by Greek city-states.

The Ionian Revolt
Lasting from 499 to 493 BC, the Ionian revolt saw the Greek-city of Asia Minor revolt against Persian rule.

Sardis
The capital of Lydia which, after it was conquered by Cyrus the Great, was made into the administrative capital of the far eastern reaches of the Persian Empire.

Reading Comprehension Questions

1. What was Persia like under King Darius? How big was the empire? What bound it together?

2. Where was Ionia? Why did such a large population of Greeks live under the rule of the Persian Empire?

3. What was the Ionian Revolt?

4. What was Sardis, and who burned it? Why did they burn it?

The Battle of Marathon / 490 BC / Persian Wars

IN 491 BC, Darius sent envoys to Athens and Sparta and demanded they surrender. When they refused, Darius invaded mainland Greece. Darius wanted to conquer Athens first to punish this city-state for their assistance in the Ionian Revolt. The Persian navy landed at a site called Marathon, a distance of about twenty-six miles from Athens.

The Bay of Marathon could accommodate the Persian fleet but the ground surrounding the Persian beachhead was swampy, uneven, and unsuitable for Persian cavalry. A plain led out from the beachhead, but the Athenian *hoplites*, supplemented by a band of soldiers from Plataea, blocked the entry and exit points out of it. The Persians were thus pinned down near their beachhead, but they possessed an army of 25,000 troops and enough cavalry to turn the tide of any battle in their favor.

The Athenians sent word to Sparta requested their assistance. Sparta had the most experienced and disciplined army in Greece, but the Spartans replied they could not come to their aid, not until the end of a religious festival ten days hence.

The Athenian army was commanded by a group of ten **strategoi**, generals elected from each of the ten tribes. The *strategoi* voted each day whether or not to engage the Persians. Half the Athenian *strategoi* favored waiting, afraid of the Persian military. One *strategos* named **Miltiades** lobbied the other *strategoi* to attack quickly, for the Persians had grown overconfident from years of victories and knew little of Greek tactics. Moreover, Athens could not survive a Persian siege, so such a victory was their best option.

Then, for reasons not entirely understood, the Persians pulled their cavalry. According to Herodotus, Militiades came to another influential *strategos*, Callimachos, and gave the following speech:

> *With you the matters rests, Callimachos, for we may bring Athens under slavery or leave her free. Today, if we fight, we can leave a memorial for all time.*
>
> *For now, the Athenians have come to the greatest danger which we have ever faced.*
>
> *On the one hand, if we submit to the Medes, we know what misery awaits us, but if this city shall gain the victory, it may become the first of the cities of Hellas.*
>
> *How this may happen and how it comes to thee of all men to have the decision of these matters, I am now about to tell. Of us the generals, who are ten in number, the opinions are divided. One party urges that we fight and the others that we do not.*
>
> *If we do not, I expect great strife will fall upon the Athenians and so shake them until they submit to Persia. Yet, if we fight before any unsoundness appear in any part of the Athenian people, then we may gain the victory in the fight, if the gods grant equal conditions. These things depend on you, for if you attach yourself to my opinions, you will both a fatherland which is free and a native city which shall be the first among the cities of Hellas.*

Vocabulary

Marathon
Fought in 490 BC, Athens defeated a much-larger army of Persian soldiers and was the first upset in a series of upsets by the Greeks over the Persians. The Athenians considered their victory over Persia to have preserved their city, their way of life, and the unique civic freedoms and opportunities that life in Athens gave to its citizens.

Strategoi
The generals in charge of the Athenian army, of which there were ten in total. One *strategos* was elected from each of the ten tribes of Athens.

Miltiades
Of of the ten Athenian *strategoi* in command at Marathon, Miltiades urged his colleagues to attack the Persians as soon as possible.

With that, the Athenian phalanx began their assault on the Persian army, beginning with a slow march that broke off into a full run until at last, the Athenians slammed into the Persian troops. The fighting was most intense in the center, but at last the Persian troops broke ranks and fled back to their ships. In the swamps and marshlands at Marathon, Persian troops were cut down in huge numbers by the attacking Athenians.

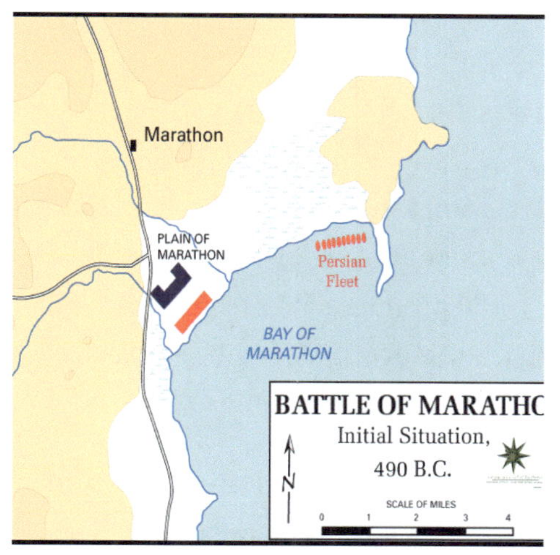

THE BATTLE OF MARATHON / TERRAIN AT MARATHON
A diagram of the combatants at Marathon with Athens in blue *and Persia in* red *(left); swamps besides the plain of Marathon (right).*

According to Herodotus, the Athenians had suffered almost 200 casualties whereas the Persians had suffered 6,400 casualties and the loss of seven ships. Later, the Greek historian Plutarch reported that a herald from Marathon ran the twenty-six miles back to Athens to report of the Athenian victory over the Persians. At his announcement the herald, named Pheidippides, died of exhaustion. From this story we derive the name for the modern twenty-six mile race, the marathon.

The Athenians considered the victory at Marathon to be of inestimable importance. The very survival of Athens and of all Greece depended on pushing the Persians out of mainland Greece and had the Athenians lost, the Persians would have most likely besieged and ultimately conquered Athens herself.

The Athenians viewed their victory as the triumph of Greek independence over the autocratic and somewhat cruel reign of Darius I, a king who would stop at nothing to bring Greece into his domains.

XERXES I / 518 - 465 BC

A relief carving of a Persian king, most likely Xerxes I

More than that, the Athenians and hoplites from the nearby village of **Plataea** defeated the Persians all on their own without aid from Sparta, showcasing that the civic freedoms Athens enjoyed could produce soldiers as hardy and accomplished as the Spartans. All in all, the victory at Marathon showcased the superiority of a system that gave its citizens more freedoms,

social mobility, and opportunities for their professional and spiritual advancement. The voctory at Marothon was held in such high regard that the Greek tragedian Aeschylus, a poet who won Athens' City Dionysia many times and produced some of the best examples of Greek tragedy, wrote nothing about his accomplishments. Instead, he mentioned only that he fought at Marathon (Pomeroy 142-144).

The great king made preparations to raise an even larger army and invade Greece again. But Darius was set back in his efforts to punish Greece by two different events. First, a revolt broke out in Egypt that required his immediate attention.

The second event that kept Darius from invading Greece was, well, his own death. In 486 BC, Darius the Great died of natural causes at the age of sixty-four. Darius' tomb was carved into a cliff, located at modern-day Naqsh-e Rostam, and his son, **Xerxes I** prepared to take the throne from his father. Darius' son, the grandson of Cyrus the Great, would carry on his father's legacy.

Xerxes, whose name means *ruling over heroes*, lived from 518 to 465 BC, and ruled the Persian Empire from 486 until he was assassinated in 465 BC. In addition to being the grandson of the founder of the Persian Empire, Xerxes was also the son of Cyrus' eldest daughter, Atossa. Atossa's influence and

Vocabulary

Xerxes I

Xerxes I was the son of Darius and Atossa and the grandson of Cyrus the Great. He is most famous for mounting a second invasion of Greece, an invasion that was ultimately unsuccessful when Xerxes and his forces were stopped at the battles of Plataea and Salamis. He lived from 518 to 465 BC.

Plataea

Plataea was a small village in Boeotia that earned much glory for itself during the Persian Wars. First, hoplites from Plataea were the only other people to aid Athens at the Battle of Marathon in 490 BC, and Plataea was the site of the final victory over Persia in 479 BC.

authority helped provide Darius with the legitimacy he needed when he became king in 522 BC.

Upon Darius' death, Xerxes moved quickly to consolidate power and stop revolts from breaking out. He put down the rebellion in Egypt first, then moved to crush another rebellion in Babylon, destroying the city's defenses and the all-important statue of Marduk. Those actions prevented Xerxes from ever "clasping the hand of Marduk," a ceremony important for recognizing the king's right to rule the Babylonians.

Now with the rebellions quashed, Xerxes' counselors urged him to make war on the Greeks and punish them for burning Sardis, humiliating the Persians at Marathon, and defying the king's right to rule. Speaking to an assembly of Persian noblemen, Xerxes said thus:

> *I design to yoke the Hellespont with a bridge, and to march an army through Europe against Greece, in order that I may take vengeance on the Athenians for all the things which they have done both to the Persians and to my father.*
>
> *You saw how my father Darius purposed an expedition against these men; but he did not succeed in taking vengeance upon them.*
>
> *On behalf of my father and of Persia, I will not cease until I have conquered Athens and burnt it with fire, for all the wrong done to me and to my father* (Book VII, Chapter 8).

And so, Xerxes raised an army and prepared to crush the Greek city-states, once and for all.

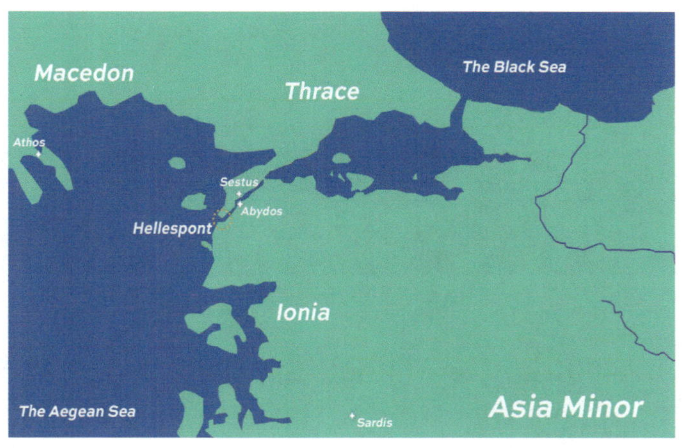

THE HELLESPONT

The cities of Abydos and Sestus lie on opposite side of the straits of the Hellespont, a waterway that separates Europe from Asia.

XERXES WHIPPING THE HELLESPONT

Xerxes' troops punish the Hellespont for its disobedience.

Reading Comprehension Questions

1. According to Militiades, what was at stake for Athens? According to Militiades, what could happen if they fought? If they did not fight, what would most certainly happen?

2. What was at stake at the Battle of Marathon? Why did the Athenians consider this battle to be such an important victory for them?

3. What were Xerxes' reasons for invading Greece?

Primary Source Analysis / Herodotus' *Histories*

Description: Herodotus wrote his *Histories* in and around 430 BC, two decades after the end of the Persian Wars. That would have been enough time for Herodotus to gather his source material and write his narrative, as well as provide some context on these seminal historical events.

The *Histories* is the earliest example of what we would consider historical narrative, so much so that Herodotus has been described as the "father of history". Indeed, Herodotus opens his *Herodotus* stating his purpose in writing is so that "the deeds of men may not be forgotten by lapse of time" and "the works great and marvelous, some of which have been done by the Greeks and others by Barbarians, may never lose their renown.

In this passage, Herodotus described the actions of Xerxes and his army in crossing the Hellespont, the straits that separate Europe from Asia. At first glance, Xerxes' actions may not seem that consequential. The crossing of so large an army is impressive but may not seem worth writing about in the kind of detail that Herodotus provides, but it is the moral that Herodotus draws out from this episode that is so important for historians: take heed, lest you fall. This text comes from Book VII, Chapter 32 of Herodotus' *Histories*, translated by George Macaulay.

Xerxes Crosses the Hellespont

32. Having arrived at Sardis, Xerxes proceeded first to send heralds to Greece, to ask for earth and water. He also gave notice that these cities prepare meals for the king. He did not send heralds sent to Athens or Sparta to ask for earth—only to the other city-states in Greece. The reason why he sent the second time to ask for earth and water was this: those cities had not given earth and water when Darius sent for them. Thus, Xerxes thought they would certainly submit to Persia rule now on account of the might of the Persians: this matter it was about which he desired to have certain knowledge, and he sent accordingly.

33. After this, he made his preparations intending to march to Abydos. First, they built a bridge over the Hellespont stretching Asia to Europe. Now there is in the Chersonese of the Hellespont between the city of Sestos and Madytos, a broad plain running down into the sea right opposite Abydos; this is the place where no long time afterwards the Athenians under the command of Xanthippos the son of Ariphron, having taken Artaÿctes a Persian, who was the governor of Sestos, nailed him alive to a board with hands and feet extended.

34. The Persians began making their bridges starting from Abydos, the Phoenicians weaving with ropes of white flax and the Egyptians ropes made of papyrus rope. Now from Abydos to the opposite shore is a distance of seven furlongs. But when the strait had been bridged over, a great storm came on and dashed together all the work that had been made and broke it up.

Then when Xerxes heard it he was exceedingly enraged. He ordered his troops to scourge and whip the Hellespont with three hundred strokes of the lash. Then, they cast into the sea a pair of fetters. Indeed, I have even heard further Xerxes sent branders also with them to brand the Hellespont. However this may be, he ordered them, as they were beating the waves of the Hellespont, to say such barbarian and presumptuous words as follows:

> *You bitter water, I, Xerxes, your master, lay upon you this penalty. This I do because you have wronged me, yet you have suffered not a wrong from me.*
>
> *I, Xerxes, the king will pass over you whether you want to or not, and see to it no man will ever sacrifice to you, as you are nothing but a foul and treacherous stream!*

The sea he purposed to punish in this way, and then he ordered the execution of the engineers appointed with building the bridge over the Hellespont.

36.Thus then the men did, to whom this ungracious office belonged; and meanwhile other chief-constructors proceeded to make the bridges. And in this way, they made them: They put together fifty-oared galleys and triremes, three hundred and sixty in all, to be under the bridge towards the **Euxine Sea**, and three hundred and fourteen to be under the other, the vessels lying in the direction of the stream of the Hellespont (though crosswise in respect to the Pontus), to support the tension of the ropes. Having done this, they proceeded to make the ropes as tight as they could, winding them with wooden windlasses. They gave to each bridge two white flax ropes and four papyrus ropes to give the bridge added strength.

When the passage was bridged over, they sawed up logs of wood. They cut the logs equal in length to the breadth of the bridge and laid them above the stretched ropes.

They fastened them above the stretched ropes in the same way. When this was done, they piled brushwood on the bridge, and having set the brushwood also in place, they carried on to it earth; and when they had stamped down the earth firmly, they built a barrier along on each side, so that the baggage-animals and horses might not be frightened by looking out over the sea.

37. And so construction of the bridges was finished.

Vocabulary & Annotations

...ask for earth and water
The Persians asked for *earth and water* as signs of submission, indicating that the village or city in question had yielded control of their land to the Persians.

Abydos
Abydos is a city in Asia Minor, close to the Hellespont.

The Athenians
Herodotus relates a story in which the Athenians captured and crucified Artaÿctes, who was the tyrant of the city of Sestos in Ionia.

The Phoenicians
The Phoenicians had been impressed into the Persian army to serve as sailors, as well as in other tasks in which they had more specialized knowledge than did the Persians.

...seven furlongs
A *furlong* is a distance of about 220 yards, so that a distance of *seven furlongs* is 1540 yards, or more than 15 football fields.

Euxine Sea
The Euxine Sea is an alternative name for the Black Sea.

Athos
Athos is a mountain in northern Greece, around which Xerxes built a canal.

38. They also built embankments about the mouths of the channel. That way, the mouths of the channel and the channel itself might not be filled up during high tide. When all this was finished, along with the works at Athos, they spent the winter at Sardis. At the beginning of spring, the army set forth from the city fully equipped and marched to Abydos. Just as the army had set out in march, the Sun left his place in the heaven and was invisible, though there was no gathering of clouds and the sky was perfectly clear.

39. Indeed, instead of day, it suddenly became night. When Xerxes saw and perceived this, it became a matter of concern to him; and he asked his wise men and counselors what the appearance meant.

40. These declared that the god foretold to the Greeks forty of their cities would leave, for the Sun predicted future events for the Greeks, but the Moon for the Persians. Having been thus informed, Xerxes proceeded on the march with very great joy.

Primary Source Questions

1. Xerxes intended to build a bridge connecting Europe to Asia so that his troops may more easily march into Greece. What happens to the first bridge?

Primary Source Questions

2. How did Xerxes respond? Why did he respond this way?

3. How does Xerxes compare with prior kings in the Persian Empire? Would Cyrus the Great have responded in this way?

Primary Source Questions

4. What character traits does Xerxes show in his response to the rough waves of the Hellespont?

5. As a historian, why might Herodotus include this story in his account of the Persian Wars? What might he be communicating to his readers?

The Coming of Persia / 480 BC

XERXES HAD PREPARED THE LARGEST invasion force by land and sea up until that point. But of course, the Athenians had been busy, too. After the Battle of Marathon, the Athenians made slight changes to the Athenian constitution and the way important leaders were chosen. Those who would hold the office of *archon* would be chosen by lot—essentially, at random. In a democratic state like Athens, the people were expected to hold power so, theoretically, any Athenian citizens could hold that office. They still vetted each candidate, but the change meant that a wider number of individuals could hold such an office and participate in government. The change meant that ambitious Athenians sought the office of *strategoi*, or the generals in charge of Athens' *hoplite* troops. This development was all the more important in the event of the looming war with Persia.

THEMISTOCLES / 524 - 459 BC
Athenian strategos *and a kind of "father" for the Athenian navy.*

Secondly, the Athenians began a new practice known as **ostracism**. In the same way a student may feel *ostacized* by a group of friends in the lunch room, the Athenian Assembly would vote to exile, rather than just ignore, people in Athens who could be causing trouble. The Athenian Assembly would conduct such a vote by writing a person's name on a piece of *ostraka*, or broken pottery. If some Athenian politician looked as if he wanted to become a tyrant, the assembly wrote his name on a piece of broken pottery. If that person received enough votes, he was kicked out of Athens for a period of ten years.

More significant, though, was the chance discovery of silver in the mountains of Laurium. The Athenian Assembly had to decide what to do with this huge quantity of silver, which came down to two possibilities. The *strategos* Aristides argued for the money to be shared among Athenian citizens, presumably for buying armor and weapons.

In contrast, **Themistocles** (above), another *strategos*, argued Athens should build a fleet. Both men had served as *strategoi* at Marathon and enjoyed reputations as honorable men, but the debate grew increasingly heated. Themistocles argued the fleet could help Athens defeat the city of Aegina, their great rival, and the Assembly voted in favor of his proposal. Then in 482 BC, the Assembly voted to ostracize—that is, exile—Aristides from the city.

That left Themistocles the most influential and powerful leader in Athens as construction on the fleet began and Xerxes readied his invasion force (Pomeroy 144-145).

Vocabulary

Ostracism
In Athens, the Assembly could vote to *ostracize*, or exile, any citizen who appeared ambitious and had designs on becoming a tyrant. The policy is named for the broken pieces of pottery called *ostraka* upon which a person's name may be written.

Themistocles
A Greek politician and general who led Athens during the Persian Wars. He argued that the proceeds from the silver mines at Laurium be used for constructing a naval fleet. He lived from 524 to 459 BC.

Hellenic League
The Greek city-states that fought against the Persian Empire, with Athens, Corinth, and Sparta being the foremost cities in the League. The league formed in 481 BC.

THE SPARTANS & PERSIA'S ENVOYS

The Hellenic League

As Herodotus recounted in the *Histories*, the Persian king Xerxes sent heralds throughout Greece demanding *earth and water*. These were signs of submission from a city or kingdom, in that they freely yielded their land and seas to Persia. Many city-states in Greece yielded to Xerxes and joined the Persian invasion force.

But not Sparta or Athens: Sparta threw the Persian diplomats into a well, saying they could find the earth and water for themselves at the bottom. The Athenians, meanwhile, cast the envoys into a gorge. Athens, Sparta, Corinth, and other city-states that would not submit to Persia met at Corinth in 481 BC. There, they formed an alliance now called the **Hellenic League**. As part of their pact, they vowed to cooperate with each other, resist Xerxes and the Persian invaders, and follow the military leadership of the Spartans.

The odds seemed stacked against them. Xerxes ruled an empire that stretched from the Libyan Desert in the west to the Hindu Kush Mountains in the east, an empire that now included many Greek city-states who had sided with Persia. Even the Oracle at Delphi, perhaps the most respected institution in ancient Greece, urged the Greeks not to resist Persia.

The priests at Delphi predicted that Sparta would survive only by the death of their king, and the Athenians only if they took cover behind their wooden walls. Neither oracle spoke of good tidings or an easy victory over Xerxes and the thousand nations of the Persian Empire. Undeterred, the Spartans marched to one location in Greece where Persian numbers counted for little: Thermopylae.

A Closer Look at Thermopylae

THERMOPYLAE IS YET ANOTHER high point in a war of high points. At **Thermopylae,** an army of Spartans and Thespians (they came from the *polis* of Thespis) held off an army approximately ten times their size, composed of battle-hardened troops of Persian infantry. For numbers, the Spartans fielded an army upwards of 7,000 troops and the Persians somewhere between at 200,000 to 300,000 troops, including the elite heavy infantry unit known as the Immortals at 10,000. So how did the Spartans do it?

Look over the photos and illustrations on the next page, then write your answer in the space below. In this exercise, you are only responsible for using your *historical imagination*, your ability to put yourself in the minds and predicaments of ancient heroes, long since past, and recreate what they could do. The story of the Battle of Thermopylae in the following pages will explain the strategy and how King Leonidas of Sparta and his *hoplite* army held off for one week the largest and most formidable army the world had seen up until that point.

Closer Look Questions

1. How did an army of 7,000 soldiers manage to hold off an army upwards of 300,000 troops?

GREEK HOPLITE SOLDIERS FIGHTING

HOT SPRINGS AT THERMOPYLAE

The springs smelled so foul the Greeks believed they led to the Underworld.

XERXES' ROUTE THROUGH GREECE

Xerxes marched along the coastline, close to the ships supplying his troops. But did he have to march through Thermopylae?

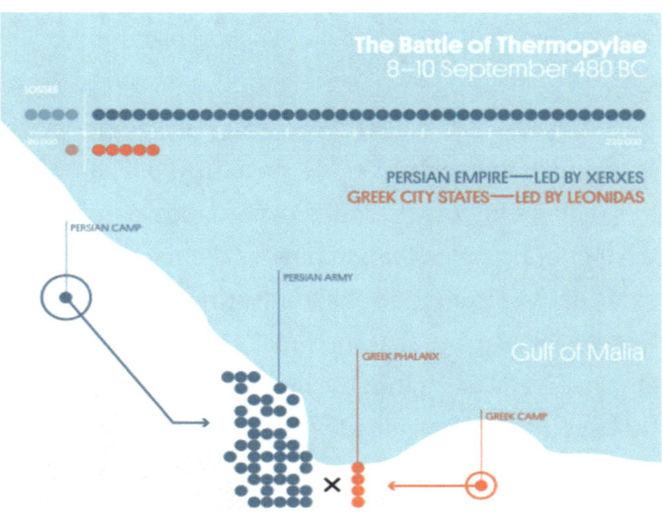

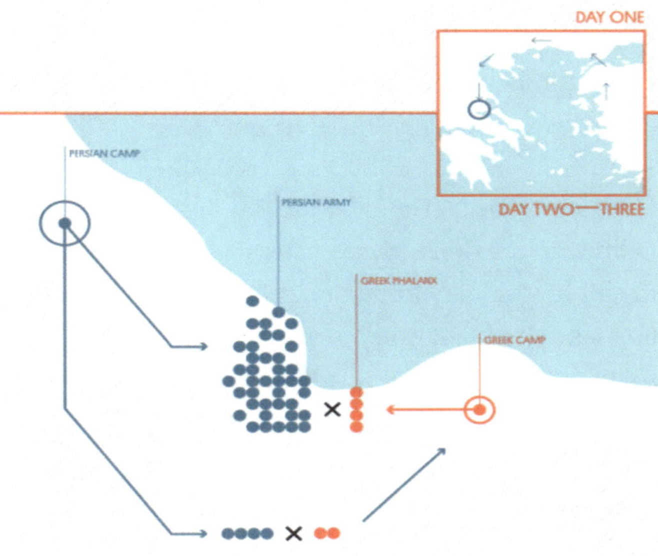

THE PERSIAN AND SPARTAN TROOPS

Notice that the Malian Gulf is on the right side of the Spartans, while moutains are on their left.

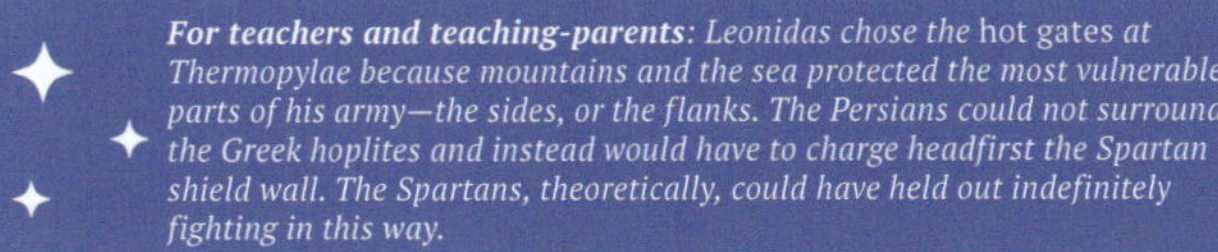

***For teachers and teaching-parents**: Leonidas chose the hot gates at Thermopylae because mountains and the sea protected the most vulnerable parts of his army—the sides, or the flanks. The Persians could not surround the Greek hoplites and instead would have to charge headfirst the Spartan shield wall. The Spartans, theoretically, could have held out indefinitely fighting in this way.*

Thermopylae, Salamis, & Mycale / 480 to 479 BC

THE BATTLE OF THERMOPYLAE, Thermopylae meaning "hot gates" in Greek, is a narrow pass between the Malian Gulf and the Balkans, the modern name for the mountain range that dominates the region. The name derives from the hot sulfur springs in the area that smelled so foul that the Greeks believed that Thermopylae leads down into the underworld of Greek mythology. The Spartan king **Leonidas** led a group of 300 Spartan hoplites and 700 soldiers from the Greek city of Thespis, as well as soldiers from other Greek city-states to make up a force of about 7,000 troops. Leonidas chose Thermopylae because here, the Persians had to march through the narrow passageway at Thermoplyae en route to Attica and the Peloponnese.

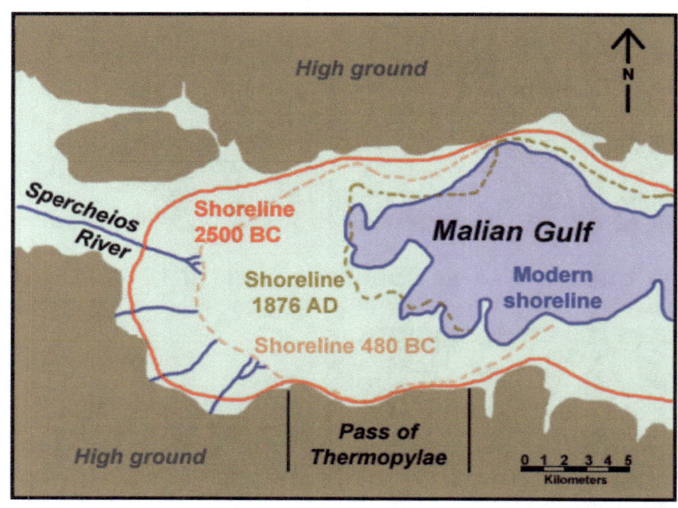

|| MAP OF THERMOPYLAE / CREATIVE COMMONS

More importantly, Thermoplyae was best suited for fighting in the Greek *phalanx*. Recall that the Greeks fought in a military formation called a *phalanx*, which is essentially a tank composed of people. In the *phalanx*, soldiers form a shield wall and hold spears in between the heads of the soldiers in the front row. Each *hoplite* carries a shield with which he covers half of his own body and half of the body of the hoplite to their right. The *phalanx* works excellently when engaging an enemy head-on, and the Persians had to engage the Greeks head-on at the pass at Thermoplyae. But the *phalanx* falls apart when the enemy army attacks it from the sides (called the flank in military terms) or from the rear.

Leonidas' plan was to block the advance of the Persian army long enough for the Athenian naval fleet to destroy the Persian fleet at nearby **Artemisium**. Herodotus estimated the Persian army numbered upwards of 2,000,000 soldiers, but he most likely mistook the population of the entire Persian Empire for that of the Persian army. Instead, the Xerxes possessed an army of 120,000 to 300,000 troops, numbers that included the **Immortals**, a group of heavy infantry. The name Immortals came from the fact that should any member of their unit die in battle, they were immediately replaced by another. The number of the Immortals would always equal 10,000 soldiers, no more, no less.

As Leonidas anticipated, the narrow passageway of Thermoplyae protected the flanks of the *hoplites*. The Persians engaged the Greek hoplites for seven days with three days of intense fighting. Each day, the Persians were beaten back, unable to pass through the "hot gates" of Thermoplyae. The Spartans might have held off indefinitely, but a local resident informed Xerxes of a path around Thermoplyae. That way, Xerxes could attack Leonidas and the Spartans from behind and render the Spartan shield wall useless. Upon learning that the Persians were marching to encircle them, Leonidas dismissed the bulk of the Greek troops back to their home city-states. Then Leonidas and a band of

Vocabulary

Thermopylae
Fought at a narrow passage called Thermopylae in 480 BC, an army of 7,000 Greek troops managed to hold off a Persian army of 120,000 to 300,000 troops.

Leonidas
The king of Sparta, whose most famous accomplishment was leading the band of Spartan hoplites at Thermoplyae. He lived from 540 to 480 BC.

Artemisium
Fought in 480 BC, this battle was a naval battle between the Athenian navy, commanded by Themistocles, and the Persian fleet. A storm destroyed much of the Persian fleet before the battle.

Immortals
The Immortals were a group of elite soldiers in the Persian army, whose name derived from the fact that their numbers always equaled 10,000 soldiers.

Trireme
A Greek warship so-named for the three banks of oars that powered them. They also were equipped with a bronze prow used for ramming enemy ships.

‖ THE PERSIAN WARS / 499 TO 449 BC

300 Spartans, 700 Thespians, and auxiliary troops fought the Persians to the death. The last stand of the hoplites under Leonidas was commemorated by the poet Simonides:

Go tell the Spartans, stranger passing by,
That here, obeying their commands, we lie.

Salamis & Plataea

Once Xerxes found the body of Leonidas, he had the Spartan king decapitated and impaled as a warning against future resistance. Then the Persians marched straight to Athens to destroy the city as their punishment for burning Sardis a decade earlier. The Persians burned the Athenian Acropolis while the Athenians, under the command of Themistocles, watched the destruction from the nearby island of Salamis.

Prior to the Persian invasion, the Delphic Oracle had counseled the Athenians they would survive only by hiding behind their wooden walls. Now, the meaning of the Oracle was made plain: the wooden walls was not an actual wall, but the massive fleet of almost three hundred **triremes** now at the command of the Athenians. Just after Marathon, the Athenians had discovered a rich vein of silver in the Mountains of Laurium and, at the urging of Themistocles, had constructed a naval fleet. That fleet lay anchored in Salamis, ready to engage the Persian fleet. Had Themistocles not won that debate, the Athenians would not have had such a force with which to cripple the Persian invasion.

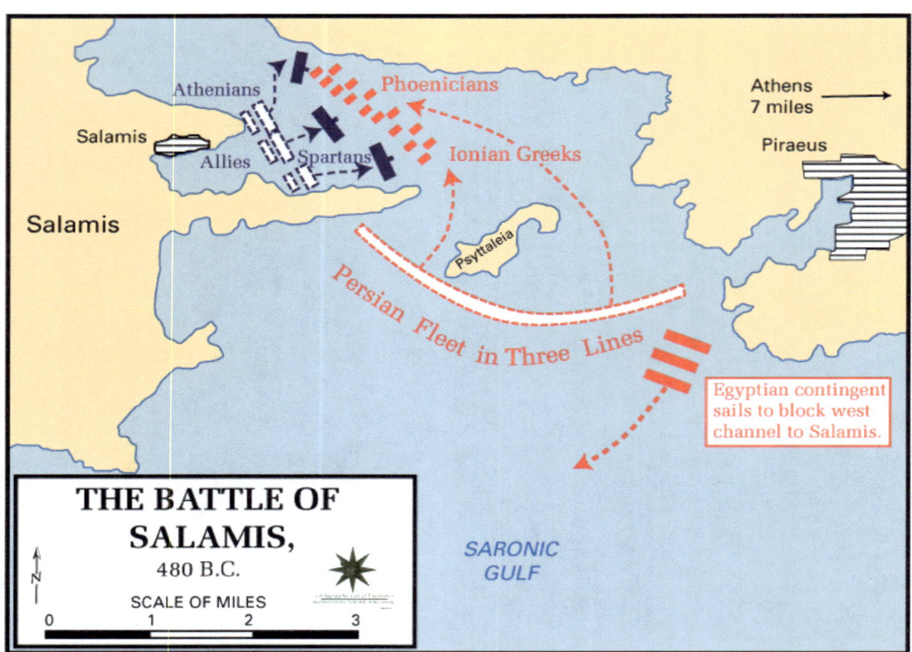

THE BATTLE OF SALAMIS / 480 BC

Notice the narrow waterways in and around the island of Salamis, difficult for even an experienced crew to navigate through.

A trireme is named for its three banks of oars. Each bank or level of oars contained upwards of 30 oars, so that the entire trireme had upwards of 180 men to move the warship forward. Every oarsmen had to row in unison if the ship was to move quickly and conduct complicated turning maneuvers in battle. But the last and most formidable feature on a trireme was its sharp, bronze prow. With that bronze prow, triremes rammed enemy vessels, punctured their hulls with the prow, and sent those ships to the bottom of the sea. This action the Athenians did at the Battle of Salamis in numbers large enough to destroy the Persian Navy.

Xerxes ordered his fleet, manned by Egyptian and Phoenician sailors, to engage the Athenians at Salamis. The Persian ships were too large and cumbersome, and its sailors too untrained, to conduct the intricate turning maneuvers needed to navigate the narrow straits at Salamis. The Athenians were perhaps the best sailors in Greece and had already mastered such maneuvers.

The Athenians rammed and stove in—that is, they sank—one Persian ship after another, many of which were manned by Persian crew members who, growing up in the mountains, could not swim. Once their ships sunk, the sailors drowned, further weakening the Persian navy.

By the end of the battle, the Persians had lost two hundred ships. To make matters worse, Xerxes executed the Phoenician captains for cowardice, further crippling his ability to make war upon the Greeks.

Vocabulary

Battle of Salamis
Fought in 480 BC in the narrow straits between the island of Salamis and mainland Greece, the Athenian navy crippled the Persian fleet.

Mardonius
The Persian general in charge of the invasion of Greece.

Battle of Platae
Fought in 479 BC in Boeotia, a region to the northeast of Athens, a coalition of Spartan, Athenian, Megaran, and Corinthian troops destroyed the whole of the Persian army still left in Greece.

Battlae of Mycale
Fought in 479 BC, the Athenian navy destroyed the remaining ships of the Persian fleet. From this point forward, the Persian Empire can no longer threaten the Greek city-states on the mainland or in Ionia.

THE TRIREME
A Greek warship, so-named for its three banks of oars

After this defeat, Xerxes journeyed north to Thessaly and camped for the winter. When spring arrived and campaigning became possible again, Xerxes sent his general **Mardonius** and the Persian army south into Greece. The final decisive battles came soon after, both of which, according to legend occurred on the same day. First, at the **Battle of Plataea**, hoplites from the Greek cities of Athens, Sparta, Corinth, and Megara faced off against a larger, but not unbeatable, Persian army.

The Greek avoided battle for upwards of eleven days, hoping to keep from being encircled by the Persian cavalry. When battle finally started, the Greeks overwhelmed the Persian center and forced them to retreat. Ultimately, the Greek army trapped a huge number of Persian troops in their camp and cut them down to the last man, destroying almost the entirety of the Persian army.

And across the Aegean Sea, the Athenian navy defeated the last remnants of the Persian fleet at **Mycale**. With the Persian fleet destroyed, the Greeks were at last safe from the threat of Persian invasion. Xerxes returned home to Persia to finish the myriad building projects his father, Darius I, had begun. These buildings included many of the most magnificent and beautiful public buildings at Persepolis, including the Apadana.

For the Greeks, the Persian Wars helped them to forge a powerful sense of national identity and civic pride. Together, the Greeks had stood against the most powerful empire in the world, one that had crushed kingdoms far larger and more powerful than any of the Greek city-states. For Athens and Sparta, their victory helped prove the superiority of their respective systems, as well as the general conviction that a people fighting for freedom and independence could topple foes as fearsome as the Persian Empire.

The Persian Wars had heroes whose leadership inspired not only the Greeks but generations of students who read of their exploits: the last stand at Thermopylae, the sacrifice of King Leonidas, who died seemingly in fulfillment of the Delphic Oracle's prophecy, Themistocles and the *wooden walls* of the Athenian fleet, and upsets at Marathon, Plataea, Salamis, and Mycale.

THE PERSIAN WARS / BATTLES
The Greeks won a series of surprising victories at Marathon, Salamis, and Mycale, and even the loss at Thermoplyae has become one of the most significant battles in world history.

Yet, as we have said, the Persian Wars constitute the high point of Greek culture and civic life, the moment when they banded together to defeat a foe more powerful than anything they had experienced before. But while the Greeks would enjoy some peace following the defeat of Persia, a much larger and more destructive war loomed on the horizon.

And, in this conflict, the Greeks would not be fighting an outside power—instead, they would be fighting themselves.

Reading Comprehension Questions

1. How did the Spartans temporarily hold off a much larger army at the Battle of Thermopylae?

2. How did the Athenians hold off a much larger army at the Battle of Salamis?

3. Why are the Persians so significant for the Greeks but also Western history and culture?

4. Can you hypothesize how would the Greek city-states turn on each other, following the Persian Wars?

ACTIVITY

Direct Instruction Review

The hardest part about history is memorizing all those facts, dates, and events. To make this process easier, we have included this short section called *Direct Instruction Review*. Direct Instruction (or DI) is a powerful pedagogical tool whereby teachers ask students a series of *call-and-response* questions, and students respond back with the aim of learning this material to *mastery*. Teacher's lines are in **bold**; student's lines in *italics*.

Who were the main combatants in the Persian Wars? *The Empire of Persia and the city-states of Greece, led by Athens, Sparta, and Corinth.*

What started the Persian Wars? *The Greek city-states in Ionia, the west coast of Asia Minor, revolted against the Persian Empire and, with help from Athens, burned down the Persian capital at Sardis.*

How did the Persian king, Darius I, respond to the burning of Sardis? *With rage! He invaded mainland Greece, intent on conquering and destroying the city of Athens.*

So what happened to Athens? *They stood up to the Persians and, at the Battle of Marathon, defeated a much larger Persian army in a stunning upset in 490 BC.*

Did Darius keep up his invasion of Greece? *No! Darius died shortly after, and his son, Xerxes, readied a new invasion force.*

And what year did Xerxes invade Greece? *Xerxes began his invasion in 480 BC, crossing the Hellespont and marching through Macedon, Thessaly, and Thrace en route to mainland Greece.*

Did the Greek city-states surrender to Xerxes? *No way! The Spartans, under King Leonidas, met Xerxes at the "hot gates" of Thermopylae.*

What happened at Thermopylae? *Leonidas knew the Persians would have to march through Thermopylae; if he and his* hoplite *soldiers got there first, the mountains and the sea would protect his flanks.*

And then what happened? *The Battle of Thermopylae took place in 480 BC with an army of 7,000 Greek* hoplites *holding off an army upwards of 100,000 to 300,000 troops for almost a week.*

Why is the Battle of Thermopylae significant? *The Greeks under Leonidas fought to the last man, making it one of those heroic last-stand-battles that inspired generations of students and leaders henceforth.*

Did Xerxes go home after the Battle of Thermopylae? *No! Xerxes marched his army south to Attica.*

What did Xerxes do once he arrived in Attica? *He burned the Athenian Acropolis as punishment for their role in destroying Sardis in 490 BC.*

ACTIVITY

Direct Instruction Review (Cont.)

If Athens was destroyed and occupied by the Persians, what had happened to the people living in Athens? *They had already retreated to the island of Salamis, taking cover behind the* wooden walls *of the Athenian navy.*

Wooden walls? What are these wooden walls? *The Delphic Oracle said Athens should take cover behind their wooden walls which Themistocles, an Athenian* strategos, *interpreted as being the Athenian fleet of 300 triremes.*

Having punished Athens, did Xerxes finally go home to Persia? *No! He brought out the Persian navy to crush the Athenians, encamped on the nearby island of Salamis.*

And did he crush them? *Nope! The Athenian navy sunk a large number of Persian ships at the Battle of Salamis in 480 BC.*

Having been defeated once again, did Xerxes finally go home to Persia? *No! He encamped for the winter, then engaged the Greeks once again in the spring of 479 BC.*

And what happened in 479 BC? *Xerxes lost his army at the Battle of Plataea and his navy at the Battle of Mycale and, with his forces destroyed, he returned home to Persia.*

So, why are these wars significant? What happened to Greece during the Persian Wars? *The Greeks developed a strong national identity and civic pride for having defeated the world's most powerful empire.*

Why are these wars significant for us today? *The Persian Wars provide us with stories of great heroism and sacrifice and preserved for us the treasures of Greek literature, culture, and civilization.*

ACTIVITY

Map Practice: The Persian Wars

Instructions: Carefully look over the map below, which are identical to maps provided in the rest of this chapter. However, there is one crucial difference: these maps have blanks in the place of the name of a sea, a region, or a site. Fill in the appropriate blank with the term list provided above each map.

The Persian Wars: Bodies of water such as the Hellespont and the Aegean Sea; the cities of Athens, Sparta, Corinth, and Miletus; and the Battles of Mycale, Thermopylae, Plataea, Salamis, and Marathon.

Want to study this map online? Type in the link below or scan the QR code to access an interactive diagram: **https://bit.ly/3okSogF**

ACTIVITY

Timeline Practice / The Persian Wars

The hardest part about history is memorizing all those facts, dates, and events. To make this process easier, check out the timeline below—well, technically, there are *two* timelines. Some entries are missing dates, and others are missing the event that occurred on that date. With the information available from both timelines, fill in the missing blanks to get a better sense of the timeline for this chapter.

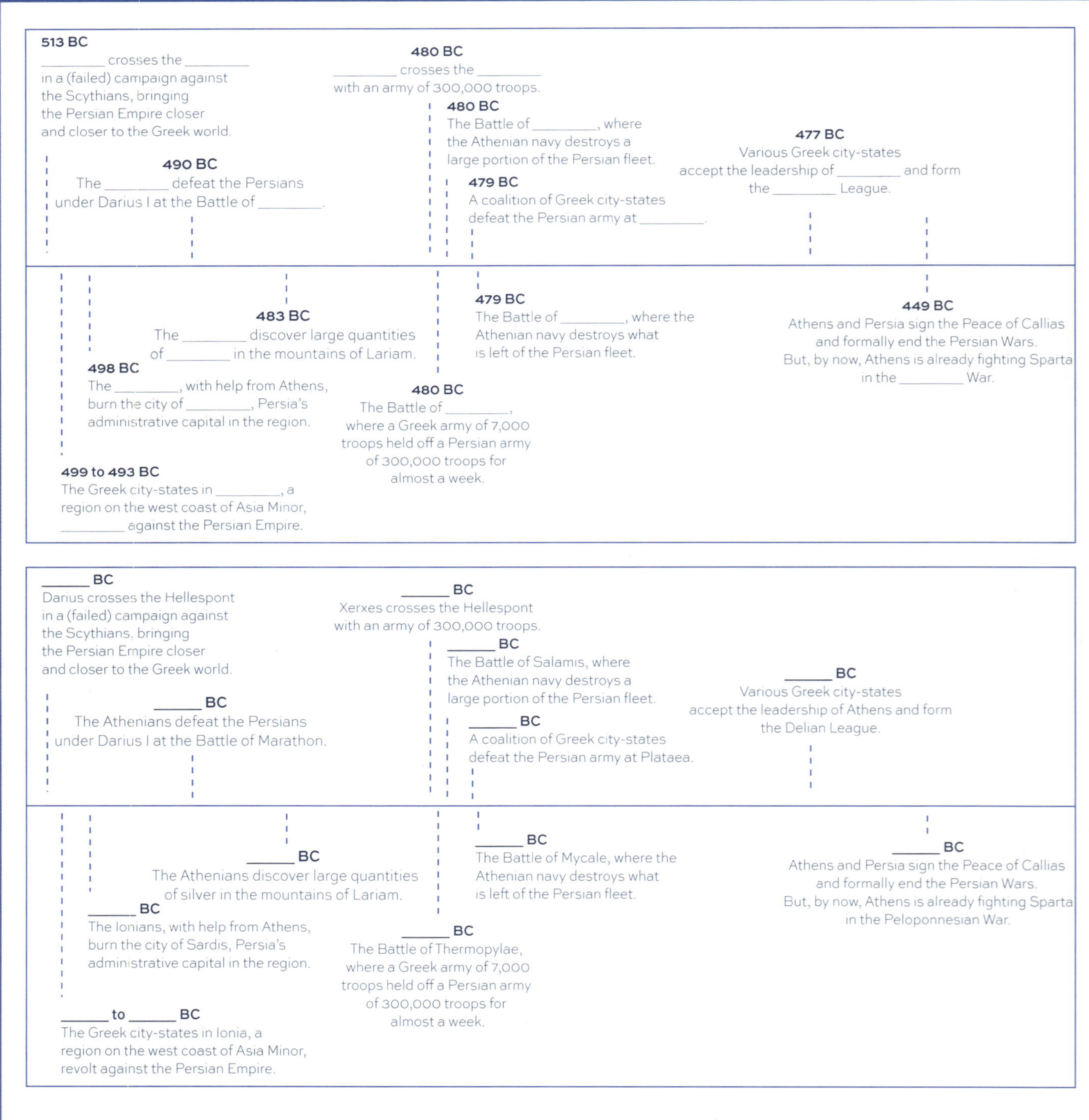

WRITING

Writing Prompt

Writing is thinking, so we will spend considerable time this year writing and thinking about history. In the space provided, write a short essay answering the question: *Why were the Persian Wars so significant to the Greeks and to Western culture in general? What kind of values and lessons can we draw from the wars of the Greeks against the Persian Empire?*

THE ACROPOLIS / ATHENS

Photo by Sergio García

Classical Greece

ROADMAP

- Examine the opening chapter from Thucydides' *History of the Peloponnesian War* and learn how a historian carefully and systematically examines sources, weighs pieces of evidence, and tries to find as accurate an explanation as possible for the events that happened.
- Learn about the age of Classical Greece, a golden age of Greek history and culture and the incredible contributions the Greeks made to drama, philosophy, and architecture.
- Take a closer look at Greek architecture and the three orders of Classical Greek temples.
- Learn about the outbreak of the Peloponnesian War and why war came down upon Athens, Sparta, and the leading city-states of Greece.
- Read selections from Plato's dialogue the *Phaedrus*, as well as excerpts from Thucydides.
- Practice our knowledge of maps and chronology, as well as our writing skills through reading comprehension questions and an essay.

THALES OUTCOME

Nº 4

A Truth Seeker *critiques a variety of truth statements and/or observations through research and scientific methodology.*

In this chapter, we turn to the Peloponnesian War that lasted from 431 to 404 BC and was fought between Athens and Sparta and their respective allies. We know much about this war thanks to Thucydides, an Athenian general who wrote an influential work of history on the war. As a historian, Thucydides is an excellent example of what it means to be a **Truth Seeker**: he sought out the causes of why the war happened, carefully evaluated his sources and in this way, wrote a book that would be a "possession for all time".

Opening Question

1. How do you think a historian should go about checking their sources when writing their work of history?

The Science of History / Thucydides' *History of the Peloponnesian War*

Description: The Greek historian **Thucydides** lived from 460 to 400 BC. We have looked at various samples from the historian Herodotus, who is credited as the *Father of History*. We look to Thucydides, though, as the father of *scientific history*, because Thucydides was far more careful in citing sources and more exact in determining the causes and motivations behind the actions he described in his history book, which covers a devastating war between Athens and Sparta.

In the opening to *The History of the Peloponnesian War*, Thucydides includes this description of the Peloponnesian War, his methodology in writing it, and what separated it from other conflicts.

Book I, Chapter 1

01 Thucydides, an Athenian, wrote the history of the war **between the Spartans and the Athenians**, beginning at the moment that it broke out, and believing that it would be a great war and more worthy of relation than any other war that had preceded it. This belief was not without its grounds. The preparations of both the Spartans and the Athenians were, in every regard, staggering, having developed such resources to prolong the war indefinitely. Moreover, the whole of the Hellenic race took sides in the quarrel; those who delayed doing so long-contemplated what side to join. Indeed this was the greatest movement yet known in history, not only of the Greeks as a whole, but of a large part of the barbarian world—I had almost said of mankind. For though the events of remote antiquity, and even those that more immediately came before the war, cannot be clearly ascertained due to the long time between the time of writing and the time of the events. Yet, the evidences which an inquiry carried as far back as was possible leads me to trust, all point to the conclusion that there was nothing on a great scale, either in war or in other matters.

02 In regards to the history of the Greeks, I grant that readers will find it difficult to believe every particular detail. The way that most men deal with traditions, even traditions of their own country, is to receive them

Vocabulary & Annotations

...between the Spartans and the Athenians
Thucydides refers to the Peloponnesian War, which lasted from 431 to 404 BC and was fought between Athens and Sparta and their respective allies.

...any critical test
Thucydides refers to the human tendency to believe something without really testing that idea to see if it corresponds to reality.

...the Lacedaemonian kings
The Lacedaemonian kings refer to the two kings who ruled over Sparta. Thucydides cites this as an example of the kind of statements people take at face value.

...turning from these
Thucydides separates the task of writing a historical account from that of composing an epic poem, like that of the Homeric epics. This passage criticizes the approach of Herodotus, the "prior historian" who wrote a thrilling narrative in *The Histories* but was not as thorough in its attention to detail.

...reference to the speeches
Thucydides explains his method in recreating the speeches in the work.

all alike as they are delivered, without applying **any critical test whatever**. Such are the many unfounded ideas current among the rest of the Hellenes, even on matters of contemporary events, which have not been made more difficult to understand by time. For instance, there is the notion that **the Lacedaemonian kings have two votes each**, even though they have only one.

03 So little pains do common people take in the investigation of truth. Instead, they immediately accept the first believable story that comes to hand. On the whole, however, the conclusions I have drawn from the proofs and evidence I have quoted, I believe, is sound and may be trusted. On the other hand, the songs of a poet displaying his skill but exaggerating human events, or the compositions of prior historians who are attractive at the expense of the truth, would not disturb many readers.

04 The subjects they treat are often beyond the reach of evidence, and time has robbed most of them of historical value by enthroning them in the region of legend. **Turning from these**, we can rest, satisfied that we have proceeded upon the clearest data. Indeed, we have arrived at conclusions as exact and thorough as we can expect in matters of such antiquity. And now to this war, for despite the known tendency of the combatants in a struggle to overrate its importance, and when it is over to return to their admiration of earlier events, yet an examination of the facts will show that it was much greater than the wars which preceded it.

05 With **reference to the speeches** in this history, some were delivered before the war began, others while it was going on. I heard some speeches myself, whereas others I got from various quarters. It was in all cases difficult to carry them word for word in one's memory, so my habit has been to make the speakers say what was in my opinion demanded of them by the various occasions. Of course, I stuck as closely as possible to the general sense of what they really said. And with reference to the narrative of events, I did not allow myself to write such events down from the first source that came to hand. Nor did I did trust even my own impressions. Instead, my account rests partly on what I saw myself and partly on what others saw for me, the accuracy of the report being always tried by the most severe and detailed tests possible.

06 My conclusions have cost me some labor from the lack of coincidence between accounts of the same occurrences by different eye-witnesses. At times, their accounts differ on account of imperfect memory, other times from undue partiality for one side or the other. The **absence of romance** in my his-

tory will, I fear, detract somewhat from its interest. But if my work be judged useful by those inquirers **who desire an exact knowledge** of the past as an aid to the interpretation of the future, which in the course of human things must resemble such things even if it does not reflect it, I shall be content. In fine, I have written my work, not as an essay which is to win the applause of the moment, but as a possession for all time.

07 The Persian Wars, the greatest achievement of past times, yet found a speedy decision in two actions by sea and two by land. The Peloponnesian War was prolonged to an immense length, and, long as it was, it was short without parallel for the misfortunes that it brought upon Greece. Never had so many cities been taken and destroyed, here by the barbarians, here by the parties contending (the old inhabitants being sometimes removed to make room for others).

08 Never was there so much banishing and blood-shedding whether on the field of battle or in the strife of faction. Old stories of occurrences handed down by tradition, but rarely, if ever, confirmed by experience, suddenly ceased to be incredible. There were earthquakes of unparalleled extent and violence; eclipses of the sun occurred with a frequency unrecorded in previous history; there were great droughts in various places and consequent famines. And there was that most terrible and horrifically fatal visitation, **the plague**.

09 All this came upon them with the late war, which was begun by the Athenians and the Spartans by **the dissolution of the thirty years' truce** made after the conquest of Euboea. To the question why they broke the treaty, I answer by placing first an account of their grounds of complaint and points of difference, that no one may ever have to ask the immediate cause which plunged the Hellenes into a war of such magnitude.

10 The real cause I consider to be the one which was formally most kept out of sight. The growth of the power of Athens, and **the alarm** which this inspired in Sparta, made war inevitable. Still it is well to give the grounds alleged by either side which led to the dissolution of the treaty and the breaking out of the war...

A·Z

Vocabulary & Annotations

...absence of romance
The word *romance* is used more in reference to an adventure story, told in the style of the Romans, than of a modern "romantic" novel about love and relationships.

...who desire an exact knowledge of the past
Thucydides' words are often cited as the point of writing and studying history.

...the plague
Thucydides refers a plague that struck Athens circa 430 BC, which Thucydides himself contracted.

...the dissolution of the thirty years' truce
In 446-445 BC, Sparta and Athens signed a peace treaty ending what was called the First Peloponnesian War. That war lasted from 460 to 446 BC and is not the subject of Thucydides' *History* apart from providing context. The word *dissolution* means "dissolving" or "breaking", so that the treaty that made peace between Athens and Sparta was no longer in effect.

...the alarm
That is, Athens had grown so powerful they challenged Spartan leadership and influence over the rest of Greece.

Reading Comprehension Questions

1. Why did Thucydides want to write a history of the Peloponnesian War?

2. When presented with a story or an account of event, what do most people do with that information? According to Thucydides, do they test that information?

3. What did Thucydides do with any information he was given in writing his *History*?

Reading Comprehension Questions

4. How did Thucydides recreate the speeches in his work?

5. Why did the Peloponnesian War last for so long?

6. Why did the Peloponnesian War start?

ACTIVITY

The Greek World . . . In Two

Instructions: As previously mentioned, the Peloponnesian War is something of a civil war between the various city-states in Greece. Look at the map below and answer the following questions in regards to that map. Which sides, Athens or Sparta, controls which territory, and why?

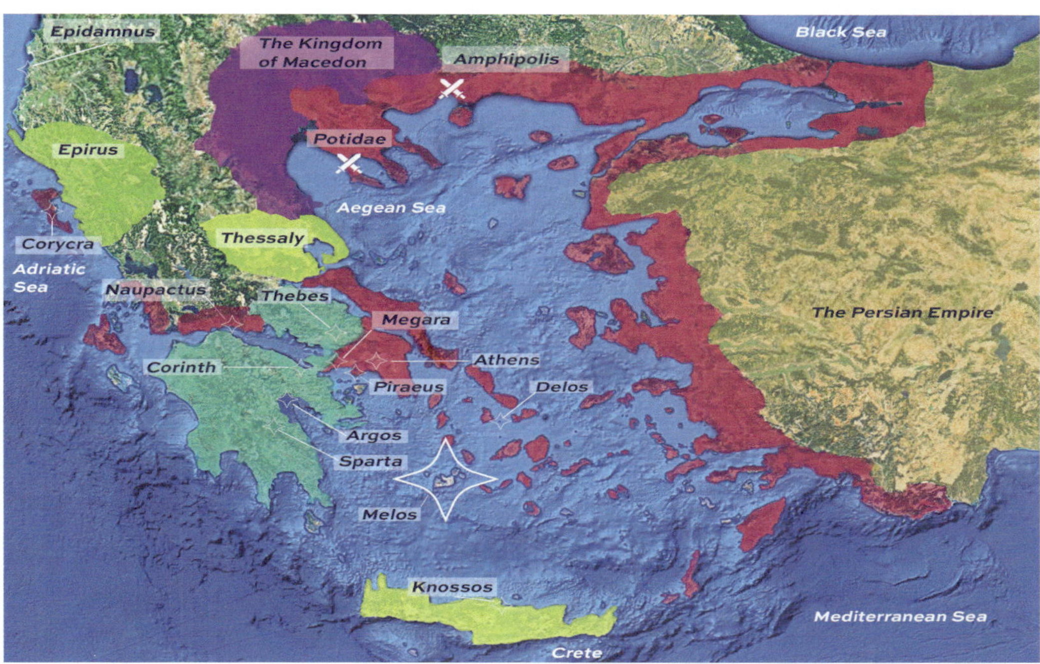

1. What "color" is Sparta and her allies? Explain your reasoning.

2. What "color" is Athens and her allies? Explain your reasoning.

Athens & Classical Greece / ~479 to 323 BC

Following the Persian Wars is the age of **Classical Greece**. The period of Classical Greece lasts from the end of fighting in the Persian Wars circa 479 BC to the death of Alexander the Great in 323 BC. This time period included the horrible and destructive Peloponnesian War but was also a time of dazzlingly creativity, producing great works in philosophy and history, drama and poetry, art and architecture. This period also produced philosophers like Socrates, Plato, and Aristotle, historians like Herodotus and his successors, Thucydides (460 to 400 BC) and Xenophon (430 to 354 BC). Accordingly, historians use the word **golden age** to refer to Classical Greece.

The term golden age refers to a time in which a people or a city produced so many cultural treasures that their accomplishments inspire generations to follow their example. Such was the time of Classical Greece with works as monumental and influential as the Parthenon, Sophocles' plays, Plato's dialogues, and everything in between. At times, this period is also called the **Age of Pericles**, named for the Athenian politician Pericles who, as Athens' leading citizen, was responsible for many achievements during this time.

Indeed, the Persian Wars and the age of Classical Greece are a high point for the Greeks. However, this high point was followed by a period that was notably worse. Events went downhill faster than any Greek *strategos*, sage, or statesmen could handle. In Classical Greece, despite the great cultural achievements of the age, the Greek city-states began fighting with each other almost as soon as the threat to their respective freedom disappeared. Athens and Sparta united together in the face of a common foe like Persia, but they turned on each other in a war that decimated Greek culture and civilization: the **Peloponnesian War**.

The Peloponnesian War lasted from 431 to 404 BC and was fought between Athens and Sparta. The Peloponnesian War so weakened the Greek city-states they were easy prey for other ambitious kingdoms such as Macedon to the north and Rome to the west. As the war dragged on, Macedon, a region to the north of Greece and populated by tribes distantly related to the Greeks, accomplished what no Persian king could do: conquer the Greek city-states. Later, when Rome conquered Macedon, they absorbed the Greek city-states into their growing empire. But before these later conquests occurred, the Greek city-states had already become their own worst enemies.

Lasting from the Persian Wars to the death of Alexander the Great, Classical Greece was wealthy and prosperous, producing many beautiful works of literature and art. Yet at the same time, the Greek city-states grew jealous of each other and came to blows in the Peloponnesian War, demonstrating that both suffering and prosperity may do much to tear a civilization apart.

Vocabulary

Classical Greece
Lasting from 479 to 323 BC, the age of Classical Greece produced philosophers such as Socrates, Plato, and Aristotle, playwrights like Sophocles and Aeschylus, and monumental architecture like the Parthenon.

Golden Age
A period of great cultural and artistic achievements and great material and economic prosperity.

Age of Pericles
At times, the world of Classical Greece is called the Age of Pericles because this influential Athenian statesman was responsible for so many of Athens' great accomplishments and institutions.

The Peloponnesian War
The Peloponnesian War lasted from 431 to 404 BC and was fought between Athens and Sparta and their respective allies.

City Dionysia
Areligious festival held each year in Athens to honor the god Dionysus. Since Dionysus was the god of comedy, revelry, and the theater, the City Dionysia featured Greek playwrights' newest works.

Dionysus
The Greek god of wine, revelry, and the theater.

THE THEATRE OF DIONYSUS / ATHENS

Before we examine how and why the city-states of Greece made war upon each other, let's look at their accomplishments in drama, architecture, and philosophy.

Greek Theater and the City Dionysia

The movies, television shows, and plays we watch all have their origins in ancient Greece. Terms commonly associated with theatre are rooted in the rocky soil of Greece: the word *theater* comes from the Greek word "theatron", meaning "a seeing place," and our word *thespian*, meaning "a talented actor," comes from the Greek figure Thespis. Thespis is said to have written the first tragic play and invented Greek drama.

These plays have their roots in the worship of the Greek god Dionysus. Each year, the city of Athens held a festival called the **City Dionysia** in honor of **Dionysus**, the god of theater, comedy, and tragedy, as well as wine and partying. Athens performed them in a theatre cut into the hillside of the Acropolis overlooking the city.

The theatre thus provided a beautiful backdrop for the plays being performed such as a valley or the sea. People from all over the region came to Athens to watch these plays, so that Athens and the City Dionysia helped to unify Attica with Athens as a kind of cultural capital similar to the influence that New York City and Broadway has on the country today. Later, other Greek cities throughout the Mediterranean built theaters of their own. Indeed, some of the most beautiful theaters are not in Greece but in North Africa, Sicily and southern Italy, and Turkey.

THE THEATRE AT TAORMINA / SICILY

Athens exported its culture aboard to places like southern Italy, the coast of North Africa, and here in Sicily, an island in the very center of the Mediterranean.

The City Dionysia featured two types of plays: comedies and tragedies. A comedy begins in misfortune but ends in happiness (and are generally funny), whereas a tragedy begins in happiness but ends in misfortune. Plays were chosen by lot and performed all in the course of one day with a winner chosen at the end of the day's festivities.

Figures like Aeschylus, whom we have mentioned as one of the soldiers at Marathon, and Sophocles are often cited as having won the City Dionysia in one year or another. The actors wore masks, and special effects were exceedingly limited. As such, the plays had to be relatively simple and straightforward for the audience to understand them.

The Greek philosopher **Aristotle** (384 to 322 BC) wrote that the plot of a play should not change scenes or take place within a time frame longer than an hour. That way, the audience had little chance of being confused by the actions taking place on stage. And the playwrights could display greater skill by working within such rules.

These plays served several important purposes for Athenians. First, Athens lacked the deep, mythological traditions of their neighbor Sparta to the south or Thebes, the dominant city in nearby Boeotia. Athens had great heroes, but Thebes and Sparta had a lot more of them. For instance, Sparta sent many warriors of great renown to the Trojan War, whereas Athens is barely referenced in either of Homer's great epics. These plays included figures famous in Greek mythology but were also connected to Athens or explained

Vocabulary

Aristotle

A Greek philosopher whose works entitled *Politics, Poetics, Physics, Metaphysics,* and *Rhetoric* form the basis for much of the Western canon. He lived from 384 to 322 BC.

the origins of some institution in Athens. In this way, Greek tragedies tried to explain Athens' place in the Greek world and connect Athenian institutions to deeper traditions in Greek mythology.

More importantly, these Greek playwrights retold and updated these myths to suit an audience of everyday Athenian theatergoers. They knew the stories, the characters, and the struggles before the play even began. What mattered more was the moral lesson that the playwright drew from the lives of Greek heroes like Oedipus, Agamemnon, or Orestes.

The plays also provided an important moral lesson for the audience. For example, the Greek playwright Aeschylus (525 to 455 BC) wrote a series of plays about the death of Agamemnon, the king of Mycenae. Agamemnon was the leader of the Greeks fighting in the Trojan War who displayed unbelievable ruthlessness to achieve his ambition. As part of the punishment for his hubris, his own wife Clytemnestra murdered him upon his return home from Troy. Plays like these would have shocked and frightened the Athenians in attendance, reminding them the gods punish wrongdoers one way or another. Of course, the audience may miss such lessons, if they grew rowdy enough. It ws not uncommon for viewers to throw fruit or pistachio shells at actors if they were unhappy with a performance!

These plays continued into the years of the Peloponnesian War. Indeed, one of the most famous plays from Greek tragedy—Sophocles' *Oedipus Rex*—was performed following the outbreak of a terrible plague in Athens. The events of *Oedipus Rex*, which itself opens with a plague, must have seemed eerily similar to the circumstances in which the Athenians found themselves.

Reading Comprehension Questions

1. How long did the age of Classical Greece last? What do you think were the two most important features of Classical Greece?

Reading Comprehension Questions

2. People speak of Classical Greece as a "golden age". How was it a "golden age"?

3. What was the City Dionysia? What kinds of activities happened during this event?

4. How did the City Dionysia bring the people of Attica, the region of which Athens was the principal city, together? What was the purpose of these plays?

Architecture & Philosophy / Classical Greece

The Age of Classical Greece is also famous for its monumental architecture. The two most prominent examples are the **Parthenon** in Athens and the **Temple to Zeus at Olympia** at the foot of Mount Olympus. Both temples were built with the immense wealth from into Athens following the conclusion of the Persian Wars. The city-state grew rich from looting the Persian camps after the war, trade throughout the Aegean world, and the money sent in by states from the Delian League for building ships, money which, as those states complained, was used to beautiful Athens and *not* always for their defense.

The Athenians built the Parthenon on top of the Acropolis, the towering, rocky outcrop in the middle of the city. Normally, a city's acropolis contained a citadel used to defend the city during a siege, but during the Classical age, the Athenians repurposed their Acropolis. Since the Persians had destroyed their Acropolis in 480 BC, the Athenians decided to build a magnificent temple on the site dedicated to the goddess Athena, the patron deity of the city. Indeed, the word Parthenon means "maiden" in Greek and refers to Athena herself. The Parthenon is a temple built in the **Doric order**, named for the Doric columns suporingt the temple's massive roof.

Unlike today's churches, a temple was not built to accommodate a large number of people. Instead, temples were built more like houses for the god or goddess who lived there, tended to by a small number of priests. The **idol**, a statue made of wood, stone, or in the case of many Classical Greek idols, ivory and gold, "lived" in a central chamber surrounded by columns. Only the priests could come near the idol of the god or goddess which resided in the center of the temple.

VARVAKEION ATHENA / 2ND C. BC
The original statue was destroyed, but this Roman copy from the second century is said to be the most faithful and accurate representation of the original statue.

The Greek world's grandest temples contained statues almost as tall as the temple itself, and the Parthenon contained such a statue dedicated to the goddess Athena. Built by the sculptor **Phidias**, the statue of Athena Parthenos was almost thirty feet high and covered in ivory and gold. Moreover, the statue "lived" in the center of the Parthenon, where the rays of the rising sun would strike the idol and make it appear beautiful and radiant. The Parthenon featured other decorations such as its elegant friezes—carvings with scenes from Greek mythology running just below the roof of the temple.

THE TEMPLE TO ZEUS AT OLYMPIA / MOUNT OLYMPUS

The temple boasted one of the seven wonders of the ancient world: a 41-foot statue of Zeus.

Construction on the temple began in 447 and was completed in 432 BC, only a few years after the Peloponnesian War had begun.

We often speak of works from the ancient world withstanding the test of time. The Temple to Zeus at Olympia is not one of those works, for this massive temple survives today only in ruins. The temple was most famous for its statue of Zeus, sitting on his throne. The Greek sculptor Phidias built statue of Zeus by first constructing a wooden frame, then overlaying the frame with gold and ivory. The statue was originally over forty feet in height, but it has not survived to the present day. The statue was an architectural marvel, included amongst the **Seven Wonders of the Ancient World**, a list that includes the Lighthouse at Alexandria, the Great Pyramid at Giza, and other examples of monumental architecture.

The Temple to Zeus helped bring the Greeks together. The temple would have been the site of religious festivals and sacrifices conducted prior to the Olympic Games, held every four years at Mount Olympus. The Parthenon, in contrast, was not such a structure. Construction on the Parthenon was ordered by the Athenian statesman **Pericles**, who lived from 495 to 429 BC and was the most influential politician at the onset of the Peloponnesian War.

In the years following the Persian Wars, the Greek city-states gave money to Athens to help outfit a navy that could protect them all from another Persian invasion. Pericles, the unofficial ruler of Athens, used that money not only to build ships but also to build the Parthenon and other projects. These projects beautified Athens at their allies' expense. Such actions helped divide the Greek city-states and encouraged them to turn on each other as the goodwill of the Persian Wars waned and rivalry between the city-states drove them to make war upon each other.

Vocabulary

Parthenon
A temple built on the Athenian Acropolis and dedicated to the goddess Athena. Construction began in 447 and was completed in 432 BC.

The Temple to Zeus at Olympia
A Doric temple built near Mount Olympus.

Idol
A statue made of wood, stone, or in the case of many ancient Greek idols, ivory and gold. In the ancient world, these objects were worshiped by people who believed they represented the god or goddess it imaged. Only Jews and Christians did not engage in this practice.

Phidias
A Greek sculptor and architect who built the massive statue of Zeus at Olympia and the statue of Athena in the Parthenon. He lived from 480 to 430 BC.

Seven Wonders of the Ancient World
The Seven Wonders of the Ancient Wonder are ancient architectural masterpieces.

Doric Order
One of the three architectural orders of Greek temples, marked by a simple but commanding style, and is named for the Dorians, the people of the Peloponnesus known for their stern, reserved character.

Greek Philosophy: Socrates and Plato

We celebrate the age of Classical Greece because of what the age contributed to our modern world: democratic institutions, great works of tragedy and comedy, and the development of a literary tradition we call philosophy. The word **philosophy** means literally "the love of wisdom", and the study of philosophy focuses on the kinds of questions that provide meaning and value to life. These questions focus on how human beings should live, the fundamental nature of reality, and the nature of **virtue**, a word that refers to the habits of moral excellence that individuals should try to develop for themselves. Philosophy focuses on how people should treat their fellow man, how we should view the world in which we live, and the ends for which we should live our lives. The sheer act of meditating on these questions can add joy to life not found in other pursuits.

Of course, the Greeks did not necessarily invent the idea of philosophy. To think about how we should live, and to write down the answers to such questions, is not unique to the Greeks. The ancient Sumerians and Egyptians had their philosophy and wisdom literature, and the Hebrew Bible contained books like the Proverbs of Solomon and the treatise of Ecclesiastes that explored these same questions. The Greeks are not the first people to deal with these questions, but they often get the most credit because Greek philosophy directs almost all of its attention to the **good life**, a life spent in contemplation of ideas like justice, virtue, and beauty. Moreover, Athenian philosophers wrote so many books that Western philosophy has often been described as a series of footnotes to figures like Plato and Socrates. These figures are just a few of the Western canon's most famous writers coming from ancient Athens.

The study of philosophy as we previously described here began in Athens for several reasons. First of all, Athens was a wealthy, vibrant city, and that wealth helped create the leisure time needed to think about philosophical questions. Athens had a large population of slaves, many of which had been captured in the Persian Wars. This large class of slaves also helped create the leisure time needed to produce works of art, literature, and philosophy. Athens had grown wealthy through trade, and it is trade that helps cities find the newest and best ideas and put them into practice. The hardships caused by the Peloponnesian War forced many Greeks to reconsider many of their most basic assumptions about the world, since these assumptions helped, in part, to bring on this devastating war.

SOCRATES / 470 - 399 BC

1st c. AD Bust (Louvre)

But the most important reason why philosophy started in Athens began with **Socrates**, who lived from approximately 470/469 to 399 BC. Socrates initially worked as a stonecutter, and like his fellow Athenians he fought in the Peloponnesian War. After the war, one of Socrates' friends went to the Oracle of Delphi to inquire who was the wisest man in Athens, and the oracle pronounced Socrates to be the wisest. Socrates, naturally, thought the oracle had made a mistake since Socrates claimed he knew nothing. To test the oracle, Socrates went about the city of Athens interviewing people whom he thought were wiser than himself.

He asked them questions about the purpose of life, the emptiness of riches and power, and the pursuit of the

PLATO (428-348 BC) / ARISTOTLE (384-322 BC)
Plato was the student of Socrates, and Aristotle was the student of Plato.

good life. Eventually, Socrates realized that these individuals were merely arrogant, unconcerned with living a life marked by goodness or virtue. The Delphic oracle pronounced Socrates to be the wisest man in Athens because only Socrates recognized how little he actually knew. Socrates interviewed many of the leading men in Athens in his pursuit of wisdom. He asked them questions that made them re-evaluate the things for which they were living, and he sometimes challenged people on their preconceived, unexamined assumptions about the world.

But in so doing, Socrates actually made many enemies. Socrates embarassed many of Athens leading citizens that a group of them brought charges of "impiety" and of "corrupting the youth of Athens" against Socrates, hoping to shut him up. They even managed to have Socrates condemned to death, ultimately forcing Socrates to drink poisonous hemlock as the penalty for seeking after the good life.

Socrates' life and death profoundly affected his followers, all of whom were deeply saddened at the unjust execution of their teacher. Chief among his followers was **Plato**, who was born into a wealthy, well-connected Athenian family during the Peloponnesian War.

Like Socrates, the Peloponnesian War forced Plato to re-evaluate everything he thought they knew about the world. Plato eventually wrote over forty dialogues, literary works featuring extended conversations between Socrates and one or two other individuals about the nature of truth and goodness, beauty and morality, human flourishing and the ends for which individuals should live their lives.

Many of these dialogues focus on the nature of justice and morality since such questions arose from the Peloponnesian War's brutal realities and the relentless fighting that took place year after year.

Vocabulary

Philosophy
Literally, the "love of wisdom," philosophy is the academic subject that treats certain overarching questions of the human condition.

Virtue
From the Latin *vir* for "manliness", the word "virtue" refers to a series of habits of moral excellence individuals should strive to develop for themselves.

Socrates
A Greek philosopher and *gadfly of Athens* whose incessant questioning about the nature of the good life led to his execution in 399 BC.

Good Life
A life spent in contemplation of ideas like justice, virtue, and beauty.

Plato
An Athenian philosopher whose writings serve as the basis for much of Western philosophy. He wrote dialogues that explored the fundamental nature of reality, morality, and the value of believing in ideas like truth, goodness, and beauty.

Reading Comprehension Questions

1. What did Greek architecture look like during Classical Greece?

2. Why did philosophy, as we know it, begin in ancient Athens and not elsewhere?

3. Who was Plato? Who was Socrates? How did Socrates get "started" as a philosopher?

A Closer Look at Greek Architecture

IMAGINE WALKING THROUGH Greece today and seeing the ruins of these once grand temples. Structures such as the Parthenon, the Temple to Zeus at Olympia, the Temple to Artemis at Ephesus, and other examples of monumental architecture once dominated the skylines of ancient Greece, but these magnificent buildings have not withstood the test of time. Some of these structures may once have ranked amongst the Seven Wonders of the World, such as the Temple to Artemis and the Temple to Zeus, but today they are little more than stones scattered and half-exposed in an archaeological park.

Greek temples employed a simple, grand system called **post and lintel**. In such a system, a horizontal element—the lintel—is placed on top of a vertical element —the post—with gaps large enough for windows or doors. The result is a kind of square that extends along the length of the building that may be as simple as the buildings at Stonehenge, a Neolithic example of post and lintel building. When such a system is combined with soaring columns and elaborate decorations, the result is the beautiful temples we have seen thus far in ancient Greece. Most temples in Athens were built of marble excavated from Mount Pentelikon just north of Athens and thus called **Pentelic marble**.

In Classical Greece, architects placed great attention to the columns used in the temple, which are called by the name **orders**. There are three principal orders in Greek architecture: Doric, Ionic, and Corinthian, with the names derived from regions in which these styles originated or became popular. The very top of the

STONEHENGE / POST & LINTEL CONSTRUCTION

column was called the **capital**, and each kind of capital assigned to a specific order. Above and below the capital were other architectural features meant to beautify the temple and show off the skill of the architects and craftsmen building this monumental structure. In all, these temples demonstrated the Greek values of order and beauty, for these temples commanded the attention of viewers and brought them to marvel at a temple's size, balanced proportions, and symmetrical designs. See the diagram below for the architectural terms, where they appear on a term, and a definition of their role in supporting or beautifying the temple itself.

Let's take a closer look at Greek architecture now and learn the defining features of each order of architecture.

The Doric Order

The Dorians believed they had descended from Heracles himself, who himself was the son of Zeus and one of the greatest heroes in Greek mythology. Greek historians like Thucydides wrote that the Dorians invaded the Peloponnesse sometime after the collapse of Mycenae, and that peoples like the Spartans were descendants

Vocabulary

Post and Lintel
An architectural system composed of horizontal beams resting on vertical supporting beams. Large gaps exist in between the vertical beams.

Pentelic Marble
A marble of high quality mined in Mount Pentelikon, north of Athens. This marble was famously used in the Parthenon and other famous sculptures from Antiquity.

Order
The word refers to different conventions of Greek architecture.

Capital
The top of a column where the column meets the roof of the temple.

Doric
An order characterized by a simple, strong, imposing capital and little ornamentation at the top and base of each column.

Ionic
An order characterized by the appearance of a *volute*, a scroll-like ornament found at the top of the column.

Corinthian
The most decorative and elaborate of the three orders, the capital of a Corinthian column was carved to look like acanthus leaves pushing through a basket.

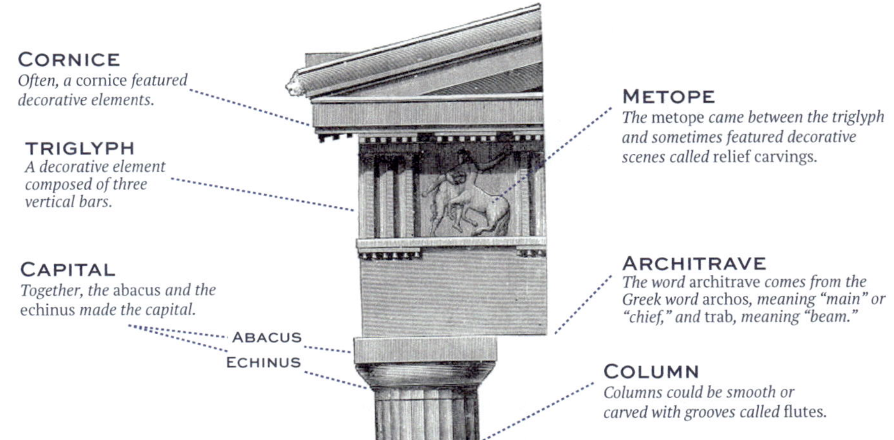

DORIC COLUMN / DIAGRAM

of the Dorians. Such details about the Dorians are important because Doric architecture is very much like the Dorians themselves: simple, strong, and imposing. First made in mainland Greece, Doric columns have a simple, undecorated capital and are fixed to the tops and bottoms of the temple structure with little ornamentation.

DORIC (LEFT), IONIC (MIDDLE), AND CORINTHIAN (RIGHT)

The Ionic Order

The Ionic Order originated in the region of Ionia, the coastline of Asia Minor that included Greek city-states like Ephesus and Miletus. The dominant feature on an Ionic column was the *volute*, a scroll-like decorative feature at the top of each column.

The Corinthian Order

The Corinthian Order was the most decorative and elaborate of the three Greek orders. Acanthus plants are flowering, nectar-bearing plants found on lands surrounding the Mediterranean Sea. According to legend, the sight of acanthus leaves breaking through a basket provided the inspiration for the capital of a Corinthian column, which is decorated with rows of acanthus leaves. Corinthian columns developed in Corinth, one of the wealthier cities in Classical Greece. Corinthian columns originated in the Hellenistic age, the period following Classical Greece.

ACTIVITY

Closer Look at Greek Temples & Orders

Instructions: Each row contains a photograph of a particular Greek temple. Each photograph could be of a temple built according to ***Doric, Ionic,*** or ***Corinthian,*** order of architecture. In the space provided, identify the order of architecture for each photo.

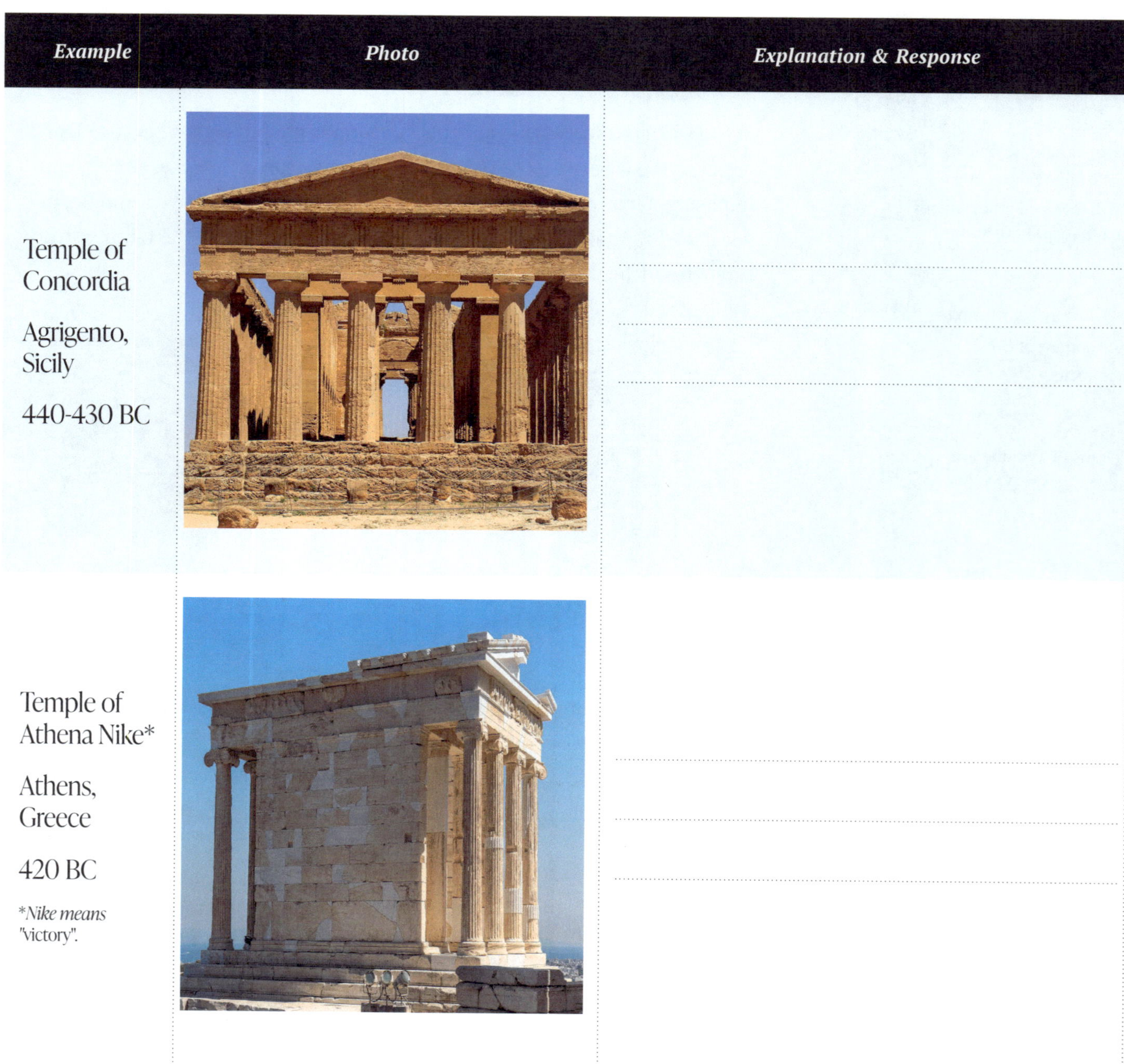

Example	*Photo*	*Explanation & Response*
Temple of Concordia Agrigento, Sicily 440-430 BC		
Temple of Athena Nike* Athens, Greece 420 BC **Nike means "victory".*		

Greek Temples & Orders (Continued)

Example	*Photo*	*Explanation & Response*
Maison Carrée *Nîmes, France* *1st c. AD*		
Parthenon Athens, Greece 437-432 BC		
Erechtheion Athens, Greece 421-406 BC		

Greek Temples & Orders (Continued)

Example	Photo	Explanation & Response
Temple of Juno Agrigento, Sicily ~ 450 BC		
Temple of Garni Garni, Armenia 1st c. AD		
Temple of Bacchus Bekaa Valley, Lebanon 2nd c. AD		

Closer Look at Greek Temples & Orders / Answer Key

The Temple of Concordia: *The Doric order of Greek architecture.*

The Temple of Athena Nike: *The Ionic order of Greek architecture.*

Maison Carrée: *The Corinthian order of Greek architecture.*

The Parthenon: *The Doric order of Greek architecture.*

Erechtheion: *The Ionic order of Greek architecture.*

The Temple of Juno: *The Doric order of Greek architecture.*

The Temple of Garni: *The Ionic order of Greek architecture.*

The Temple of Bacchus: *The Corinthian order of Greek architecture.*

While the Greeks built their temples to showcase the superiority of their respective cities, these temples (as with all architecture) also communicated the values the Greeks considered important. In Classical Greece, their temples convey the principles of order, harmony, and beauty, and as such, these monuments not only survive, albeit in ruins, but still inspire all those who look upon them.

Primary Source Analysis / Plato's "Ring of Gyges"

Description: What if Socrates died at the siege of Potidaea? The famed Greek philosopher served with distinction during the siege, even saving the life of an ambitious aristocrat named Alcibiades, a relative of Pericles, who would one day become one of Athens' leading politicians. Today, we know Socrates as one of the founders of philosophy.

Socrates had a relatively boring upbringing. He was born around 470/469 BC, and since most Athenians had to learn a trade to earn a living, Socrates initially worked as a stonecutter. Like his fellow Athenians he fought in the Peloponnesian War. After the war, Socrates' life changed forever as the result of a visit to the oracle at Delphi. At these sites, people could ask questions of the priests and priestesses serving the Greek god Apollo. One of Socrates' friends visited the Oracle at Delphi and inquired of the priestesses there, "Who is the wisest person in all of Greece?"

The Oracle replied it was Socrates, and when Socrates heard this answer, he couldn't believe it! The Oracle couldn't be wrong, but all the same, Socrates could not believe he was the wisest person in Athens. To test the oracle, Socrates went about asking his fellow Athenians questions about the nature of wisdom and the good life, questions that made them re-evaluate the things for which they were living.

As Socrates went about asking such questions, he inevitably alienated many people in Athens who believed he was mocking them and encouraging the youth to reject the gods. Ultimately, these enemies accused Socrates of corrupting the youth of Athens and managed to get him convicted of the crime. As his punishment, Socrates drank poisonous hemlock and died in 399 BC, but that is not the end of the story.

SOCRATES / 470 - 399 BC
1st c. AD Bust (Louvre)

That's because many people loved Socrates. The most significant of these students was Plato, who wrote over forty dialogues featuring Socrates as his main character, recreating some of conversations Socrates really had and inventing others in his immense collection of dialogues. Plato was born in Athens into a wealthy, well-connected Athenian family during the Peloponnesian War. Plato studied under Socrates, and then Plato started a school called the **Academy** to teach others about Socrates' ideas.

Vocabulary & Annotations

Academy
The philosophical school started by Plato.

Dialogue
A literary work in which two or more speakers discuss a topic of great philosophical significance.

Lydia
This Lydia is the same Lydia conquered by Cyrus the Great in 538 BC. King Croesus was an ancestor of the king of Lydia at the time of this story.

...Gyges
The story of Gyges was originally found in Herodotus' *Histories*, for Gyges was an ancestor of the more famous (and more ric) king Croesus.

...pocketing it
If this story seems similar to *Lord of the Rings*, it is because author J.R.R. Tolkien loved this story and wove its elements into his fantasy novels.

SOCRATES AT HIS DEATH
Jacques Louis-David's The Death of Socrates *(1787)*

Little is known about Plato outside of the autobiographical details he includes in his dialogues, of which Plato wrote over forty. A **dialogue** is a literary work wherein two or more speakers discuss a topic of great philosophical significance, and the person at the center of Plato's dialogues was the inquisitive, sometimes exasperating philosopher, Socrates.

Here, we feature a selection from a dialogue called the *Republic*. This dialogue focuses on the nature of justice, a virtue regarding how we treat our fellow man. Justice can be described as the midpoint between being so weak you let others walk on you and so overbearing and proud that you walk on everyone else. A precise and exact understanding of justice is needed, but given how hard it is to put such ideas into words, Plato, by way of Socrates, offers the following story.

Plato's *Republic*: The Ring of Gyges

01 Long, long ago, in a kingdom far far away called **Lydia**, there was a shepherd named **Gyges**. One day, while Gyges was tending his sheep, an earthquake struck. The ground shook, rocks tumbled down the mountainside, and the very earth opened up beneath Gyges' feet.

02 When the earthquake was over and the ground was still again, Gyges found himself in a deep, dark cavern. He stumbled to his feet and walked ahead but stopped short when he saw a most terrible sight before him: the skeleton of a great king who must been buried in the cavern generations earlier.

03 Gyges approached the skeleton and noticed a most beautiful golden ring on the skeleton's long, bony finger. Slipping the ring off the skeleton's finger

and **pocketing it**, Gyges began the long climb up to the world above, with this delightful new ring in his possession. Now on solid ground again, Gyges slipped on the ring and to his astonishment, he became invisible! He tested out his newfound power, slipping the ring on and off at his house and the marketplace. No one could see him, and he could do practically anything and everything he wanted. What would he do with this newfound power?

04 Whereupon Gyges hatched the following plan. He got himself chosen as a messenger to the court of Candaules, king of Lydia. Once Gyges arrived, he seduced the queen. With her help, **Gyges conspired** against the king, slew him, and took the kingdom.

05 Suppose now that there were two such magic rings, and the just put on one of them and the unjust the other; no man can be imagined to be of such an iron nature that he would stand fast in justice.

06 No man would keep his hands off what was not his own when he could safely take what he liked out of the market, or go into houses and lie with any one at his pleasure, or kill or release from prison whom he would, and in all respects be like a god among men.

Then the actions of the just would be as the actions of the unjust; they would both come at last to the same point. And this we may truly affirm to be a great proof that a man is just, not willingly or because he thinks that justice is any good to him individually, but **of necessity**, for wherever any one thinks that he can safely be unjust, there he is unjust.

07 For all men believe in their hearts that **injustice is far more profitable** to the individual than justice, and he who argues as I have been supposing, will say that they are right. If you could imagine any one obtaining this power of becoming invisible, and never doing any wrong or touching what was another's, he would be thought by the lookers-on to be a most wretched idiot, although they would praise him to one another's faces, and keep up appearances with one another from a fear that they too might suffer injustice. Enough of this.

A·Z

Vocabulary & Annotations

...Gyges conspired

In telling this story, Socrates assumes that murder and adultery are both acts of injustice. Under normal conditions, a person would not commit such acts for fear of punishment. Justice and personal integrity determinewhat a person does when no one is watching them.

...of necessity

The man who is truly just believes that justice is good in and of itself and ought to be pursued for that reason, not because he may gain from his actions in any way, shape, or form.

...injustice is far more profitable

Acts of injustice, such as seizing the throne of a great kingdom, may be "profitable" in the short term since one may become rich. In the long term, these deeds do great harm to one's soul and are thus very unprofitable.

Reading Comprehension Questions

1. Who is Gyges? Where does he live? What is his occupation?

2. What does Gyges find? What new powers does this item give him?

3. What temptation does this item give to Gyges? Does he give into it?

4. How does this story illustrate the nature (and importance) of justice? What does justice look like based upon this simple but profound tale?

The (First) Peloponnesian War / 460 - 434 BC

THE AGE OF CLASSICAL GREECE was the highpoint of Greek culture and civilization. Yet during this period, problems between the Greek city-states had begun to brew beneath the surface. One might think that a war like the Peloponnesian War started for more practical causes but at its heart, the two largest city-states went to war because they did not trust each other. Sparta feared Athens' rising power while Athens refused to accept a second-place status to Sparta among the Greek city-states. As one Greek historian wrote, "the real cause" of the Peloponnesian War was "the one which was formally most kept out of sight. The growth of the power of Athens, and the alarm which this inspired in Sparta, made war inevitable."

That historian, and our primary source for this conflict is the Athenian Thucydides, who lived from 460 to 400 BC. Thucydides served as a general in the Peloponnesian War, experiencing the war firsthand. He even contracted and survived the terrible plague that struck Athens in 430 BC. As a general, he had performed poorly during a siege of the strategic city of Amphipolis in northern Greece. The Athenian assembly blamed him for its loss, and they exiled him from Athens.

Thucydides spent the rest of the war in Sparta, Athens' enemy. Thucydides' time in Sparta gave him even more experience and sources to consult when writing his history. Such access was crucial to Thucydides' great work, for as he states in the introduction to *The History of the Peloponnesian War*, a historian has to evaluate sources carefully and make sure each event is represented truly and accurately. These sources would be of invaluable importance to Thucydides, who tended to be much more thorough and precise with his sources than his predecessor, Herodotus. Indeed, Herodotus' *Histories* may be the first work of history, but Thucydides set the standard for **scientific history**, an approach to history that attempts to recreate the past with exacting detail and to find real causes for human events rather than attributing such causes to the gods or the fates. Thucydides also helped establish an idea in political theory called **realist theory**. Realist theory claims that states, such as Athens and Sparta, pursue their own rational self-interest and are ultimately concerned with their own survival. Under this framework, states behave more like animals than like people.

Thucydides' time in both Sparta and Athens gave him access to sources and interviews that would have been difficult for anyone else to access, and the result was

Fearing Athens' growing power, the Peloponnesian War began as Sparta hoped to contain Athens and keep them from becoming the new dominant state in Greece. Wars often break out in this way as the rise of a new superpower (like Athens) hallenges the reigning superpower (Sparta), who go to war to protect their position.

Vocabulary

Scientific History
History is a narrative about past events; scientific history is an effort to recreate the past as accurately as possible in terms of dates, source material, and other available pieces of evidence.

Realist Theory
This theory states that in politics and international relations, states pursue their own rational self-interest. At times, this self-interest may seem amoral at best but the state is concerned with its own survival.

Pausanias
A Spartan general who commanded Greek forces in Asia Minor following the Battle of Plataea; he was accused by his fellow Greeks of acting too "Persian" and was conspiring with the Persian king Xerxes I.

Delos
An island in the center of the Aegean Sea, where the gods Apollo and Artemis were born and where Athens formed the Delian League.

The Delian League
An alliance between the Greek city-states for protection against Persia. Under Athens' leadership, a Greek fleet patrolled the Aegean Sea and kept it clear of Persian ships. The members of the alliance contributed either ships or money to help maintain the fleet.

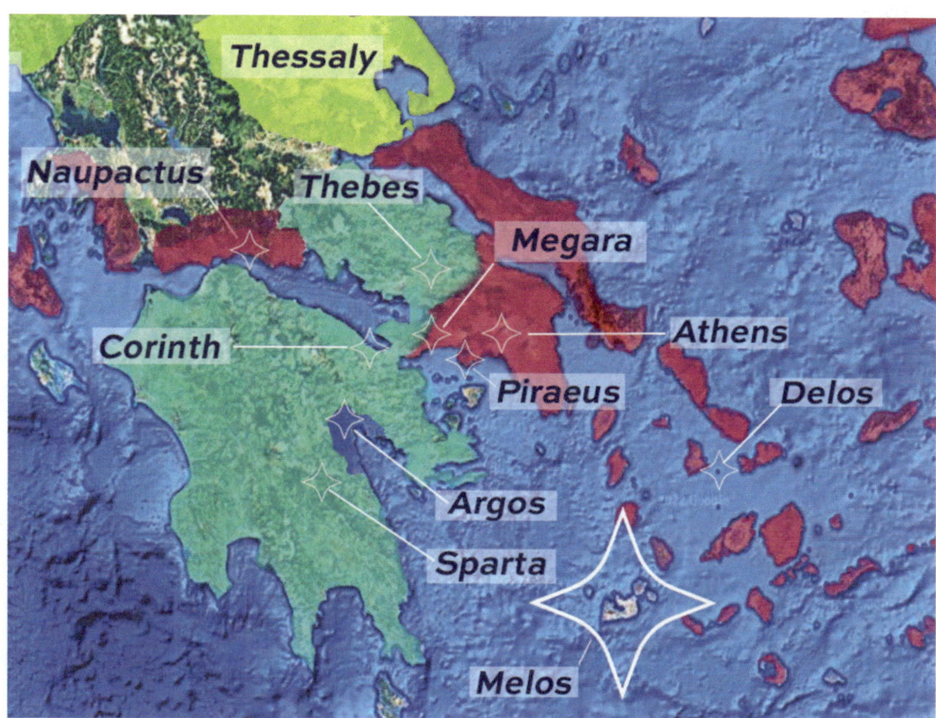

GREEK CITIES & REGIONS / THE PELOPONNESIAN WAR

a work that has withstood the test of time. The work is significant because, in addition to writing a thorough history of the war, Thucydides connected these events to larger issues within the human condition.

The alliance between Athens and Sparta unraveled soon after the defeat of the Persians. In 478 BC, following the victories at Plataea, Salamis, and Mycale, the Greek fleet was patrolling the eastern Aegean Sea and expelling what was left of Persia from the region. The fleet was commanded by a Spartan named **Pausanias**, but Pausanias angered the Greeks under his control by his conduct, his manner, even his dress, all of which seemed too "Persian" for his fellow Greeks.

When Pausanias hired Egyptian bodyguards, it seemed as if he was preparing to seize power for himself in a Peisistratus-like coup. (Another Athenian named Peisistratus had also hired bodyguards he used to seize control of the Areopagus.) As a result, some of the leading Greeks under Pausanias asked Athens to assume control of the fleet and the various Greek city-states contributing resources to the fleet, believing the Athenian leaders to be more trustworthy. Naturally, Athens agreed to the proposal.

In 477 BC, Athens and other leading city-states met on the island of **Delos** and formed the **Delian League**. Athens possessed the largest fleet of triremes, great Greek warships equipped with a bronze prow for ramming enemy ships, so Athens assumed control of the league. The league contained about 150 other cities who would contribute either ships or money to Athens. Athens, then, added the ships to their fleet or used the money to maintain ships in service. Under the control of the Athenians, the Greek fleet would patrol the Aegean Sea and protect the Greek world from any future Persian invasion.

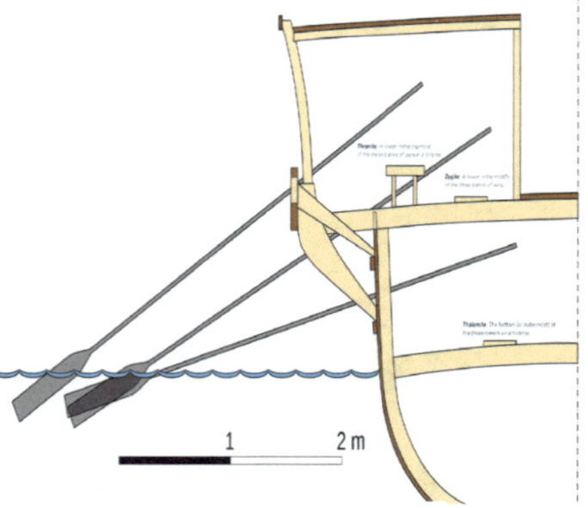

‖ RECONSTRUCTION OF A TRIREME / DIAGRAM OF A TRIREME

The treasury was held on the island of **Delos**, already sacred to the Greeks as the birthplace of Apollo and Artemis (Pomeroy 155-157). But problems appeared in the Delian League, too. Sometimes, they forced islands to either join the Delian League or kept other islands in the league so they could contribute their resources to Athens' increasing number of ships.

During this time, Athens became increasingly democratic which, on the surface, seemed like a positive thing. In Athens, the privilege of serving in government came from one's ability to purchase hoplite armor. The poorest Athenian male citizens still had some privileges, but not as many as those citizens who could afford hoplite equipment. The growth of the Athenian navy also required these privileges be given to the rowers on board Athenian triremes—after all, the rowers on board were risking their lives just like the hoplites did on land. At this time, the rise of Athenian democracy and the increased political privileges given to Athenian rowers seem to go hand-in-hand. The rowers on these warships were often poorer, and they wanted more political privileges and influence to keep them rowing. But, their relative poverty meant they were less-educated. Those poorer Athenians might be more easily swayed to attack a city or deal heavy-handedly with members of the league.

Themistocles, an Athenian who urged his countrymen to look to their *wooden walls* as a fleet of triremes, still held great influence in Athens. Themistocles urged more democratic reforms in the city of Athens and spoke out against Sparta's assumed leadership over the Peloponnesse. As a result of all these factors, the Athenian government became more and more unstable and less rational. The Athenian Assembly could make a decision one day and immediately reverse it the day after—something that happened during the Peloponnesian War on one occasion (Pomeroy 158-159).

For example, Athens' rowers, who had voting rights, would benefit from conquering a neutral island or a region from their rivals, the Spartans. After all, any land or treasure won in such a conquest would be distributed amongst them, the people of Athens. These benefits made it all the more likely that they would vote in favor of such a proposal, even if it was unjust. Knowing

Vocabulary

Peloponnesian League
An alliance system composed of states from the Peloponnesian Peninsula, with Sparta being the dominant city-state in the league.

Sphere of Influence
A sphere of influence refers to territory controlled by a larger, more powerful state, who consider it a necessity to guard their territory from rivals.

Megara
A city near Athens which had long been Athens' rival. In the years following the Persian Wars, Megara made an alliance with Athens to protect itself from Corinth.

First Peloponnesian War
A relatively short conflict fought between Athens and Corinth, but is not the same Peloponnesian War immortalized by Thucydides.

The Long Walls
A series of defensive that connected Athens to the port of Piraeus, located on the Saronic Gulf. The Long Walls made sure Athens would still have access to the sea during a siege and make Athens all but impossible to conquer.

that common people were easier to sway, politicians crafted arguments to move the hearts of the masses, a phenomenon commonly known as demagoguery, which we will take a closer look at in the following pages.

The (First) Peloponnesian War: 460 to 445 BC

The suspicion of Sparta and Corinth made war between the largest of the Greek city-states more and more likely. Sparta was at the head of a defensive alliance known as **Peloponnesian League**, a loose grouping of city-states in the Peloponnesse who pledged their support in times of crisis. Corinth was the second most-powerful member of the Peloponnesian League, and both city-states were alarmed at Athens' growing power and influence. Athens dominated the Delian League, controlled a massive fleet, and could draw resources from islands and cities across the Aegean world. And to Sparta, Athens was converting its defensive alliance—the Delian League—into an Athenian Empire, the likes of which had never existed before in Greece. Shouldn't Sparta do *something* before Athens grew too powerful to be stopped?

And Corinth also had good reason to feel threatened by Athens. Corinth owed its wealth and status to its position on the Gulf of the Corinth and the Isthmus of Corinth, which allowed it to dominate trade coming from one end of the Greek world to the other. Increasingly, Athens' expansion came at the expense of Corinth, who resented Athens' growing power and wealth as much as Sparta feared it. In the decades following the Persian Wars, Athens expanded into Corinth's **sphere of influence**. A sphere of influence refers to the territory controlled by a great power, and they consider it their right to defend such territory from rivals. For example, Corinth considered its colonies and the area around the Isthmus of Corinth part of its sphere of influence, and they believed any powers coming into this area threated their interests.

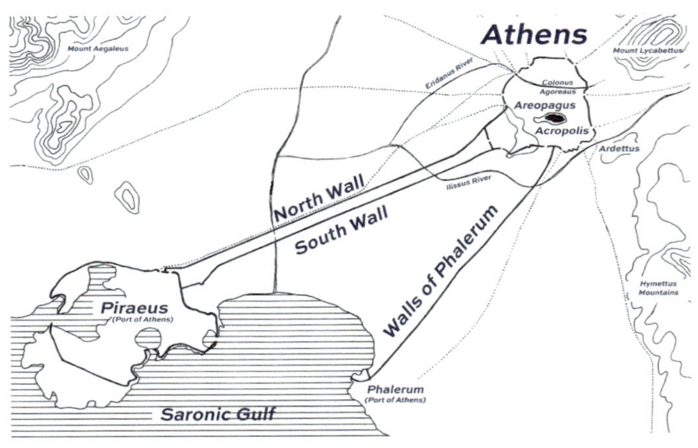

ATHENS & THE LONG WALLS

Thus, as Athens expanded into Corinth's sphere of influence, it angered Corinth. First, Athens made a formal alliance with **Megara**. Megara sits on the other side of the isthmus, and Corinth tried to conquer the territory itself. An alliance with Megara could allow Athens to cut into Corinth's prosperous trade across the land bridge joining the Peloponnesse to the Greek mainland—something Corinth could not tolerate. Even worse, Athens allowed the survivors of a failed slave revolt against Sparta to live just across the gulf from Corinth at a city called Naupauctus. That threatened both Corinth and Sparta. The Spartan system produced soldiers to force the helots, the population of slaves living in nearby Messania who had just revolted, to do all of the farming and produce all of the food the Spartans lived on. The Spartans feared revolts amongst the helots more than anything else, and anything that might encourage the helots to fight for their freedom the Spartans had to oppose.

To stop Athens from becoming too powerful, Corinth attacked Athens in what was known as the **First Peloponnesian War**, which lasted from 460 to 445 BC. The war did little to check Athens' growing influence and naval strength. In response, Athens took more steps to protect itself. Athens built **the Long Walls**, the map for which is depicted below, protecting a path the city of Athens to the valuable portside town of Piraeus on the Bay of Salamis. Athens moved the treasury from the island of Delos—a neutral island in the Aegean, famed as the birthplace of Apollo and Artemis—to the city of Athens.

Reading Comprehension Questions

1. Who was Pausanias, and how did he initially help drive Sparta, Athens, and their respective allies apart from each other?

2. Why did the various islands in the Aegean form an alliance with Athens?

3. What did the cities in the Delian League have to give to Athens in exchange for protection?

4. Why did Corinth resent the rise of Athens so much?

The (Famous) Peloponnesian War / 431 - 404 BC

AT THIS POINT, ATHENS became the empire that Sparta and Corinth feared so much. But they could do little to stop it, and the First Peloponnesian War ended in a draw with both sides keeping their respective spheres of influence. Now that the First Peloponnesian War was over, we can move to the more famous Peloponnesian War immortalized by Thucydides.

This second conflict broke out again on account of the longstanding feud between Corinth and Athens, beginning at the city of **Epidamnus** Epidamnus. Located on the Adriatic Sea, Epidamnus was a colony founded by **Corcyra**, and Corcyra was a colony founded by Corinth. Epidamnus began feuding with Corcyra, which had long resisted control from the mother city of Corinth.

Corcyra allied itself with Athens. This alliance embarrassed Corinth, who considered Corcyra part of its sphere of influence. Athens knew this fact, and they knew that an alliance with Corcyra would anger Corinth but made it anyway. That way, Corcyra's ships and its wealth would not fall into Corinthian hands. To punish Corcyra for their stubbornness, Corinth and her allies sent a fleet of ships to force them back into obedience. But with help from Athens, Corcyra defeated the massive naval fleet and sunk it to the bottom of the Adriatic Sea.

Soon after, another problem erupted in northern Greece at the city of **Potidaea**. Potidaea was another Corinthian colony and thus a part of Corinth's sphere of influence. Being located so far from Corinth, so close to the Aegean Sea, and so afraid of attacks from Persia, the citizens of Potidaea made an alliance with Athens. Yet Corinth still chose Potidaea's leading government officials. Circa 433 BC, the Athenians felt this arrangement no longer suited them and demanded that Potidaea dismiss any advisers or officials appointed by Corinth. When Potidaea refused to carry out Athens' demands, Athens laid siege to the city for two years.

Troubles brewed elsewhere, including the city of Megara, a city just between Corinth and Athens. Its proximity meant they both wanted it in its sphere of influence. But Megara was part of the Peloponnesian League, and to punish them, Athens took the unusual step of laying an economic embargo against the city of Megara. Athens said that Megara had taken over land sacred to Demeter close to Attica, Athens forbade any Megarian merchants from trading in Athenian-controlled ports. For Athens, the action, called the **Megarian Decree**, was meant to make it all but impossible for Megara to gain food and provisions without necessarily declaring war. Sources such as Plutarch and the Greek playwright Aristophanes blame Pericles, the leading Athenian statesman, for these actions and thus for the war in its entirety, although the Greek writer Thucydides makes little mention of it in his history.

In retaliation, Sparta declared Athens had violated the Thirty Years' Peace. Sparta then prepared to invade Attica (Pomeroy 212-213). Here, in 431 BC, the Peloponnesian War between Athens and Sparta started and lasted until 404 BC. The war goes back and forth with Sparta, a power on the land with its mighty hoplite army, gaining some victories, and Athens, a naval power, winning on the sea. Despite the fact that it occupied a relatively small space of the Mediterranean world, the Peloponnesian War is worth studying for several reasons.

First, Thucydides' *History of the Peloponnesian War* provides insights into the nature of history and the problems of the human condition. As we have read, Thucydides strives for accuracy in his writing. Beyond that, Thucydides also tries to present human nature not as poets like Homer do, where human beings are larger-than-life heroes triumphing over the odds. Instead, he presents human nature as it so often can be: mean-spirited and short-sighted. As Athens and Sparta demonstrated time and again, human beings are capable of committing the noblest acts of self-sacrifice and the most shameful deeds of injustice and oppression.

Second, the Peloponnesian War demonstrates the kind of devastation that can take place between city-states. Corinth, Sparta, and Athens each had advanced economies that could draw resources from a huge area. Athens could levy troops, sails, and swords from across the Aegean. All of Spartan society trained for warfare, and half of Greece followed Sparta and trusted Sparta's kings so much that they engaged in a decades-long war alongside her. With so many resources at their disposal, neither side gained a decisive advantage over the other.

The alliance system whereby each Greek city-state sided with either Sparta and the Peloponnesian League and Athens and the Delian League only added to the difficulties. Thucydides' *History of the Peloponnesian War* showcases the intricate political debates within Athens and Sparta, as its leaders presented the reasons why they should attack one city or another and why their respective cities may benefit from doing so.

During the course of the war, the Spartans and the Athenians tried to win more allies to their side. They did this by appealing to different factions within a particular city. Sparta was technically an oligarchy, so they tried to win over the leading citizens in a particular city and install an oligarchy. Athens, being a democracy, appealed to the common people in each city. The common people resented the rich oligarchs, who often lived in luxury and took advantage of their large landholdings and inherited wealth. But this resentment spilled over into violent bloodshed as the common people took their revenge on the wealthier members of their *polis*.

PERICLES / 495 - 429 BC

Famously, Pericles was so self-conscious about his relatively large and misshapen head, he insisted on being portrayed in his helmet to hide his embarrassing headshape.

But great heroes also emerged during the Peloponnesian War. As mentioned, the Athenian philosopher Socrates served at the Battle of Potidaea, and his time in the war encouraged him to reevaluate the things that mattered most in life. The most significant of all the players in the Peloponnesian War was the Athenian *strategos* **Pericles**, who lived from 495 to 429 BC. Pericles came from a noble Athenian family, but in his politics, he encouraged Athenians from outside the noble families to participate in civil government. He even made it possible that they might be paid, compensating them for giving up a day of working in the fields or in a craftsman's shop.

But of course, Pericles' popularity may have come from the vast sums of money he brought out from the public treasury. Then as now, many politicians try to increase

Vocabulary

Epidamnus
Epidamnus was founded as a colony by the city of Corcyra, which itself was founded by Corinth. The conflict between Epidamnus and Corcyra, and by extension with Corinth and Athens, led to the outbreak of the Peloponnesian War.

Corcyra
A colony by the city of Corinth but allied itself with Corinth's chief rival, Athens.

Potidaea
A Corinthian colony that, given its location on the Aegean Sea, entered into an alliance with Athens to protect them from Persia.

The Megarian Decree
In 432 BC, in response to Megara's incursion on land sacred to the goddess of Artemis, the city of Athens forbade any Megarian merchants and traders from operating in any ports Athens controlled.

Pericles
Pericles was an Athenian *strategos* and politician during the age of Classical Greece. As the most influential politician in Athens, Pericles oversaw the building of the Parthenon, the transformation of Athens into an empire, and its early strategy in the early years of the Peloponnesian War. He lived from 495 to 429 BC.

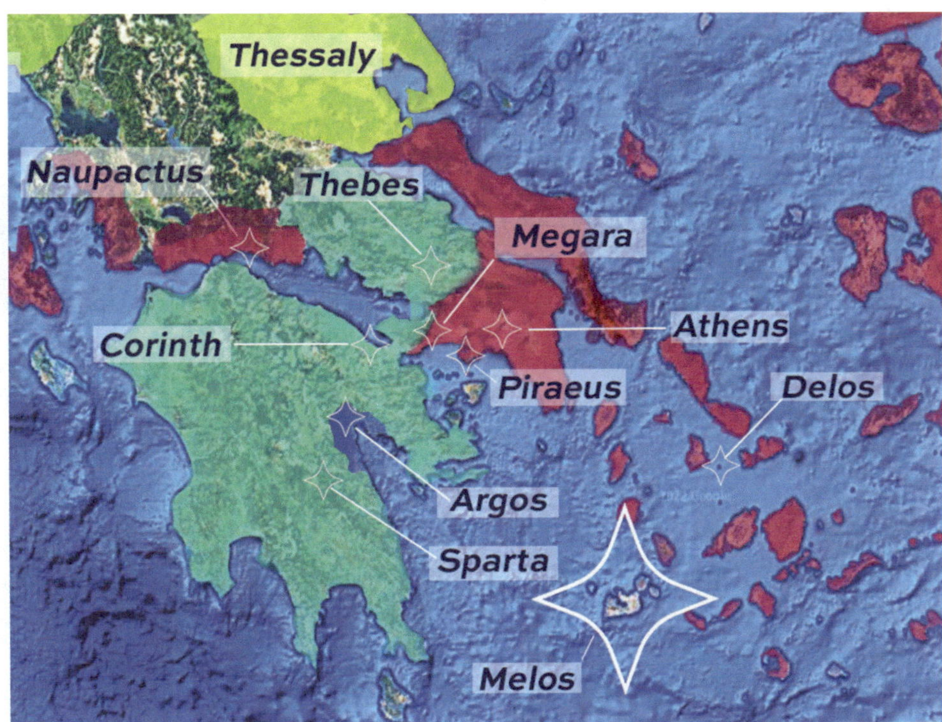

GREEK CITIES & REGIONS / THE PELOPONNESIAN WAR

The Greek world divided into Sparta and its allies in green, and Athens and its allies in red.

their power and influence by giving money from the public treasury to the voters. Often, the downfall of democratic states can be traced to the moment its citizens realize they can vote themselves money from the public treasury, and Athens had at their disposal all the tribute money pouring in from islands across the empire. They paid Athens to protect them from Persia, but such money was used to beautify the city of Athens, and Pericles likewise got the credit for it. But that money may have done more to destabilize Athens in the long run.

Pericles ranks among the very best of Athenian leaders. Not everything, though, that Pericles did helped Athens; for instance, he developed the early strategy pursued by the Athenians in the Peloponnesian War. He encouraged all the residents of Athens to bring themselves and their possessions inside the Long Walls of Athens, but the overcrowding helped a terrible plague spread in the city. Pericles himself died of the disease, and the play *Oedipus Rex* by the great playwright Sophocles, which opens with a devastating plague, may have been inspired in part by Pericles' dominance in Athenian politics. Pericles stands out as a particularly successful, practical politician as well as being one of the pivotal, once-in-a-generation statesmen.

The next few pages feature episodes from Thucydides, each of which is followed by reading comprehension questions. In our last section, we will return to the Peloponnesian War and its final years to see what effects the conflict has upon Sparta, Athens, and all of Greece.

Reading Comprehension Questions

1. What conflict broke out between Corcyra and Epidamnus? How were Athens and Corinth dragged into it?

2. How did the real Peloponnesian War, the one immortalized in Thucydides, begin? (Hint: use the name Potidaea in your answer.)

3. Why did the Peloponnesian War last for so long?

4. Who was Pericles, and what kind of impact did he have on the city of Athens?

Primary Source Analysis / Pericles' Funeral Oration

Description: Thucydides lived from 460 to 400 BC and began writing his history shortly before his exile from Athens in 424 BC. The speech, however, is Thucydides' best attempt at preserving a speech the Greek *strategos* Pericles gave in 429 BC at a state funeral.

Pericles lived from 495 to 429 BC and was the most influential politician in Athens. His influence was so great the age of Classical Greece is often known as the Age of Pericles, for it was Pericles who orchestrated the building of the Parthenon and other grand civic buildings in Greece.

And of course, one way Pericles increased his reputation in the Athenian Assembly was by his command of language and his masterful skills in public speaking. Such skills were on display in the most famous speech recorded in Thucydides, the Funeral Oration of Pericles. Each year, as a custom, Athens hosted a public funeral for those who had died fighting in the hoplite army. In this year, Pericles delivered the address, a special type of speech called a **funeral oration** characterized by its high themes, weighty subject matter (the speech is for a funeral, after all), and praise for those who were being buried.

Book II, Chapter 6: *Pericles' Funeral Oration*

01 In the same winter the Athenians gave a funeral at the public cost to those who had first fallen in this war. It was a custom of their ancestors, and the manner of it is as follows. Three days before the ceremony, the bones of the dead are laid out in a tent. Their friends bring to their relatives such offerings as they please, and in the funeral procession, coffins made of cypress are carried forth in wagons, one for each tribe, the bones of the deceased being placed in the coffin of their tribe. Among these is carried one empty coffin decorated for those missing soldiers, that is, for those soldiers whose bodies could not be recovered. Any citizen or stranger who pleases may join in the procession. The female relatives are there to wail at the burial. The dead are laid in the public sepulcher in the suburb of the city, in which those who fall in war are always buried. This is done for all with the exception of those slain at **Marathon**, who for their extraordinary valor were buried on the spot where they fell. After the bodies have been laid in the earth, a man chosen by the state, of approved wisdom and great reputation, pronounces over them an appropriate **panegyric**; after which all retire. Such is the manner of the burying; and throughout the whole of the war, whenever the occasion arose, the established custom was observed. Meanwhile these were the first that had fallen, and Pericles, son of **Xanthippus**, was chosen to pronounce their eulogy. When the proper time arrived, he advanced from the sepulcher to an elevated platform in order to be heard by as many of the crowd as possible. Pericles spoke as follows:

02 Most of the speakers who have come before me have commended him who made this speech part of the law. They tell us that it is well that it should be delivered at the burial of those who have dead in battle. For myself, I should have thought that the worth which had displayed itself in deeds would be sufficiently rewarded by the honors given to such deeds. For myself, I wish the reputations of many brave men were not to be threatened in the mouth of a single individual, to stand or fall according as he spoke good or bad. However, since our ancestors have stamped this custom with their approval,

‖ *PERICLES' FUNERAL ORATION*, PHILIPP FOLTZ (1852)

it becomes my duty to obey the law and to try to satisfy your several wishes and opinions as best I may.

03 I shall begin with our ancestors. It is both just and proper that they should have the honor of the first mention on an occasion like the present. They dwelt in the country of Attica **from generation to generation**, and handed it down free to the present time by their bravery and courage. And if our more remote ancestors deserve praise, much more do our own fathers, who added to their inheritance **the empire which we now possess**, and spared no pains to leave their acquisitions to us of the present generation. Lastly, there are few parts of our dominions that have not been augmented by those of us here, who are still more or less in the vigor of life.

04 But what was the road by which we reached our position, what the form of government under which our greatness grew, what the national habits out of which it sprang. Since I think this to be a subject upon which on the present occasion a speaker may properly dwell, and to which the whole assemblage, whether citizens or foreigners, may listen with advantage.

05 Our constitution does not copy the laws of neighboring states. Instead, we are a pattern to others to imitate than by imitating anyone else. The Athenian constitution is one that favors the many instead of the few; this is why it is called a **democracy**. If we look to the laws, they afford equal justice to everyone in their private differences. If a man has no social standing, then his advancement in public life falls to his reputation and his abilities. In this way, class considerations are not allowed to interfere with merit. And again, pover-

Vocabulary & Annotations

Marathon
Fought in 490 BC, the attle of Marathon saw Athens defeat a much larger army of Persian soldiers and was the first upset in a series of upsets by the Greeks over the Persians. The Athenians considered their victory over Persia to have preserved their city, their way of life, and the unique civic freedoms and opportunities life in Athens gave to its citizens.

Panegyric
Panegyric is the formal Greek term for a funeral oration.

Xanthippus
Pericles supported democratic institutions in Athens, but he also came from the Alcmaeonid family, one of the wealthiest and most established families in Athens.

ty does not prevent one from participating in civic life: If a man is able to serve the state, he is not hindered by the obscurity of his condition.

06 If we turn to our military policy, there also we differ from our adversaries. We trust less in system and policy than to the native spirit of our citizens; while in education, where our rivals from their very cradles by a painful discipline seek after manliness. At Athens we live exactly as we please, and yet are just as ready to encounter every legitimate danger. In proof of this it may be noticed that the Spartans do not invade our country alone, but bring with them all their allies; while we Athenians advance unsupported into the territory of a neighbor, and fighting upon a foreign soil usually vanquish with ease men who are defending their homes. With habits not of labor but of ease, and courage not of art but of nature, we are willing to encounter danger and to face them in the hour of need as fearlessly as those who are **never free from them**.

07 Nor are these the only points in which our city is worthy of admiration. We cultivate refinement without extravagance and knowledge without weakness. Wealth we employ more for use than for show, and we place the real disgrace of poverty not in owning to the fact one was born poor but in declining to struggle to escape from poverty. Our public men have, besides politics, their private affairs to attend to, and our ordinary citizens, though occupied with the pursuits of industry, are still fair judges of public matters.

08 In short, I say that as a city Athens is **the school of Hellas**. I doubt if the world can produce a man who, where he has only himself to depend upon, is equal to so many emergencies, and graced by so happy a versatility, as the Athenian. And that this is no mere boast thrown out for the occasion, but plain matter of fact, the power of our *polis*, the great city of Athens, has been acquired by these habits. For Athens alone, of all the other *poleis* in Greece, is found when tested to be greater than her

THUCYDIDES / 460-400 BC

reputation, and alone gives no occasion to her assailants to blush at the antagonist by whom they have been worsted, or to her subjects to question her title by merit to rule. Rather, the admiration of the present and succeeding ages will be ours, since we have not left our power without witness, but have shown it by mighty proofs. Indeed, we have not **needed a Homer** to write speeches celebrating our greatness, we have forced every sea and land to be the highway of our daring, and everywhere, whether for evil or for good, have left imperishable monuments behind us. Such is the Athens for which these men, in the assertion of their resolve not to lose her, nobly fought and died; and well may every one of their survivors be ready to suffer in her cause.

09 Indeed if I have dwelt at some length upon the character of our country, it has been to show that our stake in the struggle is not the same as theirs who have no such blessings to lose, and also that the bravery of those buried here today might be by definite proofs established. The Athens that I have celebrated is only what the heroism of these and their like have made her, men whose fame, unlike that of most Hellenes, will be found to be only commensurate with what they deserve.

Thus choosing to die resisting, rather than to live submitting, they fled only from dishonor.

10 These men buried here died as became Athenians. You, their survivors, must determine to have as unfaltering a resolution in the field, though you may pray that it may have a happier issue. And not contented with ideas derived only from words of the advantages which are bound up with the defense of your country, though these would furnish a valuable text to a speaker even before an audience so alive to them as the present, you must yourselves realize the power of Athens, and feed your eyes upon her from day to day, till love of her fills your hearts; and then, when all her greatness shall break upon you, you must reflect that it was by courage, sense of duty, and a keen feeling of honor in action that men were enabled to win all this, and that no personal failure in an enterprise could make them consent to deprive their country of their valor, but they laid it at her feet as the most glorious contribution that they could offer.

11 For each of them, in offering their very lives made, have received that renown which never grows old, and for a tomb, not so much that in which their bones have been deposited, but that noblest of shrines wherein their glory is laid up to be eternally remembered upon every occasion on which deed or story shall call for its commemoration. For heroes have the whole earth for their tomb; and in lands far from their own, where the column with its epitaph declares it, there is enshrined in every breast a record unwritten with no tablet to preserve it, except that of the heart. These take as your model and, judging happiness to be the fruit of freedom and freedom of valor, never decline the dangers of war.

11 Comfort, therefore, not condolence, is what I have to offer to the parents of the dead who may be here. Numberless are the chances to which, as they know, the life of man is subject; but fortunate indeed are they who draw for their lot a death so glorious as that which has caused your mourning, and to whom life has been so exactly measured as to terminate in the happiness in which it has been passed. Still I know that this is a hard saying, especially when those are in question of whom you will constantly be reminded by seeing in the homes of others blessings of which once you also boasted: for grief is felt not so much for the want of what we have never known, as for the loss of that to which we have been long accustomed.

12 My task is now finished. I have performed it to the best of my ability, and in word, at least, the requirements of the law are now satisfied. If deeds be in

Vocabulary & Annotations

...from generation to generation
At the collapse of the Bronze Age, invaders from the north attacked and displaced many of the native Greek populations everywhere except for Attica, the region around Athens.

...the empire which we now possess
At the time of his speech, Pericles considered Athens to be an empire, that of one state ruling over a wide array of territories and people.

...democracy
Pericles' explanation of a *democracy* is one of the most noteworthy elements of his speech. Herein, Pericles describes a *democracy* not simply as a constitution in which the people rule but where the rights and privileges of the common people are respected and social mobility encouraged.

...never free from them
The Spartans are never free from the fear of a revolt among the helots.

...the school of Hellas
In calling Athens the *School of Hellas*, Pericles implies that the other city-states have much to learn from the Athenian constitution and her example.

...needed a Homer
The great epic poet Homer praised heroes such as Odysseus and Priam; Pericles implies they do not need such a poet, for Athens' deeds speak for themselves.

question, those who are here interred have received part of their honors already, and for the rest, their children will be brought up till manhood at the public expense: the state thus offers a valuable prize, as the garland of victory in this race of valor, for the reward both of those who have fallen and their survivors. And where the rewards for merit are greatest, there are found the best citizens.

13 And now that you have brought to a close your lamentations for your relatives, you may depart."

Reading Comprehension Questions

1. Read over the paragraphs following Pericles' observation that "we are a pattern to others to imitate than by imitating anyone else". What policies did Athens follow that other states should imitate?

2. What kind of freedoms—civic, political, economic, or otherwise—did Athens enjoy? Why was this freedom so unique in the Greek world?

Reading Comprehension Questions

3. According to Pericles, did the freedoms Athens enjoyed make her stronger or weaker? Why or why not?

4. Why does Pericles spend his speech praising Athens, rather than the men being buried at this public ceremony?

5. Read over the paragraph beginning with Pericles' statement that " You, their survivors, must determine to have as unfaltering a resolution in the field." What does this line mean, and how might it relate to the overarching purpose Pericles has in giving this speech

A Closer Look at the Megarian Decree

IS SHUTTING OFF TRADE tantamount to an act of war? In 432 BC, shortly before the outbreak of war, Athens and their on-again, off-again rival Megara entered into another feud. Megara had trespassed on land sacred to the goddess Demeter, an act that Athens considered sacrilege and responded by imposing a trade embargo on the city. That sacred land lay in the boundary between the city-states of Megara and Athens, so Megara had effectively violated the region separating the two powers. Effectively, the Athenian navy surrounded city of Megara and prevented any supplies coming into or going out of the city, ultimately starving the city into submission.

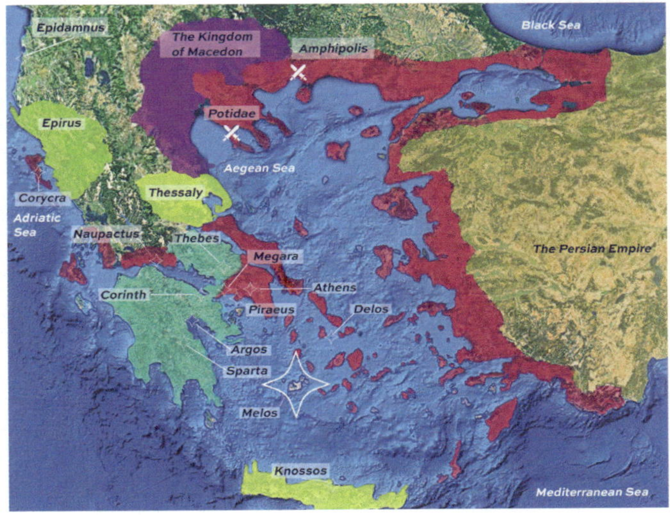

THE GREEK WORLD

Megara's position between Corinth and Sparta to the west and Athens to the east made it all-but impossible for Megara to remain neutral in the Peloponnesian War.

The Megarian Decree is an example of an *economic embargo*, the actions of one power to cut off the trade and commercial relationships of a rival. The policy is to effectively prevent rival states from obtaining the supplies and provisions they need to survive until they surrender to the state enforcing the embargo—in this case, the city of Megara would have surrendered to Athens. Moreover, Athens could have hurt Sparta, Corinth, and other members of the Peloponnesian League without violating the terms of a peace treaty Athens had signed with Sparta, the Thirty Years' Peace. Sources such as the Greek playwright Aristophanes and the Greek biographer Plutarch attribute these decisions to Pericles, the famed Athenian politician. Since Sparta cited the Megarian Decree for their justification for declaring war on Athens, much of the blame for the Peloponnesian War falls on Pericles himself.

But is an *economic embargo* equal to fighting and conflict? Was the *Megarian Decree* a sincere attempt to hold Megara accountable for violating Athens' territory—trespassing on land on the border between the two city-states which, in Athens' estimation, was sacred to Demeter—or was it a practical, calculated political decision to weaken members of the Peloponnesian League, Athens' great rival for dominance in the Greek world?

In this exercise, you are only responsible for using your *historical imagination*, your ability to put yourself in the minds and predicaments of ancient heroes, long since past, and recreate what they could do. Imagine you are the Greek statesman Pericles and debating what to do in response to Megara's actions. Knowing that your actions could very well lead to war, what should you do? As Pericles, what would you recommend the citizens of Athens to do in response?

Closer Look Questions

1. If you are Pericles, why would you fear Megara "trespassing" and coming closer to Athenian territory?

2. If you're Pericles, and you recognize you can't make open war on Megara or any member of the Peloponnesian League, what other options do you have at your disposal?

3. Can Athens really enforce an economic embargo? What would they hope to gain from preventing Megara from trading in any port that Athens controlled, of which there are many?

4. What are the trade-offs of doing nothing? What do you risk if you allow Megara to gain a foothold so close to Athenian territory?

Primary Source Analysis / The Plague

Description: In this particular excerpt from Thucydides' *History of the Peloponnesian War,* following Pericles' funeral oration, Thucydides turns to a devastating plague that struck the city of Athens. Thucydides himself suffered from this plague and provided a firsthand account of its symptoms, the hardship that struck the Athenian people, and the disparate reactions the plague on the inhabitants of the city.

The influence of Pericles extended far beyond the building of the Parthenon. Indeed, Pericles' policy may be responsible for the worst calamity that happened to Athens during the Peloponnesian War: the plague that struck Athens in the years around 430 BC. At the beginning of the war, Pericles recognized the Spartans could not be beaten on land, whereas the Athenians could not be beaten on the sea. To counter Sparta's advantage, Pericles argued the Athenians should carry all of their possessions inside the Long Walls that connected the city of Athens to its port of Piraeus on the Saronic Gulf.

With Athens protected on three sides by mountains and on one side by the gulf, which its navy controlled, Athens became, in effect, an island. The Spartans could ravage Athenian territory, but with Athens receiving supplies by the sea, the city would not be forced to submit to the Spartans. Sooner or later, the Spartans would grow tired of pillaging empty farmland and ask for a peace treaty. The people of Athens and the surrounding regions agreed to Pericles' proposal and moved themselves and all of their property inside the Long Walls. Most important, though, for our discussion is the impact this plague had on the inhabitants of Athens. For as the plague ran its course, Thucydides describes the manifold effects the plague wreaked upon the Athenians. This selection comes from Book II, Chapter 7 of Thucydides, translated by Richard Crawley.

History of the Peloponnesian War: The Plague

01 Such was the funeral that took place during this winter, with which the first year of the war came to an end. In the first days of summer the Spartans and their allies, with two-thirds of the Spartan army as before, invaded Attica, and destroyed the countryside. Not many days after the arrival of the Spartans outside Athens the plague first began to show itself among the Athenians.

It was said that it had broken out in many places previously in the neighborhood **of Lemnos** and elsewhere; but a pestilence of such extent and mortality was nowhere remembered. Neither were the physicians at first of any service, ignorant as they were of the proper way to treat it, but they died themselves the most thickly, as they visited the sick most often; nor did any human art succeed any better. Supplications in the temples, divinations, and so forth were found equally futile, till the overwhelming nature of the disaster at last put a stop to them altogether.

02 It first began, it is said, in the parts of **Ethiopia** above Egypt, and thence descended into Egypt and Libya and into most of the King's country. Suddenly falling upon Athens, the plague first attacked the **population in Piraeus**—which was the occasion of their saying that the Peloponnesians had poisoned the reservoirs, there

being as yet no wells there—and afterwards appeared in the upper city, when the deaths became much more frequent. All speculation as to its origin and its causes, if causes can be found adequate to produce so great a disturbance, I leave to other writers, whether they are laymen or professionals. For myself, I shall simply set down its nature, and **explain the symptoms** by which perhaps it may be recognized by the student, if it should ever break out again. This I can the better do, as I had the disease myself, and watched its operation in the case of others.

03 That year then is admitted to have been otherwise unprecedentedly free from sickness; and such few cases as occurred all determined in this. As a rule, however, there was no observable, obvious cause. But people in good health were all of a sudden attacked by a violent fever in the head, followed by redness and inflammation in the eyes and the inward parts like the throat or tongue, becoming bloody and emitting an unnatural and fetid breath.

04 These symptoms were followed by sneezing and hoarseness, after which the pain soon reached the chest and produced a hard cough. When the plague fixed itself in the stomach, it upset it; and **discharges of bile** of every kind named by physicians ensued, accompanied by very great distress. In most cases also an ineffectual retching followed, producing violent spasms, which in some cases ceased soon after, in others much later. Externally the body was not very hot to the touch, nor pale in its appearance, but reddish, livid, and breaking out into small pustules and ulcers. But internally it burned so that the patient could not bear to have on him clothing or linen even of the very lightest description.

05 What they would have liked best would have been to throw themselves into cold water; as indeed was done by some of the neglected sick, who plunged into the rain-tanks in their agonies of unquenchable thirst; though it made no difference whether they drank little or much. Besides this, the miserable feeling of not being able to rest or sleep never ceased to torment them. The body, meanwhile, did not waste away so long as the distemper was at its height, but held out to a marvel against its ravages.

06 But while the nature of the illness was such as to baffle all description, and its attacks almost too grievous for human nature to endure. Some died in neglect, others in the midst of every attention. No remedy was found that could be used to help anyone: the good medicine had upon one person did harm when used on others. Strong and weak individuals proved equally incapable of resisting the plague—all alike were swept away even if they lived with

Vocabulary & Annotations

...of Lemnos
Lemnos is an island in the northern reach of the Aegean Sea.

Ethiopia
The Greeks were aware of the kingdom of Ethiopia, sometimes called *Cush*. Ethiopia was connected to the Mediterranean world via the Nile River which, because the Nile flowed south to north, is *above* Egypt although it is *south* of Egypt.

...population in Piraeus
Piraeus was the main port of Athens.

...explain the symptoms
True to his craft as a historian, Thucydides attempts to present the events of the Peloponnesian War in as realistic and exacting detail as he can. Thucydides also contracted the plague himself.

...discharges of bile
We know *bile* as a chemical secreted by the liver, but writers in the ancient world used *bile* to refer to the different bodily fluids.

...lawless extravagance
The residents of Athens were so broken physically and spiritually by the plague and resolved to live however they wanted to since they could contract the plague and die at any moment.

the utmost precaution. Even the birds and beasts that prey upon human bodies either kept from touching the dead (as there were many lying unburied), or died after tasting them. In proof of this, it was noticed that birds of this kind actually disappeared. Such birds avoided the bodies, or indeed to be seen at all.

07 By far the most terrible feature in the plague was the sadness that ensued when any one recognized themselves getting sick. The despair that gripped them took away their power of resistance and left them a much easier prey to the disorder. Besides that, there was the awful spectacle of men dying like sheep, having caught the infection in nursing each other. This caused the greatest mortality. And aggravating everything else that afflicting Athens was the arrival of so many people from the country into the city. As there were no houses to receive them, they had to live during the hot summer months of the year in stifling cabins, where the disease raged without restraint. That left bodies of dying men laying one upon another, half-dead creatures reeling about the streets and gathering round all the fountains desperate for water.

08 The sacred places also in which they had quartered themselves were full of corpses of persons that had died there, just as they were. For as the disaster passed all bounds, men, not knowing what was to become of them, became utterly careless of anything and everything, both sacred and profane. All the burial rites before in use were entirely disregarded, and they buried the bodies as best they could. Sometimes, they threw dead bodies upon a stranger's pyre and ignited it. Other times, they tossed the corpse which they were carrying on the top of another pyre that was burning and so went off.

09 Nor was this the only form of **lawless extravagance** which owed its origin to the plague. Men now coolly, without any real thought, attempted deeds they would have only done under the cover of darkness. They lived however they wanted, seeing the rapid transitions pro-

MICHAEL SWEERTS, "PLAGUE IN AN ANCIENT CITY" (1652-54)

duced by persons in prosperity suddenly dying and those who before had nothing succeeding to their property. So they resolved to spend quickly and enjoy themselves, regarding their lives and riches as alike things of a day. Perseverance in what men called honor was popular with none, it was so uncertain whether they would be spared to attain the object; but it was settled that present enjoyment, and all that contributed to it, was both honorable and useful. Fear of gods or law of man there was none to restrain them. As for the first, they judged it to be just the same whether they worshiped them or not, as they saw all alike perishing; and for the last, no one expected to live to be brought to trial for his offenses, but each felt that a far severer sentence had been already passed upon them all and hung ever over their heads, and before this fell it was only reasonable to enjoy life a little.

10 Such was the nature of the calamity, and heavily did it weigh on the Athenians; death raging within the city and devastation without.

Primary Source Questions

1. From where did the plague come?

2. Why did the plague strike Athens so particularly hard?

3. What were the symptoms of the plague? What physical effects did it have on the people of Athens?

Primary Source Questions

4. What were the spiritual and emotional effects of the plague?

5. As a historian, and once he survived, do you think Thucydides was happy he had survived the plague? Why or why not?

6. If you got so sick, as those individuals did during the plague, how would you respond? Would you respond with despair, or would you endure? Could you endure?

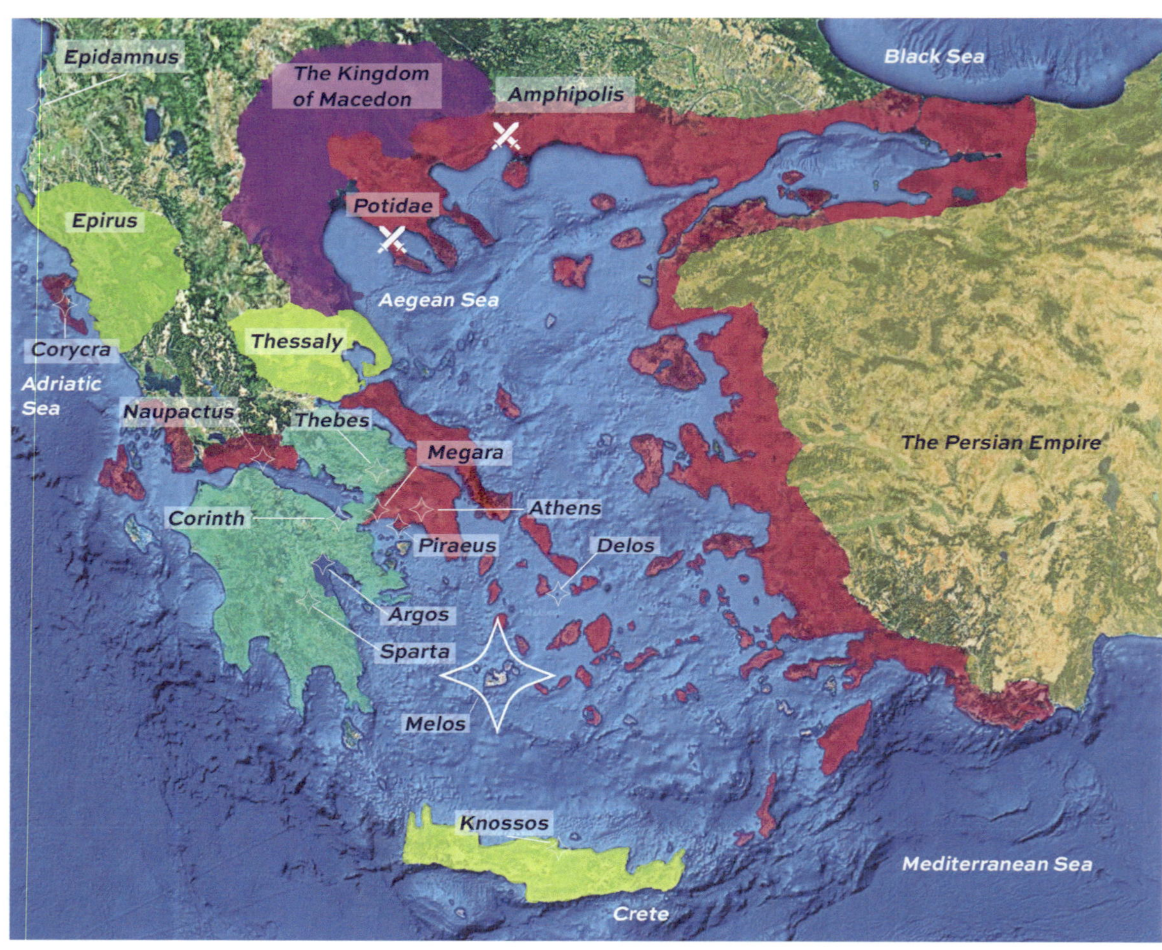

Closer Look Questions

1. Looking at the map above and imagine you are an Athenian statesman: what about this map would give you the most concern? What is one thing—and perhaps the easiest thing—you would want to change?

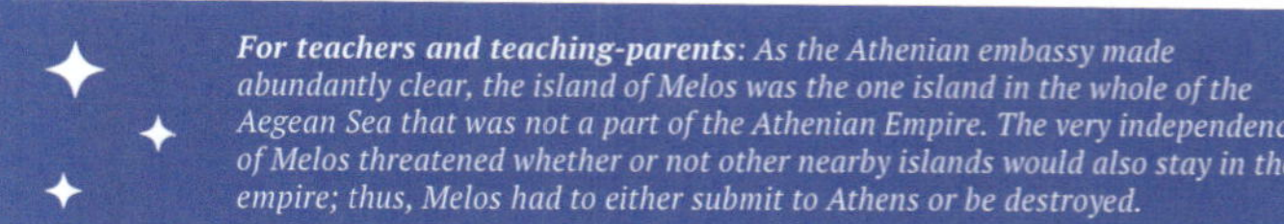

***For teachers and teaching-parents**: As the Athenian embassy made abundantly clear, the island of Melos was the one island in the whole of the Aegean Sea that was not a part of the Athenian Empire. The very independence of Melos threatened whether or not other nearby islands would also stay in the empire; thus, Melos had to either submit to Athens or be destroyed.*

Primary Source Analysis / The Melian Dialogue

Description: The Athenians surveyed the extent of their domains and saw immediately one problem: the tiny island of Melos was not part of it. Melos was a small island in the Aegean Sea and up until 416 BC, had maintained their independence during the Peloponnesian War. Like the Spartans, the people of Melos were Dorians, a tribe that claimed descendence from no less a hero than Heracles. Thucydides identified Melos as a colony of Sparta, suggested they had close cultural, diplomatic, and ethnic ties even if the Melians were not necessarily apart of the Peloponnesian League, the alliance-system headed by Sparta. Nevertheless Melos was an island in the Aegean, and every other island in the Aegean was a part of the Athenian Empire. How could Athens let so small and so insignificant a power as Melos remain independent and neutral?

In 416 BC, the Athenians sent a delegation to Melos demanding they become part of the Athenian Empire. Thucydides recreated (or imagined) the meetings between the Athenians and the Melians to the best of his ability, and this piece of historical writing has become one of the more famous parts of Thucydides' *Peloponnesian War*. Thucydides was not present for the conversation between the Athenians and the Melians, so the section is more like the kind of plays produced in ancient Athens. Thucydides uses the conversation between the Athenians and the Melians to demonstrate the cold, stark realities of a world in which only the strong (Athens) survive and the weak (Melos) have to submit or face ruin (Pomeroy 233-234). This text comes from Book V, Chapter 17 of Thucydides.

The Melian Dialogue

03 Cleomedes, son of Lycomedes, and Tisias, son of Tisimachus, the generals, encamping in their territory with the above armament, before doing any harm to their land, sent envoys to negotiate. These the Melians did not bring before the people, but bade them state the object of their mission to the magistrates and the few; upon which the Athenian envoys spoke as follows:

Athenians: Since the negotiations are not to go on before the people, in order that we may not be able to speak straight on without interruption, and deceive the ears of the multitude by seductive arguments which would pass without refutation (for we know that this is the meaning of our being brought before the few), what if you who sit there were to pursue a method more cautious still? Make no set speech yourselves, but take us up at whatever you do not like, and settle that before going any farther. And first, tell us if our proposition suits you.

The Melian commissioners answered:

Melians: To the fairness of quietly instructing each other as you propose there is nothing to object; but you look too armed for war for us to believe what you say. We see you are come to be judges in your own cause, and that all we can reasonably expect from this negotiation is war, if we prove to have right on our side and refuse to submit, and in the contrary case, slavery.

Athenians: If you have met to think about the possibilities of the future, or for anything else than to consult for the safety of your state upon the facts that you see before you, we will give over; otherwise we will go on.

Vocabulary & Annotations

...right to our empire
The delegates claim that because of Athens' leadership and sacrifices in the Persian Wars, they now have a right to rule over the rest of Greece.

...equals in power
In the international arena, and the interactions between states, the only thing that matters is power.

...tells our own subjects
The very neutrality of Melos may signal to other islands and states in the Athenian Empire that they, too, could be free.

...because they are strong
True to his theme, Thucydides emphasizes that power, the ability of one state (like Athens) to either defend itself or impose its will on others is all that matters—but is that all that matters?

...under the yoke
A *yoke* is placed over a team of oxen and used for plowing fields. The word *yoke* is a common metaphor to describe one state being in subjection to another.

...hope, danger's comforter
Herein, the Athenians effectively urge the Melians to give up hope and submit to Athenian rule.

...we are just men
The Melians trust that *justice*, or what is right, is on their side.

Melians: It is natural and excusable for men in our position to turn more ways than one both in thought and utterance since this is about the safety of our country. The discussion, though, if you please, can proceed in the way which you propose.

Athenians: For ourselves, we shall not trouble you with false pretenses—either of how we have a **right to our empire** because we overthrew the Medes, or are now attacking you because of wrong that you have done us—and make a long speech which would not be believed; and in return we hope that you, instead of thinking to influence us by saying that you did not join the Spartans, although their colonists, or that you have done us no wrong, will aim at what is feasible, holding in view the real sentiments of us both. Since you know as well as we do that right, as the world goes, is only in question between **equals in power**, while the strong do what they can and the weak suffer what they must.

Melians: As we think, at any rate, it is expedient—we speak as we are obliged, since you asked us to let right alone and talk only of interest—that you should not destroy what is our common protection, the privilege of being allowed in danger to speak of justice and of what is fair and right. And you are as much interested in this as any, as your fall would be a signal for the heaviest vengeance and an example for the world to meditate upon.

Athenians: The end of our empire, if end it should, does not frighten us. Yet herein, we have come here in the interest of our empire and for the preservation of your country; as we would happily exercise that empire over you without trouble, and see you preserved for the good of us both.

Melians: And how, pray, could it turn out as good for us to serve as for you to rule?

Athenians: Because you would have the advantage of submitting before suffering the worst and we should gain you as subjects by not destroying you.

Melians: So you would not consent to our being neutral, friends instead of enemies, but allies of neither side?

Athenians: No, for your very independence **tells our own subjects** of our weakness and your hatred of our power.

Melians: Is that your subjects' idea of fairness, to put those who have nothing to do with you in the same category with your own colonists or conquered, rebellious provinces?

Athenians: As far as right goes they think one has as much of it as the other, and that if any maintain their independence it is **because they are strong**, and that if we do not bother them it is because we are afraid. By securing your subjection, we would extend our empire and our security. The fact you are islanders and weaker than others makes it all the more important that you should not succeed in baffling the masters of the sea.

Melians: But do you consider that there is no security in the policy which we indicate? For here again if you keep us from talking about justice and invite us to obey your interest, we also must explain ours, and try to persuade you. How can you avoid making enemies of all existing neutrals who shall look at case from it that one day or another you will attack them? And what is this but to make greater the enemies that you have already, and to force others to become so who would otherwise have never thought of it?

Athenians: Why, the fact is that continentals generally give us but little alarm; the liberty which they enjoy will long prevent their taking steps against us. Instead, it is islanders like you, outside our empire, and subjects smarting **under the yoke**, who would be the most likely to take a rash step and lead themselves and us into obvious danger.

Melians: Well then, if you risk so much to retain your empire, and your subjects to get rid of it, it were surely great baseness and cowardice in us who are still free not to try everything that can be tried, before submitting to your yoke?

Athenians: Not if you are well advised, the contest not being an equal one, with honor as the prize and shame as the penalty, but a question of self-preservation and of not resisting those who are far stronger than you are.

Melians: But we know that the fortune of war is sometimes more impartial than the disproportion of numbers might lead one to suppose. To submit is to give ourselves over to despair, while action still preserves for us a hope that we may stand erect.

Athenians: **Hope, danger's comforter**, may be indulged in by those who have abundant resources, if not without loss at all events without ruin. But the nature of hope is to be extravagant, and those who go so far as to put their all upon the venture see it in its true colors only when they are ruined. But so long as the discovery would enable them to guard against it, it is never found lacking. Let not this be the case with you, who are weak and hang on a single turn of the scale. Nor should you be like the common people, who turn to prophecies and oracles and other such inventions that delude men with hopes to their destruction.

Melians: You may be sure that we are as well aware as you of the difficulty of contending against your power and fortune, unless the terms be equal. But we trust that the gods may grant us fortune as good as yours, since **we are just men** fighting against unjust, and that what we want in power will be made up by the alliance of the Sparta, who are bound, if only for very shame, to come to the aid of their kindred. Our confidence, therefore, after all is not so utterly irrational.

Athenians: When you speak of the favor of the gods, we may as fairly hope for that as yourselves. Neither our attitude nor our conduct is in any way contrary to what men believe of the gods or practice among themselves. Of the gods we believe, and of men we know, that by a necessary law of their nature **they rule wherever they can**. And it is not as if we were the first to make this law, or to act upon it when made: we found it existing before us, and shall leave it to exist for ever after us; all we do is to make use of it, knowing that you and everybody else, having the same power as we have, would do the same as we do. Thus, as far as the gods are concerned, we have no fear and no reason to fear that we shall be at a disadvantage.

But when we come to your notion about the Spartans, which leads you to believe that shame will make them help you, here we bless your simplicity but do not envy your folly. The Spartans, when their own interests or their country's laws are in question, are the worthiest men alive. But their conduct towards others much might be said, but no clearer idea of it could be given than by shortly saying that of all the men we know they are most obvious in considering what is agreeable honorable, and what is expedient just. Such a way of thinking does not promise much for the safety which you now unreasonably count upon.

Melians: But It is for this very reason that we now trust to their respect for expediency to prevent them from betraying the Melians, their colonists, and thereby losing the confidence of their friends in Greece and helping their enemies.

Athenians: Then you do not adopt the view that expediency goes with security, while justice and honor cannot be followed without danger. Indeed, the Spartans generally court danger as little as possible.

Melians: But they would have others to send. The Cretan Sea is a wide one, and it is more difficult for those who command it to intercept others, than for those who wish to elude them to do so safely. And should the Sparta miscarry in this, they would fall upon your land and instead of places which are not yours, you will have to fight for your own country and your own confederacy.

Athenians: Some diversion of the kind you speak of you may one day experience, only to learn, as others have done, that the Athenians never once yet withdrew from a siege for fear of anyone else. But we are struck by the fact that, after saying you would consult for the safety of your country, in all this discussion you have mentioned nothing which men might trust in and think to be saved by. Your strongest arguments depend upon hope and the future, and your actual resources are too scanty, as compared with those arrayed against you, for you to come out victorious. You will therefore show great blindness of judgment, unless, after allowing us to retire, you can find some counsel more prudent than this.

You will surely not be caught by that idea of disgrace, which in dangers that are disgraceful, and at the same time too plain to be mistaken, proves so fatal to mankind. In too many cases, the very men that have their eyes perfectly open to what they are rushing into, let the idea of disgrace lead them on to a point at which they fall willfully into hopeless disaster, and come upon disgrace more disgraceful as the companion of error, than when it comes as the result of misfortune.

This, if you are well advised, you will guard against; and you will not think it dishonorable to submit to the greatest city in Greece, when it makes you the moderate offer of becoming its tributary ally, without ceasing to enjoy the country that belongs to you. Indeed, you have the choice given you between war and security, and you should not be so blinded as to choose the worse. And it is certain that those who do not yield to their equals, who keep terms with their superiors, and are moderate towards their inferiors, on the whole succeed best. Think over the matter, therefore, after our withdrawal, and reflect once and again that it is for your country that you are consulting, that you have not more than one, and that upon this one deliberation depends its prosperity or ruin.

The Athenians now withdrew from the conference; and the Melians, left to themselves, came to a decision corresponding with what they had maintained in the discussion, and answered: "Our resolution, Athenians, is

Vocabulary

...they rule wherever they can
The Olympians like Zeus, Hera, and Apollo actually behave in the very same way the Athenians are now acting. The Athenians are merely imitating them.

...what is expedient just
The word *expedient* means an action that may be unethical and wrong but would achieve a practical end. In this case, the Athens say the Sparta are as practical and expedient as they themselves are.

...your strongest arguments
The Athenian delegates reiterate that the only thing that counts in a world is power.

THE ISLAND OF MELOS

the same as it was at first. We will not in a moment deprive of freedom a city that has been inhabited these seven hundred years. We put our trust in the fortune by which the gods have preserved it until now, and in the help of men, that is, of the Spartans; and so we will try and save ourselves. Meanwhile we invite you to allow us to be friends to you and foes to neither party, and to retire from our country after making such a treaty as shall seem fit to us both."

Such was the answer of the Melians: The Athenians now departing from the conference said: "Well, you alone, as it seems to us, judging from these resolutions, regard what is future as more certain than what is before your eyes, and what is out of sight, in your eagerness, as already coming to pass; and as you have staked most on, and trusted most in, the Spartans, your fortune, and your hopes, so will you be most completely deceived."

The Athenian envoys now returned to the army; and the Melians showing no signs of yielding, the generals at once betook themselves to hostilities, and drew a line of circumvallation round the Melians, dividing the work among the different states. Subsequently the Athenians returned with most of their army, leaving behind them a certain number of their own citizens and of the allies to keep guard by land and sea. The force thus left stayed on and besieged the place.

Primary Source Questions

1. Where is the island of Melos? Who were the Melians, and what was their role in the Peloponnesian War?

2. Why did Athens want to conquer the island of Melos?

3. The Athens told the Melians not to trust in the gods. Why would the gods not help Melos?

Primary Source Questions

4. The Athens told the Melians not to trust in the Spartans. Why would the Spartans not help Melos?

5. Instead, what did the Athenians urge the Melians to trust in?

6. The Athenians effectively define justice as being... what? What is just and right in the eyes of the Athenians? What do you believe justice should really look like?

The End of the Peloponnesian War / 421-404 BC

IN 421 BC, SPARTA AND ATHENS actually signed a peace treaty that marked the end of the First Pelopennesian War—the **Peace of Nicias**. The war had caused untold loss of life and devastation to their fields and city-life, and they were both eager to cease hostilities. The terms of the Peace of Nicias permitted Athens to retain its imperial holdings and certain strategic ports, whereas Athens was to return Spartan prisoners-of-war and ports important for Sparta as well. Sadly, the peace could not hold because Sparta's allies—Corinth, Megara, and Thebes—were not given any concessions, and they resented that the Athenian Empire had survived the war. So tensions simmered beneath the surface until hostilities broke out again shortly after the Peace of Nicias. But why would Athens go to war again, when it had effectively won?

The rise of a new kind of politician in Athens provides part of the answer: demagogues. A **demagogue** is a class of politician that arose in Athens during the age of Classical Greece. The word *demagogue* may sound like a monster from a fantasy novel—although in some ways, it is—but demagogues are politicians who use their leadership and rhetorical skills solely for their own power and influence. The word comes from the Greek *demos*, meaning "people" (as in *democracy*) and *agogos*, meaning "leader" or "driver". Thus, the name *demagogue* literally means a *driver* or a *leader of people*. The most prominent of these first *demagoges* was Cleon, whom Aristotle mocks for his "wild undertakings", for he was "the first to use unseemly shouting and coarse abuse" in the Assembly, shouting at people "with his cloak girt up short about him" (Aristotle *On the Constitution of Athens*). Often, when demagogues appear in a democratic state like that of Athens, their popularity shows something is thoroughly corrupt and rotten among the people living there. Why else would they listen to, or be swayed by, such politicians?

In 420 BC, a politician named **Alcibiades** was elected to the position of *strategos*, a general in charge of Athens' military. While Alcibiades did not shout or use wild gestures, Alcibiades urged his fellow Athenians to adopt policies much more advantageous to him than to Athens as a whole. Despite growing up under the care of Pericles and the tutelage of Socrates, Alcibiades was headstrong and ambitious. He used his considerable gifts for leadership and public speaking to benefit himself, and he saw that times of peace would not do much to advance his career. Hostilities had already broken out again between Athens and Sparta, and Alcibiades took advantage of the situation by recommending a

In 404 BC, Sparta finally defeated Athens. Athens overextended itself and invaded a region (Sicily) too far away and too powerful for Athens to conquer, whereas Sparta won by, perhaps, betraying its deepest principles and aligning itself with Persia. But in the end, both sides lost, for they were both too weak to defend themselves against the new power of Macedon, north of Greece.

Vocabulary

The Peace of Nicias

Issued in 421 BC, the Peace of Nicias ended hostilities between Athens and Sparta, but fighting resumed shortly thereafter.

Demagogue

From the Greek *demos* for "people" and *agogos* for "driver", a demagogue was a leader who uses their rhetorical and public speaking abilities to advance their own interests and not those of the broader community.

Alcibiades

Alcibiades was an Athenian politician during the Peloponnesian War. He was a relative of Pericles and a student of Socrates, but he is most remembered for his plans to invade the island of Sicily, which ended in disaster. He lived from 450 to 404 BC.

Sicily

Sicily is an island in the middle of the Mediterranean Sea that, thanks to its rich farmland and long coastlines, has long been a rich prize for neighboring empires.

Syracuse

Syracuse is a port on the island of Sicily which, thanks to its fertile plains and deep harbor, became one of the wealthiest cities in the ancient world.

GREEK CITIES & REGIONS / THE PELOPONNESIAN WAR
Unlike previous wars, the Peloponnesian War encompassed almost all of the Greek world.

new military expedition, one that, if successful, would give Athens all the resources it would need to defeat Sparta. Of course, the expedition would also give Alcibiades military glory and prestige, something Alcibiades wanted desperately. And so, Alcibiades urged the Athenian assembly to invade the island of Sicily.

Sicily is an island located off the coast of Italy. In Greek, Sicily means *fertile*, and the island's rich farmland made it an ideal place for growing grain and various fruits. The Greeks had colonized parts of Sicily, establishing new cities at one of the many harbors Sicily possessed. Sicilian cities **Syracuse** and Agrigento were some of the wealthiest ports in the ancient world. Later, Carthage and Rome considered the island so valuable they fought the First Punic War over its possession. And in 415 BC, Alcibiades pressured the Athenian assembly to invade the island, for once Sicily was conquered, Athens would have all the money and resources it needed to destroy Sparta once and for all.

Pericles had actually urged the people of Athens *not* to conquer any new lands or territories. He recognized that if the Athenians overextended themselves, they might bring about their downfall. But Alcibiades' counsel prevailed, and the assembly authorized an expedition of over 100 triremes and over 5,000 hoplite troops (Pomeroy 234-236).

The Sicilian Expedition seemed doomed from the start. In 415 BC, the night before the troops left Athens, sacred statues of Hermes (called *Hermai*), located around the city, were disfigured. The Athenian people took the destruction of the Hermai as a bad omen, and rumors circulated Alcibiades and his supporters had committed the vandalism. The Athenian assembly recalled Alcibiades from the expedition, but the troops sailed on to Sicily with the goal

MAP OF SYRACUSE / LATOMIE DEL PARADISO

After defeating the Athenian Navy in the Great Harbor, the Syracusans imprisoned 7,000 Athenians troops in the Latomie del Paradiso, a rock quarry on the outskirts of the city.

of conquering Syracuse which, being a Corinthian colony, was by default an enemy of Athens.

But upon arrival, the Athenians lost battle after battle against a coalition of Syracusans and Spartans. The biggest loss came in the Great Harbor of Syracuse, with over two hundred triremes taking part in the fighting. The ships that had not been sunk to the bottom of the sea landed on the beach, and their sailors tried to escape by land. 40,000 Athenians tried to escape, but the Syracusens and Spartans either killed them at a dangerous river crossing or captured them. The Athenian prisoners were brought back to Syracuse and thrown into massive quarry outside the city, the only place large enough and safe enough to house the 7,000 troops Thucydides estimates were captured. The Sicilian Expedition ended in 413 BC in a complete disaster, with Thucydides writing, "their fleet, their army, everything was destroyed," (Pomeroy 237-239; 7.87).

Seemingly, the Athenians had made the mistake all-too-many powerful states commit in overextending themselves. Like Xerxes a generation earlier, the Athenian people overstretched with an expedition to conquer a region, the venture fails and risked bringing down the entire state. In the Sicilian Expedition, almost all the Athenians down to the last man were killed—all except Alcibiades, who had escaped from the ship carrying him back to Athens. He spent the rest of the war in Sparta, helping the Spartans defeat the Athenians. Alcibiades, perhaps more so than anyone else in the Peloponnesian War, was responsible for the deaths of so many Athenians and the downfall of his home city of Athens.

And yet, despite this loss, no clear winner emerged until the very end of the war years in 405 BC—almost ten years later. Seemingly, Sparta or Athens could have prevailed in the conflict. Sparta had long possessed the most disciplined, formidable fighting force in Greece, whereas Athens possessed the largest navy and strong hoplite troops of its own. Each year saw some victories for Athens and some for Sparta, with each side continually wearing

Vocabulary

Lysander
Lysander was a Spartan admiral who helped secure the funds needed to build a Spartan navy. With that navy, Lysander defeated the Athenian navy at the Battle of Aegospotami.

Aegospotami
The Battle of Aegospotami was fought in 405 BC near the Hellespont, the straits that connect the Aegean to the Black Sea. The Spartan navy ensured Athens could no longer control the Aegean Sea, thus ending the Peloponnesian War.

Macedon
Macedon was a kingdom located to the north of Greece. Following the Peloponnesian War, Macedon became organized and powerful enough to conquer the entirety of Greece.

Philip II
Phillip II was the king of Macedon who transformed Macedon into the dominant power in Greece. He reigned from 359 to 336 BC.

itself down in resources and manpower. Amazingly, Athens survived for another decade until Sparta made a tremendous gamble of its own: an alliance with Persia.

The Spartans had long recognized the Athenian navy gave the Athenians a significant advantage over them. To counter Athens' advantage, the Spartans decided to build their own ships. To build ships, they needed money, and they turned to no one else but the Persian Empire for the funds. While Persia had been defeated by the Greeks nearly a century earlier, the Persian Empire was still the dominant power in the ancient Near East, the reigon to the east of the Greeks' political sphere.

The subjects of the Persian Empire sent yearly tribute to the king of kings, who was now King Darius II, who reigned from 423 to 405 or 404 BC. The Persians still longed to punish the Greeks—any Greeks, but especially Athens—for the events of the Persian Wars. And now, a friendship arose between the son of King Darius II, a Persian prince named Cyrus, and the Spartan admiral **Lysander**. Both Persia and Sparta wanted to subdue Athens, but Persian funds came with a cost: the Persians would regain their lost territories in Ionia, the west coast of Asia Minor that possessed wealthy cities like Miletus and Ephesus (Pomeroy 242-243).

The final battle came at **Aegospotami**. The naval battle saw Lysander capture over 150 Athenian triremes and the destruction of the Athenian camp, actions that effectively destroyed the Athenian fleet. Without that fleet, Athens could not control the Aegean Sea and without that control, Athens could no longer import the grain and food supplies its people needed to survive. Athens sued for peace. Lysander sailed home, stopping at the former colonies and allies of Athens and installing governments favorable to Sparta.

This time, Sparta consulted with their allies in Thebes and Corinth about Athens' fate. The Thebans and Corinthians urged Sparta to treat Athens as Athens had treated the people of Melos and others throughout the empire—that is, they wanted to punish Athens as harshly as they could. But in the end, the Spartans spared Athens the fate Athens had given to others, citing Athens' good conduct in the Persian Wars. The Spartans may have worried what could happen if Athens, long one of the most powerful states in Greece, was destroyed. Surely, Thebes or Corinth could have grown powerful enough to replace Athens and then perhaps threatened the Greeks' stability once again. In the end, Athens agreed to destroy its fortifications and especially the Long Walls that connected Athens to the port of Piraeus, as well as disbanding its navy. The Greek philosopher Xenophon wrote that people played flutes and sang and danced while the walls came down, believing that times of peace and prosperity lay ahead (Pomeroy 244-245).

PHILIP II / 382 - 336 BC

Sadly, nothing could have been further from the truth. For in the decades that the Athenians and Spartans had been fighting each other, a new power was rising to the north of Greece, one with grand ambitions of its to conquer the Greek world and make it obey. This kingdom was Macedon, known to us today as **Macedonia**, and had spent years as isolated and scattered hill tribes. But now, with the Greek mainland so weak and exhausted from the Peloponnesian War, the king of Macedon, **Philip II** set his eye (for he had only one eye) on conquering the whole of Greece.

Reading Comprehension Questions

1. Why did the Peace of Nicias last for such a short time?

2. Who was Alcibiades, and what kind of politician was he?

3. What happened in the Sicilian Expedition? Was the expedition doomed from the start?

Reading Comprehension Questions

4. Why did Sparta make an alliance with Persia?

5. How did Athens eventually lose the Peloponnesian War? What happened that kept them from fighting any longer?

6. How did the Peloponnesian War end? Was Greece in a better or a worse position long-term?

ACTIVITY

Direct Instruction Review

The hardest part about history is memorizing all those facts, dates, and events. To make this process easier, we are included this short section called *Direct Instruction Review*. Direct Instruction (or DI) is a powerful pedagogical tool whereby teachers ask students a series of *call-and-response* questions, and students respond back with the aim of learning this material to *mastery*. Teacher's lines are in **bold**; student's lines in *italics*.

What happened to the Greeks once the Persian Wars were over? *Having banded together to defeat so powerful an empire as Persia, the Greeks largely threw away all of these advantages, turning on each other and fighting each in the Peloponnesian War.*

What period in Greek history followed the Persian Wars? *The age of Classical Greece, which was a "golden age" in Greek culture thanks to Greek contributions in theatre, architecture, and philosophy.*

How long did the age of Classical Greece last? *The age of Classical Greece lasted from 479 to 323 BC, or the end of the Persian Wars to the death of Alexander the Great.*

Was the age of Classical Greece a time of great peace and prosperity? *Prosperity, yes, but peace, no, for the Greek city-states soon went to war against each other.*

What was the name of this war? *The Peloponnesian War, which lasted from 431 to 404 BC.*

And who were the combatants in the Peloponnesian War? *Athens and her allies fought against the city-state of Sparta and her allies.*

And why did they go to war against each other? *Sparta and Corinth feared the growing power and ambition of Athens, whereas Athens wanted to preserve its empire.*

What kind of a state was Athens, and what kind of a state was Sparta? What were their strengths and weaknesses? *Athens was a democracy and possessed a strong navy, whereas Sparta was an oligarchy and possessed a strong army.*

How do we know anything about the Peloponnesian War? *The Greek historian Thucydides wrote a history book detailing the events of the war and why it occurred.*

Why do we study the Peloponnesian War? *We study the Peloponnesian War because of Thucydides, whose history book helps us to understand the political theory and the workings of large states, the nature of justice, and the problems of the human condition.*

And how did the Peloponnesian War end? *The Peloponnesian War ended when Sparta finally built a navy of its own and defeated Athens at the Battle of Aegospotami in 405 BC.*

ACTIVITY

Map Practice: The Peloponnesian War

Instructions: Carefully look over the map below, which are identical to maps provided in the rest of this chapter. However, there is one crucial difference: these maps have blanks in the place of the name of a sea, a region, or a site. Fill in the appropriate blank with the term list provided above each map.

The Peloponnesian War: Bodies of water such as the Mediterranean, the Aegean and the Black Sea; the cities of Athens, Sparta, Corinth, Thebes, Epidamnus, Argos, Knossos, and Corycra; the island of Melos and Delos; the regions of Macedon, Epirus, Thessaly, and Crete; and the Battles of Potidae and Amphipolis.

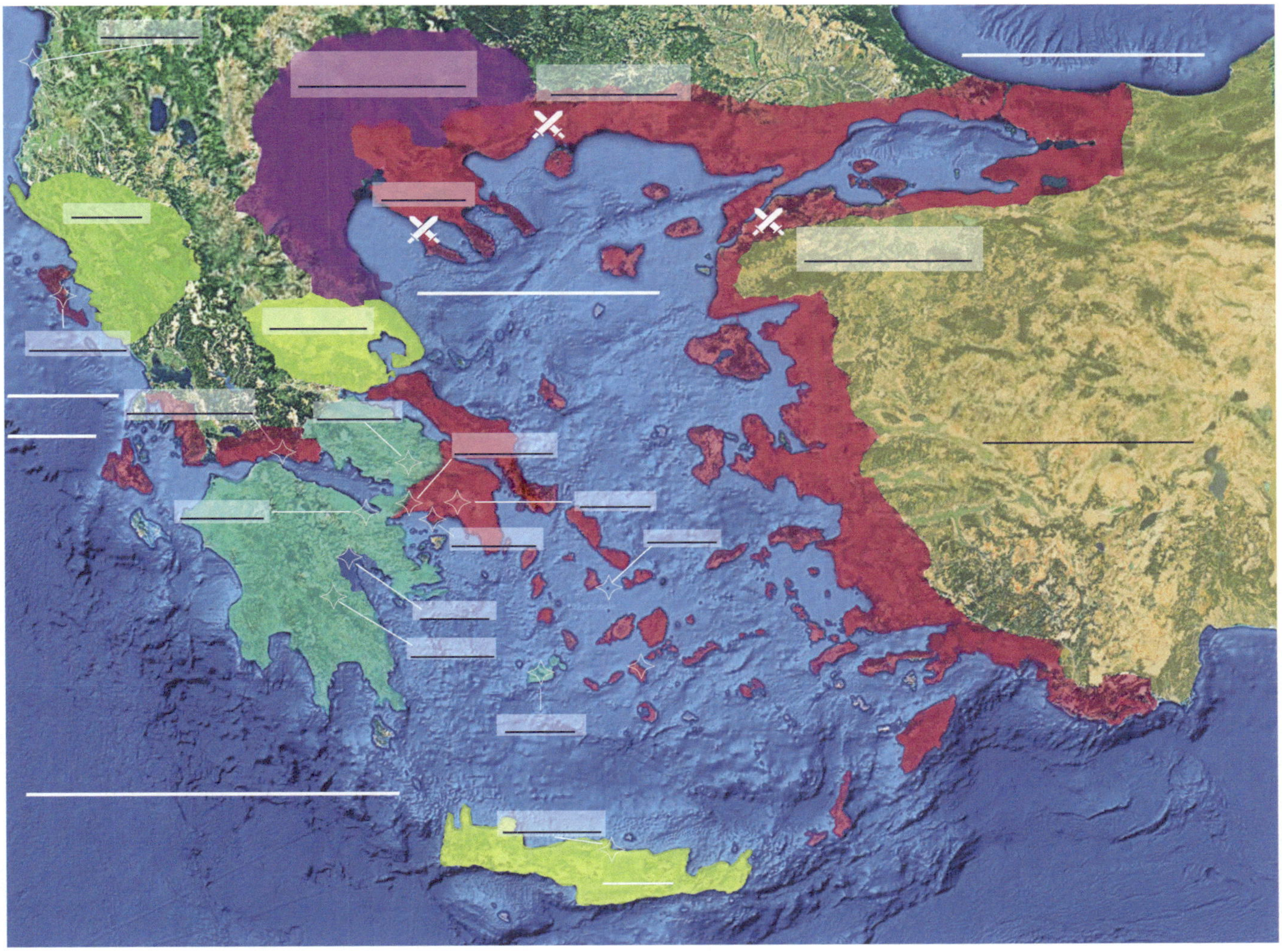

Want to study this map online? Type in the link below or scan the QR code to access an interactive diagram: **https://bit.ly/3okSogF**

ACTIVITY

Timeline Practice / The Peloponnesian War

The hardest part about history is memorizing all those facts, dates, and events. To make this process easier, check out the timeline below—well, technically, there are *two* timelines. Some entries are missing dates, and others are missing the event that occurred on that date. With the information available from both timelines, fill in the missing blanks to get a better sense of the timeline for this chapter.

480 BC
The Battle of ___________, where the Athenian navy destroys a large portion of the Persian fleet.

477 BC
Various Greek city-states accept the leadership of ___________ and form the ___________ League.

447 BC
Construction begins on the ___________ in Athens, the celebrated temple on the Athenian Acropolis.

431 - 404 BC
The duration of the ___________ War, with Athens and her allies fighting a devastating war against ___________ and her allies.

405 BC
The Spartans defeat the Athenians at the Battle of ___________, thereby ending Athens' control of the Aegean Sea.

480 BC
The Battle of ___________, where a Spartan-led army of 7,000 troops holds off a Persian army of 300,000 troops for almost a week.

449 BC
Athens and Persia sign the Peace of ___________ and formally end the Persian Wars. But by now, Athens is already fighting Sparta in the Peloponnesian War.

433 BC
Athens demands ___________ remove the ___________ officials serving in the city government. Soon, the Athenians besiege the city.

415 - 413 BC
The ___________ Expedition, wherein a massive Athenian invasion force is destroyed in a failed attempt to conquer Sicily.

404 BC
Having ___________ the Peloponnesian War, ___________ sign a peace treaty with Sparta, destroy their fortifications, and tear down the Long Wall. Herein ends the Peloponnesian War.

_______ BC
The Battle of Salamis, where the Athenian navy destroys a large portion of the Persian fleet.

_______ BC
Various Greek city-states accept the leadership of Athens and form the Delian League.

_______ BC
Construction begins on the Parthenon in Athens, the celebrated temple on the Athenian Acropolis.

_______ - _______ BC
The duration of the Peloponnesian War, with Athens and her allies fighting a devastating war against Sparta and her allies.

_______ BC
The Spartans defeat the Athenians at the Battle of Aegospotami, thereby ending Athens' control of the Aegean Sea.

_______ BC
The Battle of Thermopylae, where a Spartan-led army of 7,000 troops holds off a Persian army of 300,000 troops for almost a week.

_______ BC
Athens and Persia sign the Peace of Callias and formally end the Persian Wars. But by now, Athens is already fighting Sparta in the Peloponnesian War.

_______ BC
Athens demands Potidaea remove the Corinthian officials serving in the city government. Soon, the Athenians besiege the city.

_______ - _______ BC
The Sicilian Expedition, wherein a massive Athenian invasion force is destroyed in a failed attempt to conquer Sicily.

_______ BC
Having lost the Peloponnesian War, Athens signs a peace treaty with Sparta, destroy their fortifications, and tear down the Long Wall. Herein ends the Peloponnesian War.

WRITING

Writing Prompt

Writing is thinking, so we will spend considerable time this year writing and thinking about history. In the space provided, write a short essay answering the question: ***How do great states like that of Athens and Sparta interact with each other? What interests do they pursue in regards to each other? Do they behave like people, or more like animals? What are these states ultimately concerned with? Be sure to reference the writings of Thucydides in answering this question.***

STARO NAGORICANE / NORT

Photo by Tomica S.

CHAPTER

The Rise of Macedon

ROADMAP

- Learn about the kingdom of Macedon and its most significant rulers, Philip II and Alexander the Great.
- Study Alexander the Great's campaign against the Persian Empire and his victories at the Granicus River, the Issus River, and Gaugamela.
- Learn about the beginnings of the Hellenistic world and the expansion of Greek culture from Spain to India.
- Practice our knowledge of maps and chronology, as well as our writing skills through reading comprehension questions and an essay.

THALES OUTCOME

Nº 11

Someone with Dreams and Aspirations to Change the World *produces plans to accomplish personal and educational aspirations.*

We will conclude our study of ancient Greece studying ancient Macedon, a kingdom to the north of Greece that will come to rule over the Greek world. While the rulers of Macedon—namely, Philip II and his son, Alexander the Great—were two of the most dynamic and capable kings in world history, we want to ask ourselves, "Did they really change the world for the *better*?"

The Rising Power of Macedon / ~600s-400s BC

MACEDON MAY NOT ACTUALLY be a part of Greece. The kingdom sits too far to the north and few, if any, mythological heroes came from the area. Yet, the Macedonians ruled Greece during the last two centuries of Classical Greece, and the death of the Macedonian king Alexander the Great marked the end of the Classical period and heavily influenced the affairs of Greece. So who were the people of Macedon, and what were they like?

In a way, **Macedon** was still like the world of Homeric Greece. The Macedonians most likely spoke a dialect of Greek (we're still not sure), but the Macedonians did not live in a *polis*, the dynamic city-states that the Greeks believed separated civilized peoples from barbarians. Instead, most Macedonians lived in small villages where they eked out lives as farmers or herders.

Their Greek neighbors to the south regarded them as barbarians and criticized them for their backwardness. For example, Macedonians drank unmixed wine—i.e., wine that was not diluted with water and thus very strong—and a Macedonian boy could only become a man after killing first a boar on a hunt and then an enemy in battle. (Pomeroy 284-285).

Macedon lies in two crescent-shaped halves: long fertile plains rolling into the Aegean Sea and mountains overlooking the plains. The mountains and rivers divided the people of Macedon from each other and prevented the unified culture that characterized their Greek neighbors to the south. Macedon sits between two other regions connected to the Greek world but lacking the kind of city culture the Greeks valued so highly: to the west lay Thrace, and to the southeast Thessaly, kingdoms that threatened Macedon periodically. Macedon had immense potential with its coastline, fertile agricultural land, and mountains that possessed precious metals like gold and silver, and more practical resources for ambitious kings like iron and timber for making weapons—if only they could tap into it.

For generations, Macedon's kings were unable to do that. They died in battle or in palace coups, unable to tame the local chieftains who wielded great power over their own little corner of Macedon. The royal family, known as the **Argeads**, ruled Macedon. They claimed they came from the city of Argos in the Peloponnesse and were descended from Heracles himself. The Argeads recognized that Greek culture had its strengths and hoping to strengthen ties with the Greek world, they imitated the Greeks as much as they could. They

For centuries, Macedon existed at the edge of the Greek world. During the Peloponnesian War, Macedonian kings like Perdiccas II and Archelaus kept Macedon neutral and instead, sold Macedon's timber and grain to the highest bidder. In the end, such policies enabled Macedon to conquer regions that had for so long looked down upon them and demonstrates the wisdom of focusing on trade and diplomacy instead of outright warfare.

Vocabulary

Macedon
Macedon was a kingdom located to the north of Greece. Following the Peloponnesian War, Macedon became organized and powerful enough to conquer the entirety of Greece.

Argeads
The royal family of Macedon, who claimed descendancy from Heracles.

Alexander I
Alexander I was the first strongly-attested king of Macedon, whose reign lasted through the Persian Wars. He initially took an oath of loyalty to the Persian king Xerxes and helped him in his invasion of Greece, but he may have also given the Athenians and Spartans intelligence about Persian battle plans. He reigned from 497 to 454 BC.

Perdiccass II
The king of Macedon during the Peloponnesian War who made it a matter of policy to support neither Sparta nor Athens in the war but instead, to sell them as many goods as they needed, and thus profit off of the war. He reigned from 454 to 412 BC.

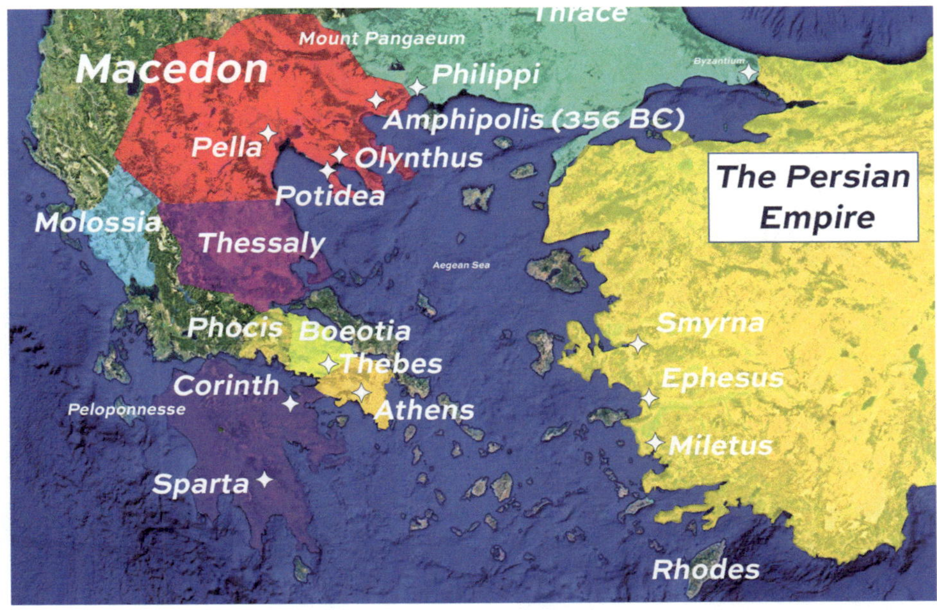

MACEDON & THE GREEK WORLD / 382 BC
At the time of Philip's birth, Macedonian territory was small and limited to northern Greece.

encouraged the Macedonian nobility to adopt Greek culture and customs, too. In principle, Macedon's kings wielded immense power: they made treaties with foreign states, they commanded the armies, and they granted land and titles to their supporters. Still, day-to-day, the kings struggled to control local Macedonian noblemen, who could refuse troops or resources for the king.

The Persian invasion of Darius I changed Macedon as much as it changed the rest of Greece. Unlike the Greeks, who resisted to the last man, the Macedonians submitted to the Persians and swore an oath of loyalty to the Persian king. As part of their status as vassals to Darius' successor, Xerxes, the Macedonians even sent troops to fight against the Greeks in the Persian Wars. Perhaps playing both sides, the Macedonian king **Alexander I** may have given the Athenians and the Spartans intelligence of Persian troop movements and battle plans. Despite their misgivings, the Greeks eventually accepted Alexander I's claim he and his royal family were Greek and welcomed them into the Greek world. The Macedonians were even permitted to participate in the Olympic Games, a privilege reserved for Greeks.

During the Peloponnesian War, Macedon enjoyed stable leadership. King **Perdiccas II**, who ruled from 454 to 412 BC, played the Spartans and the Athenians off of each other, since both sides needed timber and precious metals. Athens especially needed Macedonian grain and timber was needed for shipbuilding, and Perdiccas II sold such goods to the highest bidder without committing himself to fight for either side. During these years, Macedon also annexed regions containing valuable silver mines in the mountains and hills of Upper Macedon (Pomeroy 286-287).

Perdiccas' successor **Archelaus** continued these policies. First, the increasing trade with Sparta and Athens while otherwise remaining neutral. Second, Archelaus encouraged **Hellenization**, the process of adapting and imitating Greek culture. The art, architecture, literature and other elements of Classical Greek culture discussed in the previous chapter was seen to be superior to that of Macedon, prompting Macedonian kings to bring it into Macedon as much as they could. Accordingly, Archelaus built a new capital for the Macedonians at **Pella** and paid leading Greek artists and architects to design and decorate his new city.

He even invited playwrights to come and stay at his court, notably the Greek tragedian Euripides, among others. But Archelaus was killed on a hunt and, following his death, a series of violent assassinations took place that threatened to undo the progress all prior Macedonian kings had made in the last century (Pomeroy 287). Archelaus' son Amyntas II was caught up in the instability and reigned for only a few months in 394 BC before he was killed.

When the dust settled, Amyntas III was king of the Macedonians. Amyntas III was related by blood to the Argead family but not a direct descendant of Archelaus I. Amyntas III had to seize power through the kind of violent coup that often ruined states. In fact, peace was restored for a time, and Amyntas subdued Macedon's with a mix of diplomacy and warfare. But when Amyntas died in 387 BC, events spiraled out of control even further.

Amyntas' heir Alexander II was murdered by a Macedonian nobleman named Ptolemy of Alorus. Ptolemy seized the throne for himself and ruled as king in place of Alexander's younger brother, Perdiccas, a scenario the Macedonian nobility resented. During the chaos, the Macedonians called in representatives from **Thebes**, the leading city in the region in **Boeotia**, to help restore order. Ptolemy could rule as regent, but Perdiccas' younger brother Philip had to live in Thebes as a hostage to guarantee Perdiccass' good behavior.

When Perdiccas came of age, he murdered Ptolemy and took the throne. Perdiccas III ruled Macedon from 365 to 360 BC until he also was killed—this time in battle with the Illyrians, a tribe living north of Macedon in what is today Albania. The throne would have gone to the infant son of Perdiccas III, had it not been for Philip and his grand designs for Macedon, Greece, and indeed the whole world. The details of who overthrow whom are less important to memorize than that, one, Macedon was quietly gathering wealth while Athens and Sparta tore each other apart, and two, that it experienced dramatic political instability before rising to dominance through a ruler who united them all.

Vocabulary

Archelaus
The king of Macedon who built the capital of Pella and encouraged Hellenization amongst the Macedonian nobility. He reigned as king of Macedon from 412 to 400 BC.

Hellenization
Hellenization is the process of adapting, imitating, and spreading Greek culture beyond the borders of Attica and the Peloponnese.

Pella
Pella was the capital of the ancient kingdom of Macedon.

Thebes
Thebes was the dominant city in the region of Boeotia and a rival of Sparta, Athens, and Corinth.

Boeotia
A region in central Greece west of Athens and north of Corinth.

Reading Comprehension Questions

1. What is the geography of Macedon like? Did it help or hinder Macedon in the long run?

2. What is "Hellenization", and why did Macedonian kings encourage this process?

3. How did kings like Perdiccas II and others help Macedon in the long run?

ACTIVITY

A Closer Look at the Argead Dynasty

Instructions: The Argead dynasty claimed they descended from no less a hero than Heracles, the son of the Greek god Zeus. Their family tree can be confusing, however, given the number of assassinations, coups, and deaths-in-battle the Argead rulers suffered. Read over the family tree below and write a short description concerning the fate of each member on the tree.

The Argead Family Tree

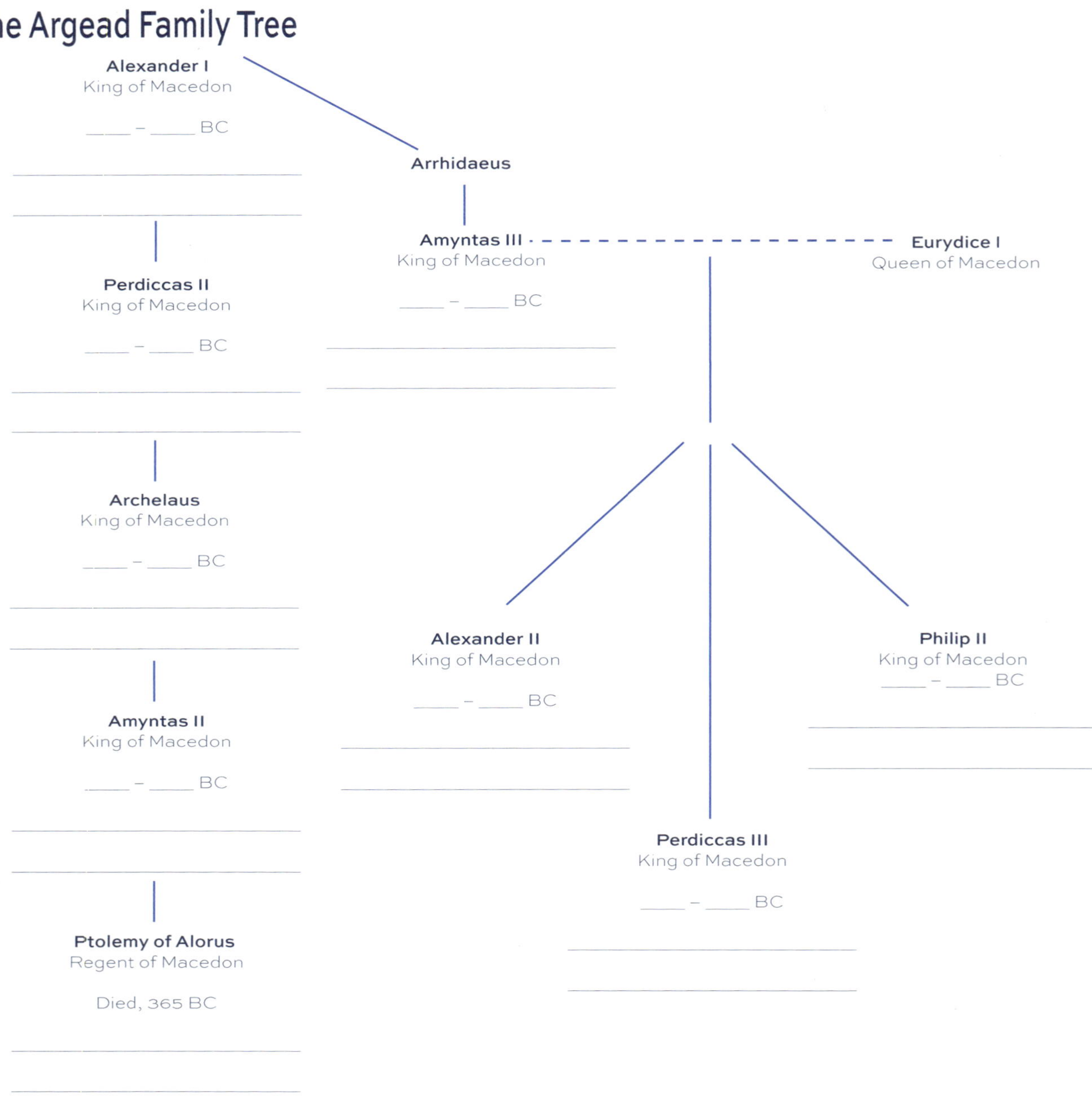

ACTIVITY

Map Practice: The Rise of Macedon

Instructions: Carefully look over the map below, which are identical to maps provided in the rest of this chapter. However, there is one crucial difference: these maps have blanks in the place of the name of a sea, a region, or a site. Fill in the appropriate blank with the term list provided above each map.

The Kingdom of Macedon: Bodies of water such as the Mediterranean, the Aegean and the Black Sea; the cities of Pella, Potidaea, Amphipolis, Byzantium, Athens, Sparta, Corinth, and Thebes; the regions of Macedon, Thessaly, Thrace, the Persian Empire, Boeotia, Phocis, the Peloponnesse, and Molossia.

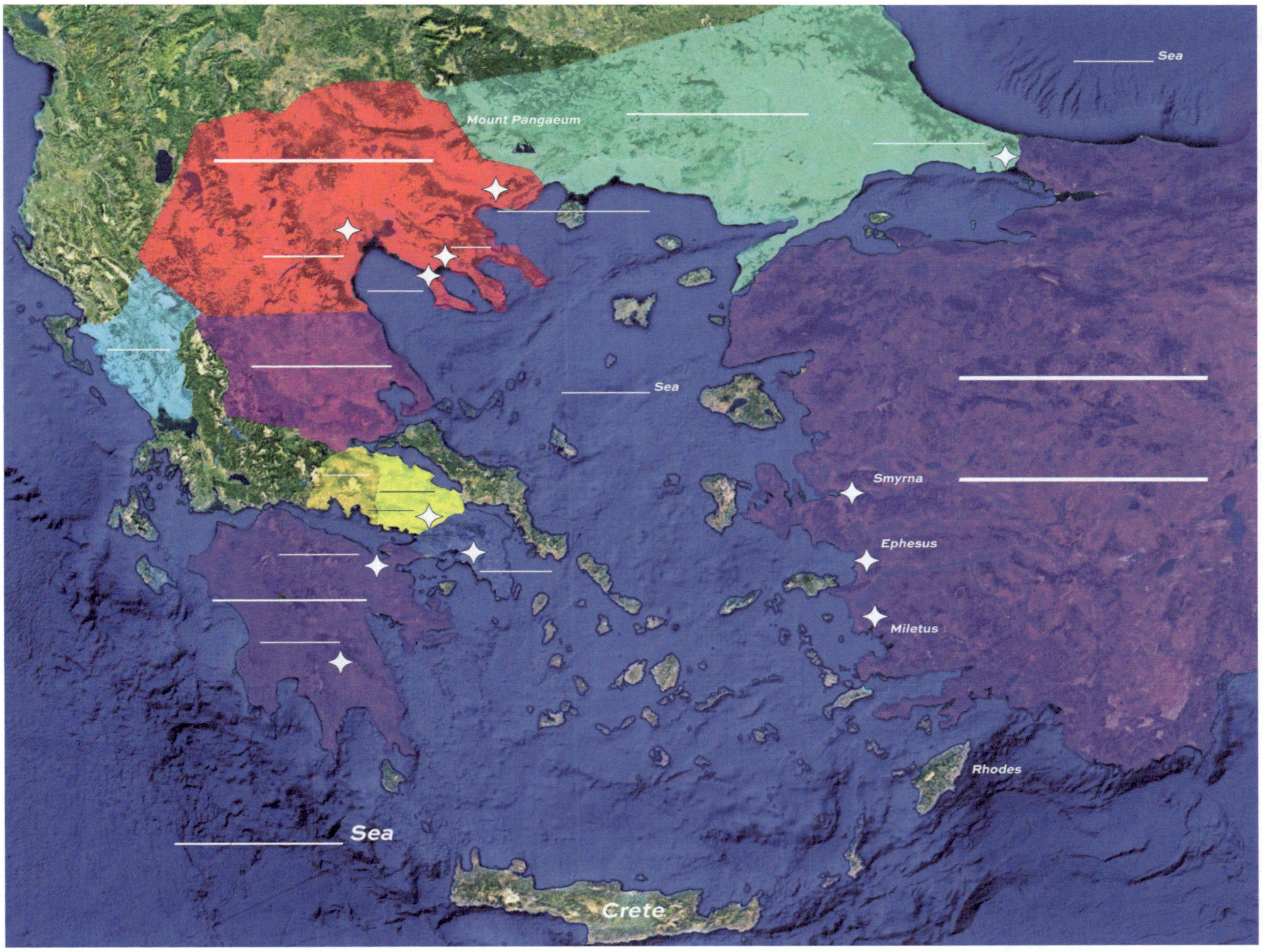

______ Sea

Mount Pangaeum

______ Sea

Smyrna

Ephesus

Miletus

Rhodes

______ Sea

Crete

The Rise of Philip II / 382 to 336 BC

PHILIP WAS BORN in 382 BC in the city of Pella. His mother Eurydice taught him to read and gave him other basic elements of a Greek education. But Philip's life changed when his brother Alexander II was murdered. As part of the negotiated peace between Ptolemy (his brother's murderer) and Pelopidas, one of the rulers of Thebes, Philip was taken to Thebes. There, Philip lived in the leading city of Boeotia from 369 to 367 as a hostage incentivising his brother Perdiccass's cooperation with the Thebans. While he was away from his home, Philip benefited immensely from the experience. Thebes, at the time, was the dominant city in Greece, and Philip absorbed many new ideas he took back to Macedon.

Thebes played a role in Boeotia not unlike that of Sparta in the Peloponnesse or Athens in Attica. Thebes, though, had sided with Persia in the Persian Wars and thus did not take part in the climatic battles at Thermopylae or Plataea. During the Peloponnesian War, Thebes sided with Sparta, fearing the rise of Athens as much as anyone else. Then, at the end of the Peloponnesian War, Sparta tried to make war on its former ally, Thebes. Led by two charismatic generals, Pelopidas and Epaminondas, Thebes defeated the Spartans handedly at the Battle of Leuctra in 371 BC (Cartwright). For a short time, Thebes became the dominant power in Greece, and it was during this period that Philip lived in Thebes. Philip received a far better education in Thebes than he would have received in Macedon—not only in Greek literature but also in Greek warfare and the strengths and weaknesses of the Greek phalanx.

THE MACEDONIAN PHALANX

Philip's older brother Perdiccas III became king in 365 BC. He reigned for five years until he was killed in battle in 360 BC, fighting a tribe known as the Illyrians. Philip returned home to Macedon and was crowned king. From there, Philip had one success after another as he subdued Macedon's customary enemies. To accomplish this subduing, Philip II either formed alliances with them or crushed them in battle. Perhaps the most significant of these alliances was with the Molossians, a tribe that lay

Philip II possessed many of the gifts we associate with virtuous leadership: he was bold and decisive, resolved to suffer hardships alongside his troops, and had the self-control to accomplish his larger goals. Yet, he did all this through means we do not find in accordance with virtue and right living: brutal warfare, selling the population of whole cities into servitude, and worse. Such ends do not justify such means.

Vocabulary

Philip II
As king of Macedon, Philip II transformed Macedon into the dominant power in Greece. He lived from 382 to 336 BC, and he reigned as king of Macedon from 359 to 336 BC.

Battle of Leuctra
Fought in 371 BC, the Thebans defeated the Spartans and became masters of Greece.

Olympias
Olympias was a Molossian princess, wife of Philip II, and the mother of Alexander the Great. She lived from 375 to 316 BC.

Alexander
Alexander was the son of Philip II and Olympias who, as prince and later the king of Macedon, would conquer the known world. Today, we know him as Alexander the Great, and he lived from 356 to 323 BC.

Sarissa
A sarissa was a twenty foot spear carried by soldiers in a Macedonian phalanx.

Pezhetairoi
The "foot companions" of the king, referring to a Macedonian soldier.

to the west of Macedon in the region of Epirus. As part of the alliance, Philip married the Molossian princess **Olympias**, who bore Philip a son named **Alexander**. On the night of their wedding, Olympias had a dream she was struck by lightning, an omen that Olympias and other soothsayers interpreted as referring to the unborn child of Olympias. Surely, one day, that child would grow up to be a great hero.

OLYMPIAS / 375 - 316 BC (*LEFT*) & PHILIP II / 382 - 336 BC (*RIGHT*)

On the battlefield, Philip made improvements to the Macedonian phalanx. Recall that a **phalanx** is a military formation, wherein soldiers fought in a tight, close-knit shield wall. They then charged the enemy and stabbed them with spears until one side broke ranks and retreated. Philip improved upon the phalanx in one significant way: huge spears. Whereas a normal spear may be taller than the height of an average man, Philip equipped the Macedonian phalanx with a twenty-foot pike called a **sarissa**. The result was that the Macedonian phalanx could stab at the enemy from a far greater distance before the enemy could get close enough to use their spears. Such a phalanx was not very mobile, so the Macedonian cavalry guarded the sides (the "flanks") of the unit.

The nobility traditionally served in the cavalry since only they could afford a horse, a privilege that gave the Macedonian noblemen special access to the king. Philip II dubbed the members of the infantry the **pezhetairoi** or "foot companions", which implied that they had a special status not unlike that of the nobles (Pomeroy 291). They were "companions" of a king who fought alongside his troops, something immediately evident in the eye Philip II lost his eye at the siege of Methone, a city on the Aegean Sea controlled by Athens.

And Philip II put those twenty-foot spears, cavalry, and foot companions to good use. The city-states of Greece were in a state of constant warfare, but now the chief source of the turmoil arose from the ambition of Phocis.

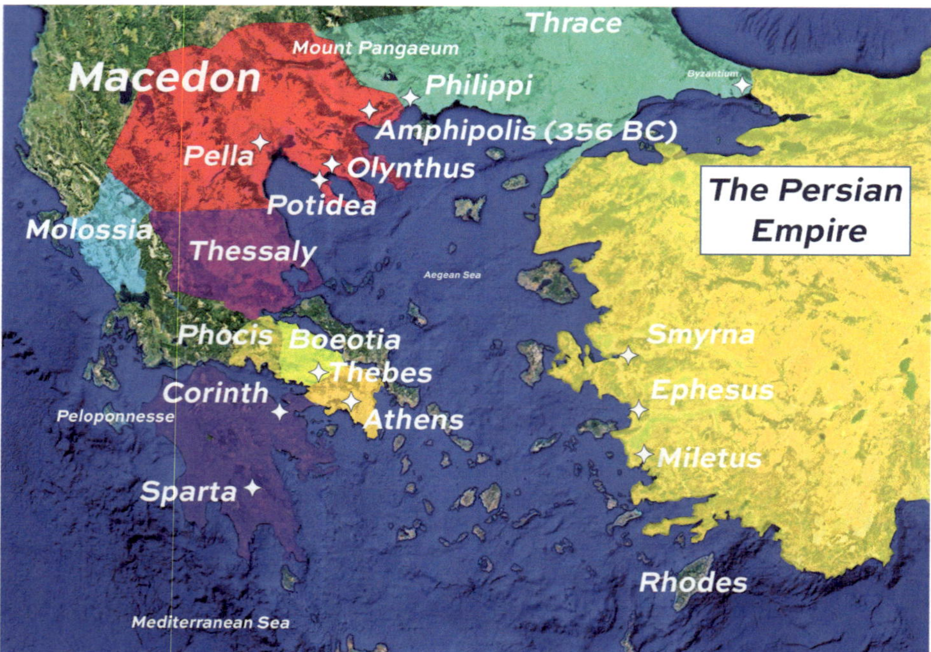

MACEDON & THE GREEK WORLD / 377 BC

During Philip's reign, the city-states of Greece were in a state of constant warfare

Phocis was a coalition of small *poleis* and villages in central Greece, and they resented Theban dominance after the Battle of Leuctra. Phocis enjoyed some early victories against Philip II, but that success came to naught: Philip II and his Thessalonian allies crushed Phocis at the **Battle of the Crocus Field**. This victory and others brought Philip II more influence and power in the region. The Thessalonians invited Philip II to be their commander-in-chief, and Philip assumed Phocis' position on the council governing the region's foreign and domestic policy.

But the rise of Macedon threatened not only Boeotia but also Athens. Macedonian territory now stretched to the very borders of Athens, and Athens relied on grain from Macedon and the Black Sea. The presence of an ambitious king like Philip II controlling Athens' grain supply abroad and threatening Athenian security at home was untenable. The Athenians recognized Philip II would not stop until he ruled all of Greece. What could be done?

Most avoided speaking out against Philip II—all except Demosthenes, an Athenian politician and orator. **Demosthenes** lived in Athens from 384 to 322 BC, and he is famous for delivering a series of speeches later called the *Philippics* that criticized Philip II of Macedon. While we remember Demosthenes for his courage in the face of the seemingly-unstoppable might of Macedon, Demosthenes' efforts came to nothing. In 338 BC, Athens, Thebes, and a few cities from the Peloponnesse met the army of Macedon at the **Battle of Chaeronea**, fought in the city of the same name in Boeotia. Athens and her allies suffered an overwhelming defeat, with Philip II's son Alexander commanding the Macedonian cavalry. Any hopes for Greek independence

Vocabulary

Battle of the Crocus Field
Fought in 352 BC, Philip II defeated Phocis and gained mastery of almost all of northern Greece.

Demosthenes
Demosthenes was a famous Athenian orator who tried, unsuccessfully, to slow down Philip II's conquest of Greece. He lived from 384 to 322 BC.

Battle of Chaeronea
Taking place in Boeotia, the Battle of Chaeronea saw Macedon crush the combined forces of Athens and Thebes.

League of Corinth
Led by Philip II of Macedon, the League of Corinth was a new alliance system, whereby all the Greek city-states pledged to work together for the common defense of Greece.

Hegemon
In Greek, the word *hegemon* refers to a single military or political leader. In political theory, the word *hegemon* refers to the dominant superpower in a regiom, similar to the position Macedon held after the Battle of Chaeronea.

were left on the battlefield along with huge numbers of Athenian and Theban hoplites.

Philip II was shrewd, and he carefully plotted his next move. While he publicly wept for Theban hoplites dead on the battlefield, he crushed Thebes nonetheless. That way, Thebes would never rise again to challenge Macedon. He demanded a large ransom for Theban soldiers, he exiled Thebes' political leaders, and he installed Macedonian troops on the Cadmea, the great citadel on the Theban acropolis. Thebes had collaborated too long with Persia, and they could not be trusted. Most Greek city-states resented Thebes' dominance in Greece and few lamented Thebes' destruction.

But with Athens, Philip II was far more conciliatory and tactful, hoping to win over the leading city in Greece. He had Alexander escort the Athenian casualties back to Athens personally and even permitted Demosthenes to give the funeral oration for them. The efforts worked, for Athens supported Philip II in his plan to bring peace and stability to the land of Greece which he called the **League of Corinth**, with himself at the head of the League.

Philip II's plans for the League of Corinth were simple. To end the squabbling between Sparta, Athens, Thebes, and any other ambitious power in the Greek world, they would all submit on relatively equal terms to Philip II. Philip would be the **hegemon**, the commander and leader of all of Greece's hoplite troops. In Greek, the word 'hegemon' refers to a single military or political leader. In political theory, the word 'hegemon' refers to the dominant superpower in a region, similar to the position that Macedon held after the Battle of Chaeronea. The League would be centered in Corinth because of Corinth's unique position on the isthmus, which allowed Corinth (or by extension, Philip) to control trade across the Corinthian Gulf and travel into and out of the Peloponnesse. Sparta was no longer a threat and was permitted to remain independent from the league.

PHILIP II'S DEATH / 336 BC

Most important, though, was Philip II's longterm plan: the invasion and conquest of the Persian Empire.

But Philip II would not live long enough to see the fulfillment of his grand ambition. Like many of his Macedonian predecessors, Philip II was assassinated—this time by a member of his own bodyguard. The assassin was a Macedonian nobleman named Pausanis, who came to loathe Philip II when Philip II did not help Pausanis with powerful members of the Macedonian nobility. The family of Philip II's seventh wife, a Macedonian princess named Cleopatra, had assaulted and insulted Pausanias, but Philip II did not want to punish the wrongdoers. Such actions would have alienated his wife's family, so as a consolation, Philip II promoted Pausanias to the coveted position of royal bodyguard. Still angry, Pausanias waited and plotted until the wedding of Philip's own daughter. There, in 336 BC, Pausanis killed the king before a crowd of shocked onlookers.

Philip II's legacy is hard to ascertain. Philip II left Macedon far more secure and politically stable than when he found it—indeed, Macedon could have been swallowed up by her neighbors had it not been for Philip II's leadership. Moreover, the city-states of Greece were also in a near-constant state of fighting, with Athens, Thebes, and Sparta not nearly powerful enough to impose a lasting peace on the whole of Greece. These states could be subdued, but they would not stay down for long. Macedonian strength and resources, combined with able leadership from a figure like Philip II, ensured such a peace would last. But to gain that peace, Philip

II razed whole cities to the ground, erasing them from the face of the earth. In his personal life, Philip II was said to have partied excessively and that he betrayed his friends, including the bodyguard (Pausanias) who ultimately assassinated him.

Despite his Philip II's shortcomings and flaws, the Macedon he left to his son Alexander was far stronger than the one Philip had inherited. Alexander quickly made plans to secure his power, and chief amongst those plans was fulfilling his father's ambition to invade and conquer Persia once and for all.

Reading Comprehension Questions

1. Why did Philip grow up in Thebes? What did he learn there?

2. Why was central Greece in a state of constant fighting and turmoil?

Reading Comprehension Questions

3. Who was Demosthenes, and what did he urge his fellow Athenians to do against Macedon?

4. What was the League of Corinth? What was its stated purpose, and what did Philip II hope the League could accomplish?

5. Does Philip II deserve a title like *the Great*, which was given to his son Alexander? Why or why not?

ACTIVITY

A Closer Look at the Invasion of Persia

Instructions: A Greek writer and teacher named Isocrates, who lived from 436 to 338 BC, had an interesting solution for the internal problems of Greece: invade Persia, a goal Philip II of Macedon adopted for the League of Corinth. For now, we won't give the answer as to why an invasion of the Persian Empire might solve these internal problems. But looking over the map of the Persian Empire, provide a list of the benefits and drawbacks if the Greek world, under the command of Macedon, invaded the Persian Empire.

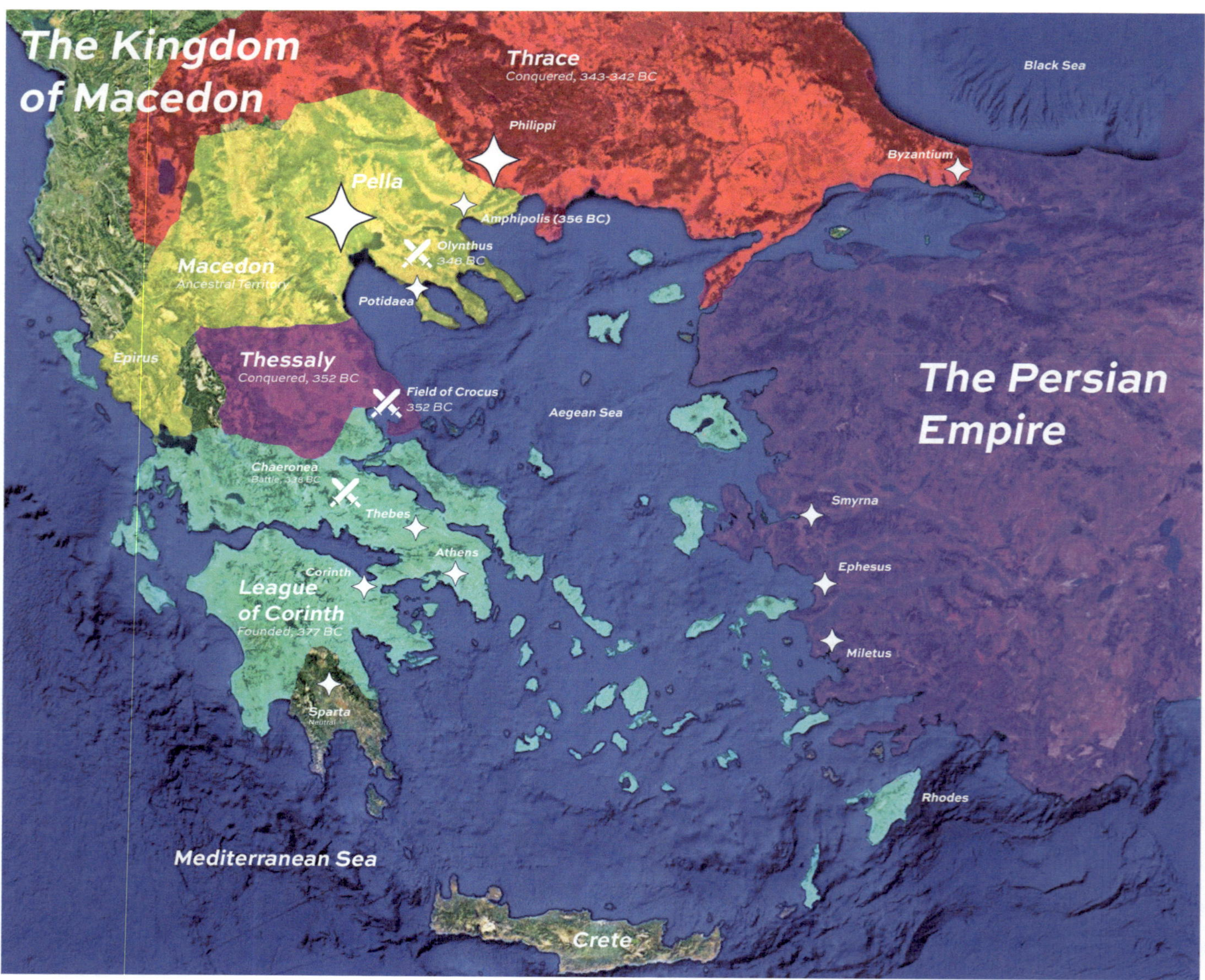

THE KINGDOM OF MACEDON / 336 BC

At the death of Phillip II, the Macedonians had conquered Greece but they, and their new Greek subjects, still feared the Persian Empire might one day again invade them.

The Invasion of Persia (Continued)

In the space below, write as many *benefits* and *drawbacks* from invading the Empire of Persia.

Benefits: What could the League of Corinth* gain *by invading the Persian Empire?	***Consequences: What could the League of Corinth* lose *by invading the Persian Empire?***
Benefit #1:	Drawback #1:
Benefit #2:	Drawback #2:
Benefit #3:	Drawback #3:
Benefit #4:	Drawback #4:

***Teachers and parents**: The Greek teacher Isocrates (436-338 BC) argued that the invasion of Persia could provide a kind of safety valve for the city-states of Greece. In his mind, Persia threatened Greek safety and this threat had to be neutralized, whereas the conquest of Persia would give the Greeks a common goal, treasure to distribute amongst the Greek people, and land the Greeks could settle* (Pomeroy 297).

Alexander the Great / 356 to 323 BC

ALEXANDER WAS BORN in Pella, capital of Macedon, in 354 BC. Alexander was the son of Olympias, a princess from the region of Epirus and the member of a tribe (the Molossians) that claimed ancestry from no less a hero than Achilles. Indeed, Olympias would tell stories about how she dreamed of being struck by lightning on the night she married Philip II, implying that their son—Alexander—was the son of Zeus, not of Philip II, and thus no mere mortal prince. That Olympias sometimes kept snakes in her bed and murdered numerous rivals to the throne of Alexander makes the story of Alexander's rise to greatness that much more intriguing (Mark, Pomeroy 301, Wasson).

Alexander's father Philip II gave him the literal best of everything. He received the kind of education reserved for the Macedonian nobility, being trained not only in horsemanship and warfare but also Greek classics, particularly Homer's *Iliad* and *Odyssey*. These works inspired Alexander to attempt such feats that would place him alongside heroes like Achilles, Diomedes, and Odysseus. Philip II even procured the Greek philosopher **Aristotle** to serve as Alexander's tutor. Aristotle was born in Stagirus, a city in Macedon, but he later studied in Athens under Plato, Socrates' prized student. Aristotle came to equal, if not surpass, his teacher Plato in his writings. Aristotle founded his own school (the Lyceum) and wrote treatises on political theory, biology, physics, and every other subject one might imagine. Having perhaps the wisest and most accomplished philosopher in all of Greece as his teacher, Alexander could not have received a better education. Better yet, Alexander's personal legend was beginning to rival that of Achilles or Jason who likewise enjoyed famous, wise tutors (albeit theirs was the wise centaur Chiron).

Indeed, the greatness that would mark Alexander showed itself early in life. When his father Phillip offered to buy him a horse, Alexander chose a beast named **Bucephalus** whom seemingly no one could tame. The steed was violent and uncontrollable, throwing off every rider who dared to break him. Phillip told his son to find another horse. Alexander looked at Bucephalus and saw its shadow on the ground, and wondered if Bucephalus was simply afraid of his own shadow. He brought the horse into the darkness and thereby tamed the horse. In this way and so many others, Alexander approached a problem that confounded others in a way no one else attempted instead of following in everyone else's footsteps (Mark).

From his father's death in 336 BC to his own death in 323 BC, Alexander conquered no less an enemy than that of Persia, ruling an empire from the Adriatic Sea in the west to the Indus River in the east. Yet, despite Alexander's bold leadership and innovative problem-solving, he could not solve the problem of how to rule his kingdom or handle the success that came from conquering the entirety of the known world.

Vocabulary

Alexander
Alexander was the son of Philip II and Olympias who, as prince and later the king of Macedon, would conquer the known world. Today, we know him as Alexander the Great, and he lived from 356 to 323 BC.

Aristotle
A Greek philosopher whose writings on *Politics, Poetics, Physics, Metaphysics*, and *Rhetoric* form the basis for much of the Western canon. He lived from 384 to 322 BC.

Bucephalus
The name of Alexander the Great's horse.

Antipater
Antipater was a Macedonian general and a close friend of Philip II, who decisively brought Alexander before the Macedonian army to proclaim him king before any rivals could appear and challenge Alexander's claim.

Satraps
The administrator of a particular province in the Persian Empire, akin to a governor.

Scorched Earth Tactics
At times, a country being invaded may destroy its own crops, resources, and infrastructure to make it as difficult as possible for the invading army to survive.

ALEXANDER THE GREAT: MOSAIC (*LEFT*) AND A SCULPTURE (*RIGHT*)
The mosaic may be the most famous representation of Alexander, coming from the House of the Faun in Pompeii.

Alexander brought this approach when he became king. Alexander was only twenty years old, and his reign may have been cut short had it not been for **Antipater**, a general and close friend of Philip II. On Philip's death, Antipater brought Alexander before the army and had them accept Alexander as their new king, a move that undercut anyone challenging Alexander's right to the throne. His father's generals urged him to move slowly and consolidate power, but Alexander refused the advice. Instead, he immediately campaigned against Macedon's traditional enemies, defeated them, and demonstrated to anyone watching that the new king was a man of war like this father.

Still, Thebes revolted. Alexander besieged Thebes and quickly conquered the city, imposing Macedonian troops on the Theban acropolis, called the Cadmea, before Thebes could rouse other Greek *poleis* to rebel. Alexander then let Thebes' neighbors decide what should happen to the defeated city. Thebes' Boeotian neighbors asked that Thebes be destroyed and its whole population—except for the family of one poet, Pindar—sold into slavery. This deed Alexander promptly did, thereby demonstrating that any other rebellious cities would receive the same fate (Pomeroy 302-303).

Then Alexander set about his grand ambition: the conquest of Persia. His father Philip dreamed of conquering the Persians, but this dream had been cut short by the assassin Pausanias in 336 BC. Thus, it was up to Alexander to lead the Greeks across the Hellespont in the same way Darius and Xerxes once led the thousand nations of the Persian Empire into Greece. Alexander divided the Macedonian army in half, leaving the bulk of the troops behind in Greece to defend the Macedonian heartland.

He took with him an army of about 35,000 hoplites and 2,000 cavalry, along with another 10,000 troops gathered from amongst Macedon's allies. In 336 BC, Alexander crossed the Hellespont and journeyed straight to the ruins of Troy. There he begged forgiveness of the long-dead Trojan King Priam for invading his ancient kingdom and sacrificed at the tomb of Alexander's

MACEDON & THE GREEK WORLD / 377 BC

At the time of Philip's birth, Macedonian territory was small and limited to northern Greece.

ancestor, Achilles. He also took the armor of Achilles that was on prominent display in a temple dedicated to Athena, goddess of wisdom, heroes, and warfare (Pomeroy 305). Then Alexander prepared for battle.

At this point, Alexander's campaign could have ended in disaster. One defeat could have encouraged more rebellion back home or cut his army off from supplies in hostile territory, if not outright destroying it. The **satraps** in the area could have destroyed the surrounding farmland and employed similar **scorched earth tactics** to weaken Alexander's army until **Darius III**, the king of Persia, arrived with his massive army.

Instead, the Persian satraps raised an army and marched out to met Alexander at the **Granicus** River in far western **Anatolia**, near ancient Troy. Their plan was to kill Alexander, an ambition Alexander made easier on them by wearing the' armor of Achilles that Alexander had borrowed from the temple to Athena. This armor choice infuriated the Persians. Indeed, the satrap Spithridates almost killed Alexander, but a commander of Alexander's cavalry named **Cleitus** cut off Sphithridates' arm just before the satrap struck the killing blow. The battle ended as the Persians retreated and the Macedonians established a much-needed foothold in Anatolia.

Alexander marched around Ionia (modern-day Turkey) and received the submission of various **satraps** once loyal to the Persian king. He also added to his growing legend the following story. In a village in Asia Minor called Gordia, the priests of the village approached Alexander with an impossible knot–**the Gordian Knot**. The priests told Alexander to try and untie the knot,

Vocabulary

Darius III
Darius III was the last king of Persia, having been defeated by Alexander the Great. He lived from 381 to 330 BC.

Granicus
Fought in 334 BC at the Granicus River in Anatolia, Alexander the Great defeated the Persian army and established a foothold in Anatolia.

Anatolia
A peninsula surrounded by the Aegean, the Black Sea, and the Mediterranean; the region is also referred to as Asia Minor. Today it corresponds to the Republic of Turkey.

Cleitus
Cleitus came from a noble family and served as a cavalry commander. His sister was also the nurse of Alexander. He famously saved Alexander's life at the Granicus River, but later, Alexander killed him in a drunken brawl.

Satraps
The administrators of a particular province in the Persian Empire, akin to a governor.

The Gordian Knot
Local legend said that whoever untied the Gordian Knot would become ruler of Asia. Alexander cut the knot with his sword.

because whoever could do so would become the ruler of all of Asia. Alexander looked at the knot, then slashed it with his sword. As with Bucephalus, Alexander solved a dilemma by rejecting the constraints under which everyone else operated.

Alexander marched south en route to Egypt. He hoped to seize Egyptian and Phoenician ships and prevent them from resupplying Darius' army. But Darius III mobilized an army large enough to attack Alexander and threaten his supply line through Anatolia and back to Macedon. So Alexander turned back to meet Darius III and his army, engaging the Persian army at Issus, a town in Syria. Darius let Alexander choose a battlefield that was too small and narrow for Darius to take advantage of his numerical superiority over the Macedonians. With the mountains to the east, the Mediterranean Sea to the east, and the river Pinarus between them, Darius III could not move his huge numbers of infantry and horses to surround the Macedonian phalanx (Mark).

At first, the Macedonians suffered heavy casualties crossing the river, but Alexander personally led a cavalry charge against the Persian lines that turned the tide of battle. The Macedonians gradually gained more and more ground until the numbers of Persian dead were so great they filled in ravines and streams, allowing the Macedonians to walk over atop of them. Finally, Darius III lost hope and fled the battlefield, leaving behind enough gold to pay for troops and provisions and even the royal family, including Darius III's wife and daughters (Pomeroy 308-309). At this point, Alexander could have pursued the Persians and defeated them once and for all. Instead of following Darius and crushing him, Alexander marched south to Egypt. Aside from the Phoenician city of Tyre, which required a lengthy siege, most cities and kingdoms in the area submitted to Alexander without trouble.

The Macedonian king received a warm and enthusiastic welcome when he arrived in Egypt, for the Egyptians

CLEITUS (*LEFT*) SAVING ALEXANDER (*RIGHT*) FROM SPHITHRIDATES (*CENTER*)

Painting by Charles le Brun

never enjoyed Persian rule and were eager for greater freedom under Alexander. Alexander made sure to honor Egyptian customs and deities on his arrival, even sacrificing to the Apis bull, since the Egyptians worshipped the Apis bull as a god. The Persian king Cambyses II had foolishly slaughtered the animal almost two centuries earlier and earned the hatred of his new Egyptian subjects. Alexander did not intend to make the same mistake. Upon receiving the submission of Egypt, Alexander founded the city of Alexandria at the mouth of the Nile River. The city would be a model of Greek city planning, boasting the world's largest lighthouse, (one of the seven wonders of the world), as well as the world's largest library. Alexandria would serve as a means for the Greeks and later the Romans to tap into the immense agricultural wealth of the Nile River valley (Mark).

But oddly, Alexander marched his army into the Egyptian desert. Alexander wanted to consult the oracle at Zeus-Ammon, an oracle similar to that of Delphi. Alexander had to know if he truly was the son of Zeus as his mother Olympias had told him, and the oracle confirmed to Alexander what he hoped: he was, indeed, the son of Zeus and that he, Alexander, was no mere mortal but a god walking among men. Like his forbearers

THE BATTLE OF ISSUS / 333 BC

Discovered at the Italian city of Pompei, the above mosaic may be the most famous artistic work of Alexander's campaigns against the Persian Empire.

Heracles and Achilles, Alexander had the blood of the gods coursing through his veins; and he began to act like it.

Yet he still had to finish the job of dismantling the Persian Empire and capturing Darius III. He and his army left Egypt and marched northwards to Mesopotamia to meet the Persian army for one final battle: **Gaugamela**, fought in 331 BC. Darius spared no expense for the battle: some 120,000 Persian troops, chariots equipped with long blades called sycthes, even war elephants. Darius forced Alexander to attack him on a plain favorable to Persian numbers where they had room to encircle the Macedonians. But the battle ended the same way: Alexander leading the cavalry in an attack on the Persians and Darius fleeing for safety, hoping to fight another day (Mark, Pomeroy 313-314).

Alexander therein conquered the great Persian cities of Babylon, Susa, and Persepolis. Alexander treated Babylon and Susa with care, even pledging to rebuild the temple to Marduk in Babylon. But Persepolis, the great ceremonial capital of the Persian Empire, received very different treatment. First, the Macedonians looted the imperial treasury, an act that required 10,000 mules and 5,000 camels to carry all the gold the Persians had amassed in three centuries of rule (Mieroop 319).

After hours of drinking and partying, Alexander and his troops set the city on fire, burning it to the ground to signal to Greece, Persia, and everywhere else that Alexander was now the undisputed ruler of both. Later, the satrap of Bactria assassinated Darius III, leaving Alexander the master of the known world. Alexander may have remained the king of Macedon and king of Persia for the rest of his life—except Alexander wanted *more*.

Vocabulary

Battle of Issus
Fought in 333 BC at the town of Issus, Alexander the Great defeated Darus III, captured Darius' family, and all-but ensured that the Macedonians would triumph over Persia.

Tyre
Tyre was a prosperous Phoenician port city that refused to submit to Alexander the Great, who then besieged and destroyed the city in 331 BC.

Alexandria
Located at the mouth of the Nile River, Alexandria was perhaps the most prosperous and successful port city in the ancient world. Alexander founded the city in 331 BC, naming the city after himself.

Battle of Gaugamela
Fought in 331 BC at the town of Gaugamela, this battle saw Alexander the Great defeat the Persian Empire for the third and final time.

Reading Comprehension Questions

1. What strange events and circumstances surrounded Alexander the Great's birth?

2. What was Alexander the Great's education and upbringing like?

3. Why did Alexander destroy the city of Thebes and sell its inhabitants into slavery?

Reading Comprehension Questions

4. What happened at the Battle of the Granicus? What were the stakes for Alexander and Darius III, if Alexander won or lost? How was Alexander almost defeated at this battle?

5. Why did Alexander march his army into Egypt? What did he hope to gain by marching into Egypt? What did he accomplish while there?

6. Do the actions of Alexander the Great remind you of Xerxes, the Persian king who invaded Greece? Why or why not?

The Death of Alexander / 323 BC

BY 331 BC, ALEXANDER'S EMPIRE stretched from the Adriatic Sea in the west to the Zagros Mountains in the east. He had accomplished more than any other king had before, conquering the most powerful empire the world had seen up until that point. He founded multiple cities in his name—even one after his horse, Bucephalus. He conquered the known world, but he put no systems into place that would determine how his empire would be governed if he suddenly died. And that is exactly what happened, although such a fate occurred years after the Battle of Gaugamela. Let's turn to the final deeds of Alexander's life and his last years on earth, 331 BC to 323 BC.

Following Gaugamela, Alexander's set his sights on consolidating his new dominions. Seeing the inevitable, the remaining satraps of the Persian Empire submitted to Alexander. One satrap named Bessus, the ruler of the far eastern province of **Bactria**, went so far as to assassinate Darius III, hoping to win Alexander's support. Alexander used Darius' death to win favor with his new Persian subjects. He arrested and executed Bessus for killing the king, thereby showing his new subjects that he would be fair and just (and perhaps giving us a warning that if we ever betray a friend, we should expect the same treatment in return).

The success that Alexander enjoyed may have changed the young king, for ruling over so vast an empire seemingly turned him into the kind of ruler the Greeks despised. The journey into the Libyan desert may have been the turning point. There, the oracle of Zeus Ammon had confirmed to Alexander that he was a god; and believing he was a god, he began not to follow the rules everyone else must obey.

The ancient world called this kind of behavior **hubris**—that is, a kind of extreme arrogance, a trait that arises when someone thinks they are better than normal people. Alexander's destruction of a grand imperial capital like Persepolis on a whim at a party certainly demonstrates this kind of arrogance—it happened without much thought after his dinner guest suggested it!

Alexander the Great also displayed this pride on his coins, which depicted him with horns like a god, in his dress (he began wearing Persian robes), and in his demeanor, even demanding that his own Macedonian subjects prostrate themselves—that is, get down on their knees before Alexander—when they entered his presence. Slowly but surely, Alexander's official policies showed the same lack of regard for the lives of the troops who had fought for him and won him this empire.

For generations, the Greeks had looked down upon the Persian Empire as a state that had been corrupted by its great power and wealth. Rulers like Cyrus the Great may have been hardy warrior-kings, but rulers like Darius III had become cruel and lazy, more concerned with taking care of themselves than their people. Yet when Alexander conquered Persia, he began to act just like them, illustrating the truth that power so often corrupts the soul.

THE EXTENT OF ALEXANDER THE GREAT'S EMPIRE / 323 BC

At its height, Alexander the Great's empire stretched from the Adriatic Sea to the Indus River Valley.

And then he married a Sogdianan princess named **Roxane**. Alexander's marriage frightened his Macedonian troops. They resented that their future kings would come from the Persian lands they worked so hard to conquer. Then came news of assassination attempts on Alexander's life, which Alexander dealt with swiftly and thoroughly—perhaps *too* thoroughly. He executed anyone connected with the plot, even a longtime friend and one of his best generals named Parmenion. Alexander discovered that Parmenion's son Philotas knew about the assassination plot but did not inform his father Parmenion or his king Alexander—so they all had to die (Mark, Pomeroy 317-318).

The worst moment was executing Cleitus the Black. Cleitus had saved Alexander's life back at the Granicus River but at a dinner party and after considerable alcohol consumption, Cleitus did the unforgivable: he criticized Alexander's Persian-like behavior. For generations, the Greeks believed they had triumphed over the Persians because the Persians had grown weak and lazy. Their great wealth kept them from working hard (why do it?) or enduring great hardships (why not pay someone?) or attempting heroic deeds (why be brave when you are already rich?). And now, having conquered Persia, Alexander was behaving just like their kings. At this criticism, Alexander threw a spear at Cleitus and killed him (Mark, Pomeroy 318).

Undeterred, Alexander planned more campaigns eastwards. He hoped to add the lands beyond the **Indus River** valley to his domains. To the Greeks, the Indian subcontinent was the ends of the earth—a desert followed by an ocean wrapping itself around the world—and the prospect of invading this desert filled Alexander's troops with unimaginable dread.

Still, Alexander marched them all through the **Khyber Pass**, a route through the Hindu Kush Mountains that Darius had taken centuries earlier in his conquest of the valley. But upon entering India, Alexander found, not a

Vocabulary

Bactria
Bactria was a former satrap of the Persian Empire Alexander populated with Greeks and Macedonians. As a result, Bactria became famous as a melting pot region of Central Asian, Greek, Indian, and Persian culture.

Roxane
A princess from the region of Sogdiana who married Alexander the Great.

Indus River
One of the two major river systems on the Indian subcontinent.

Hydaspes River
Fought in 326 BC, the battle at the Hydaspes River saw Alexander defeat King Porus. The battle is famous for its location, which was further east than any Greeks had ever gone before, the battle's use of war elephants, and that it was Alexander's last battle.

Khyber Pass
A strategic route through the Hindu Kush Mountains.

Vassal
The word *vassal* refers to someone who has taken an oath of obedience to a more powerful ruler.

Opis Mutiny
In the Opis Mutiny, Alexander's soldiers rebelled when he introduced a group of Iranian soldiers into his army and told his veteran troops they would be going home.

DEATH OF CLEITUS THE BLACK / 375 - 328 BC
Cleitus dared to criticize Alexander, who murdered his old friend at a dinner party; illustration by Andre Castaigne

desert, but a network of warring kingdoms and states as advanced and developed as those he had left behind in Greece (Pomeroy 320). Alexander moved to add these cities to his empire, but this territory would be the furthest east that Alexander would campaign.

In 326 BC, Alexander fought his last major battle at the **Hydaspes River**. His opponent was King Porus, a local ruler in the Punjab region of India. Porus assembled not only his infantry but also a pack of two hundred war elephants. Alexander won, but instead of executing Porus and his allies, he made him a **vassal**—that is, a local ruler who kept some authority but swore allegiance to Alexander. While Alexander planned further campaigns along the Indian subcontinent, his soldiers mutinied. Whether or out of fear or frustration, the soldiers refused to go any further east and demanded to return home. Alexander could not continue his conquest without an army, so he set up local rulers to administer the region on his behalf. These rulers helped spread Greek culture even as far as India. Then Alexander and his troops, whom he was slowly beginning to resent, started the return home.

For most of the journey, Alexander took the sea lanes through the Persian Gulf. But at other times, Alexander insisted on marching across Gedrosia, a dry, mountainous region capable of swallowing up whole armies foolish enough to march through it. Even Cyrus the Great lost an army marching through Gedrosia. Herein, perhaps Alexander hoped to outdo the founder of the empire he had just dismantled, or he hoped to punish his troops for not helping him in his conquest of India. Either way, Alexander's choice meant that thousands of his troops died along the way (Pomeroy 322, Mark).

GEDROSIA / MODERN-DAY PAKISTAN
Alexander lost thousands of troops (and even their families) marching through the hostile desert of Gedrosia.

Upon his return to Babylon, Alexander went about consolidating his domains. He dealt with unfaithful servants, some of whom had gone as far as looting the imperial treasury. They were dealt with accordingly. Alexander also sent home thousands of discharged soldiers back to Greece. More importantly, Alexander further reintegrated his empire, marrying more wives from conquered lands and urging members of his inner circle to marry Persian wives.

However, Alexander pushed his troops too far when he introduced a new squadron of Iranian troops whom he named the "Successors". These "Successors" were the replacements for Alexander's Macedonian troops, raised from his new domains east of the Mediterranean. At this announcement, held in the city of Opis, his soldiers mutinied and refused to obey Alexander's plan to send them home. In response to the **Opis Mutiny**, Alexander effectively shamed his troops, reminding them of how rich everyone had gotten through his campaigns in Persia. The mutiny stopped, but Alexander sent home the troops as planned (Pomeroy 323). Alexander had, at

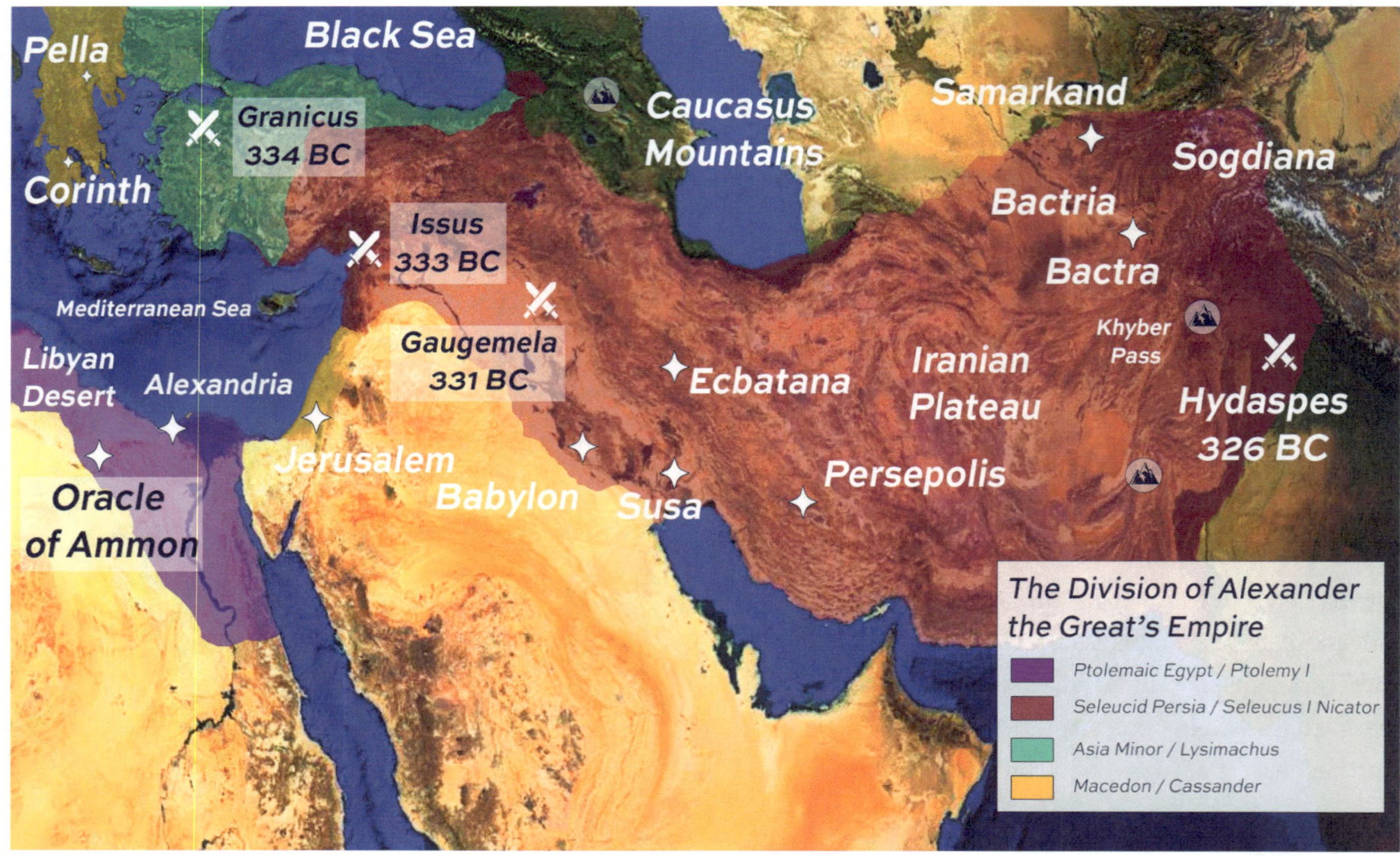

THE DIVISION OF ALEXANDER THE GREAT'S EMPIRE / 323 TO 271 BC

Ptolemy obtained Egypt (purple) Cassader obtained Macedon (purple) Lysimachus Thrace and Asia Minor (green) and Seleceus the largest prize, Mesopotamia and Persia (red).

least, some plans for his empire and his dynasty that he intended to carry out.

Alexander the Great died shortly thereafter in Babylon in 323 BC. He was young, only about thirty-three years old, but he became sick after a lavish banquet and never recovered. He caught a fever that grew worse until his death on June 10, 323 BC. While rumors circulated he had been poisoned by one of his officers, he most likely died from the hardship and fatigue he had put his body after more than a decade on campaign, coupled with the excessive banquet he threw for himself. While Alexander the Great accomplished the object of his ambition—the conquest and destruction of the Persia Empire—his success seemed to inflate his ego.

In many ways, he displayed the kind of hubris and arrogance Greek poets and tragedians had warned about. He had conquered the world, but he turned on his countrymen and even murdered his best friend in a fit of rage. Alexander's old teacher Aristotle certainly would not have approved of such actions.

Ironically, Alexander gave himself over to the kind of decadent influences long associated with the East. Greeks looked at the Persians as a warning against decadent, luxurious living that saps a country's resolve to work hard and endure great sacrifices. Long ago, before their empire, the Persians were hardy and virtuous but their success weakened the need to learn how to ride a horse, shoot a bow, or tell the truth, the ancient mainstays of Persian education. For us today, the best lesson we can draw from the life of Alexander is not how to win an empire but the need to safeguard one's personal integrity and keep from becoming too arrogant.

With Alexander's death, the Argead dynasty died with him. His sudden death in 323 BC marked the end of Classical Greece and the beginning of a new historical era—Hellenistic Greece—that in many ways was an era made in Alexander's own image.

Reading Comprehension Questions

1. Why did Alexander the Great invade the Indian subcontinent?

2. Alexander's behavior changed remarkably following his victories at Issus and Gaugamela. What did he do, and why did it raise such alarm among his troops?

3. How did Alexander the Great die? What values can we take from Alexander the Great's life and accomplishments in light of his death?

The Wars of the Successors / 323 BC

ALEXANDER DIED BEFORE he could make formal succession plans. He had succeeded in conquering the Persia Empire, bringing untold wealth into Macedon and Greece, and extended Greek culture virtually to the ends of the earth. In this way, Alexander's death serves as a convenient endpoint for Classical Greece and a starting point for **Hellenistic Greece**. The world of Hellenistic Greece is the world Alexander set in motion thanks to the cities he founded and battles he won, an age that reflected many of the qualities (for good or ill) of Alexander himself.

Yet, despite having conquered the known world, Alexander made no plans how to govern it. His wife Roxane, a Sogdianian princess, was pregnant, but Alexander had no other children to inherit the throne. He designated a trusted Macedonian official named **Perdiccas** to act as a regent, but Perdiccas was not well-liked, had many enemies, and lacked the charisma Alexander possessed. Because of the weak succession plan in place and Perdiccas' shortcomings as a leader, Alexander's empire became to fall apart.

Even before his funeral, Alexander's generals were dividing up the richest and most valuable territories for themselves. The **Diadochi** refers to the division of the empire among Alexander the Great's most powerful generals. The trouble started when **Ptolemy**, a general and close friend of Alexander's, suggested he and other close friends of Alexander divide the empire as they saw fit. With support of Alexander's inner circle, Ptolemy put his plan into place.

Hating Perdiccas, and recognizing that the body of Alexander would be an indispensable aid to help him become king of Egypt, Ptolemy took matters into his own hands. When Alexander the Great's coffin arrived in Damascus, Ptolemy simply stole the body and raced with it to Alexandria.

Upon arrival, Ptolemy buried Alexander in a grand and magnificent tomb. Then he set about consolidating Egypt as his own personal kingdom. Perdiccas sent troops into Egypt, but Ptolemy handily defeated them. War between various generals, regents, and claimants for the thrones of Alexander's sprawling empire began and lasted for thirty years.

Perdiccas did not survive the wars, while both Roxane and Alexander's infant son and heir, also named Alexander, were exiled and imprisoned, never to be seen alive again (Pomeroy 329-330).

Alexander the Great's death marked the end of Classical Greece and the beginning of the Hellenistic age when Greek culture spread all throughout the Mediterranean world. Yet for all of their accomplishments, the Greeks would soon be eclipsed by the rising power of the Romans.

Vocabulary

Hellenistic Greece
Lasting from the death of Alexander the Great in 323 BC to the death of Cleopatra VII in 30 BC, the age of Hellenistic Greece saw the spread of Greek culture, Greek language, and other expressions of Greek (or *Hellenic*) spread across the Mediterranean world and beyond.

Perdiccas
Perdiccas was a Macedonian general and a close friend of Alexander the Great, serving as a regent of Alexander's vast empire until Alexander's son came of age. He lived from 355 to ~320 BC when his soldiers revolted and murdered him.

Diadochi
Upon the death of Alexander the Great, his great empire was divided between four of his most prominent generals. The wars leading to this division are the *Diadochi*, or the Successor Wars.

Ptolemy
The Macedonian general Ptolemy triggered the wars of the Diadochi. Ptolemy ruled Egypt as his own kingdom, and he lived from 366 to 282 BC.

Pharos
The 300-foot-tall lighthouse at the harbor of Alexandria.

Museum
Named for the *Muses* of Greek mythology, the Museum was the name of massive library the Ptolemaic kings built at Alexandria.

THE FUNERAL OF ALEXANDER THE GREAT

Ptolemaic Egypt

Of the four generals, Ptolemy obtained the most valuable prize: Egypt. He made Alexandria his capital, which, being a port on the Mediterranean, ensured Alexandria and Ptolemy's kingdom would be much more Greek than Egyptian. Indeed, Alexandria became the largest and most vibrant Greek city in the Greek-speaking world. The city, too, was a melting pot of different cultures from across Greece and the Near East including Egypt, Macedon, Persia, Mesopotamia, and Greece, as well as boasting the Mediterranean's largest population of Jews living outside of Israel.

Merchants from Greece, Phoenicia, Carthage, and elsewhere came to Alexandria's harbors for grain, since the Nile River valley and the regular, predictable flooding of the Nile produced bountiful crop harvests each year. The Ptolemaic kings, moreover, had advisers and bureaucrats operating in Egyptian villages and cities to ensure a steady supply of this valuable staple crop. While Ptolemy rebuilt Egyptian temples and provided lavish donations to Egypt's priests, the Ptolemaic kings did not assimilate into Egyptian culture. In fact, the first Ptolemaic ruler to actually speak Egyptian was the famous Cleopatra VII many years later, who lived from ~ 70 to 30 BC and was a contemporary of Julius Caesar (Pomeroy 338-339, 332-343).

Beyond Egyptian grain, the Ptolemaic rulers turned Alexandria into the intellectual and cultural capital of the Mediterranean world. They built a massive, 300-foot tall lighthouse called the **Pharos**, topped with a statue of Zeus. Ptolemy's grand lighthouse was considered one of the Seven Wonders of the Ancient World (Pomeroy 343; Wasson). In addition to the lighthouse, Ptolemy I founded a library called the **Museum**, so-named for the nine Muses of Greek mythology. Ptolemy spared no expense in building this library that contained upwards of 70,000 manuscripts. In addition to manuscripts, the Ptolemaic kings also financially supported a vast network of scholars, teachers, and scribes. Their sole purpose was to study great works of literature, copy them, and then preserve them in Alexandria's great library. If ships coming to Alexandria possessed any manuscripts, they had to lend them to the library long enough for the scribes to copy them (Pomeroy 343-344; Mark).

The most famous of these scholarly efforts was the translation of the Hebrew Scriptures into Greek, a work called the **Septuagint**. According to Jewish and church tradition, King Ptolemy II tasked seventy scribes to translate the Hebrew Bible into Greek. The Hebrew Bible contains the sacred writings of the Jewish faith, beginning with the Torah and ending with the Prophets, and

LIBRARY / MUSEUM (LEFT) & PHAROS / LIGHTHOUSE (RIGHT)

The Library of Alexandria was the largest and most significant library and academic institution in Antiquity, and the Lighthouse of Alexandria was one of the Seven Wonders of the Ancient World.

Ptolemy II wanted to make these writings available to his Greek subjects as well. In the end, according to tradition, all seventy scribes produced an identical translation—hence the name *Septuagint*, Greek for 'seventy'. The Septuagint helped spread the ideas and traditions of Judaism to the Greek world and was better known and more widely-read than the Hebrew Bible in the first century AD.

Indeed, the Septuagint was the translation used by the early church at the very beginning of Christianity, something we will further address in later textbooks. All in all, the Ptolemaic kings emphasized trade, commerce, learning, and scholarship at every possible avenue they could and were rewarded for it with a long and enduring dynasty.

A·Z

Vocabulary.

Septuagint
The Greek translation of the Hebrew Bible, completed at the request of King Ptolemy II.

Reading Comprehension Questions

1. How did Ptolemy initiate the "Diadochi", or the "Wars of the Successors"?

2. What were the accomplishments of Ptolemaic Egypt? What factors made Ptolemaic Egypt so wealthy and successful?

3. Why was Ptolemaic Egypt such a center of scholarship and culture? What does this show about the relationship between civilization, leisure, and scholarship?

The End of It All / Hellenistic Greece and the Coming of the Romans

THE PROSPERITY of Ptolemaic Egypt stands in stark contrast to Mesopotamia and Persia, regions won by the general **Seleucus**. Seleucus was an elite member of Alexander's army—a member of the Silver Shields, a contingent of troops drawn from the very best of Macedon's nobility who were occasionally sent on dangerous missions. Once the war was over, Seleucus gained control of the largest, wealthiest but most difficult to govern territories: Persia and Mesopotamia. Seleucid Persia was by far the largest kingdom and had access to luxury goods from kingdoms further east in India. Moreover, cities like Babylon and Persepolis were already substantially wealthy thanks to local industries and trade routes that had operated for centuries. To aid in his rule, Seleucus founded a new capital city named **Antioch**, located in Syria, which became a wealthy and prosperous commercial center in its own right.

Because of these and other factors, Seleucid Persia had the potential to be even richer than Ptolemaic Egypt—if the descendants of Seleucus played their cards right. But they did not. Initially, Seleucus and most of the kings following him kept the Persian practice of tolerance, permitting their subjects to practice the same customs they always had as long as they remained obedient subjects. Overtime, the Seleucid kings stopped practicing this kind of toleration.

Instead, demanded their subjects worship the gods of the Greeks exclusively. In 167 BC, the descendants of Seleucus provoked the Jews living in and around Jerusalem to rebel. The Seleucid king Antiochus IV Epiphanes (215-164 BC) demanded that his subjects worship Zeus, the Greek god of thunder. He even demanded they sacrifice a pig to Zeus inside the Jerusalem Temple. Jewish food laws prohibit Jewish believers from even eating pigs, let alone sacrificing a pig inside the holiest site in all of Judaism.

As a result, a priest named Judas Maccabeus urged his countrymen to reject these pagan practices and encouraged them to join him in fighting for independence from Antiochus IV and the Seleucid kingdom. Maccabeus' revolt was successful and the event, known as the **Maccabbean Revolt**, resulted in an independent Jewish kingdom that endured until the coming of the Romans in the first century BC.

At the other end of their empire, the Seleucid kings faced threats from various Iranian tribes and states on the Indian subcontinent. Such revolts weakened Seleucid Persia internally, while fighting with the kings of Ptolemaic Egypt further weakened both kingdoms. The Seleucid Empire endured until the first century BC, when the Roman general Pompey the Great conquered the region for Rome, the region's newest imperial player. But that is a story for another book, so let's bring the story of Hellenistic Greece to a close.

In conclusion, the death of Alexander the Great in 323 BC provides a convenient end to the age of Classical Greece. Classical Greece was a golden age of Greek culture, wherein the Greeks produced a staggering array of temples, works of literature, and other magnificent achievements. Alexander's death initiated a new era for the Greeks: Hellenistic Greece.

The age of Hellenistic Greece was marked by the spread of Greek culture, language, and ideas across the Mediterranean world and beyond. The Hellenistic world was marked by a relatively common language, advanced

Vocabulary

Seleucus
Seleucus ruled over Mesopotamia and Persia and established the Seleucid dynasty that lasted until the first century BC. He lived from 358 to 281 BC.

Antioch
Founded by Seleucus I, Antioch was one of the most prosperous cities and commercial centers of the Hellenistic world. Antioch is located in Syria on the Mediterranean coastline.

The Maccabean Revolt
In 167 BC, the Jewish priest Judas Maccabeus led a revolt in and around Jerusalem against the Seleucid king Antiochus IV Epiphanes and his demands that the Jews worship Zeus, among other pagan practices. The successful revolt saw the creation of an independent Jewish kingdom that lasted until the coming of the Romans in the first century BC.

SELEUCID PERSIA / 312 TO 63 BC
Seleucus (358-281 BC) obtained the largest and most difficult-to-govern kingdom in Alexander's Empire. To aid in governing the territory, Seleucus founded the city of Antioch on the coastline of the Mediterranean.

trade routes and commercial networks, and the melding of religious ideas and traditions and gods from Spain to India, all of which produced something profoundly new in the Hellenistic world.

Yet even as Greek influence extended east and westward, the center of power was moving further and further west. Two new powers—the cities of Rome and Carthage—were fighting for mastery in the western Mediterranean. And once that contest was decided, the victor would be coming for the Greeks and their domains.

Hellenistic Greece: Wealth & Culture

Until the coming of the Romans in the third century, Greek influence, economic power, and military might were all still strong. We can chart the spread and development of Hellenistic Greek culture across the Mediterranean world in terms of Greek colonies, the Greek language, and Greek philosophy and art.

The Greeks had long established colonies throughout the Mediterranean world. Those colonies existed on the coastlines of what is today Spain, France, Sicily, and Italy—indeed, the region of southern Italy had so many Greek cities it was called **Magna Graecia**, or "Greater Greece". These colonies had long served as places for the Greeks to extend their culture and language further afield. The Greeks built theaters in these new colonies, exported their books, plays, and poems, and mingled their religious customs with those of the native peoples. The conquests of Alexander the Great continued this process further, albeit eastward and not westward.

Across the Mediterranean as far as the Hindu Kush Mountains, groups of Macedonians and Greeks often lived side-by-side with the peoples of Egypt, Israel, Italy, Syria, Mesopotamia, Bactria, Persia, and India. Often, Greek religious traditions and mythology mixed with that of the polytheistic religions

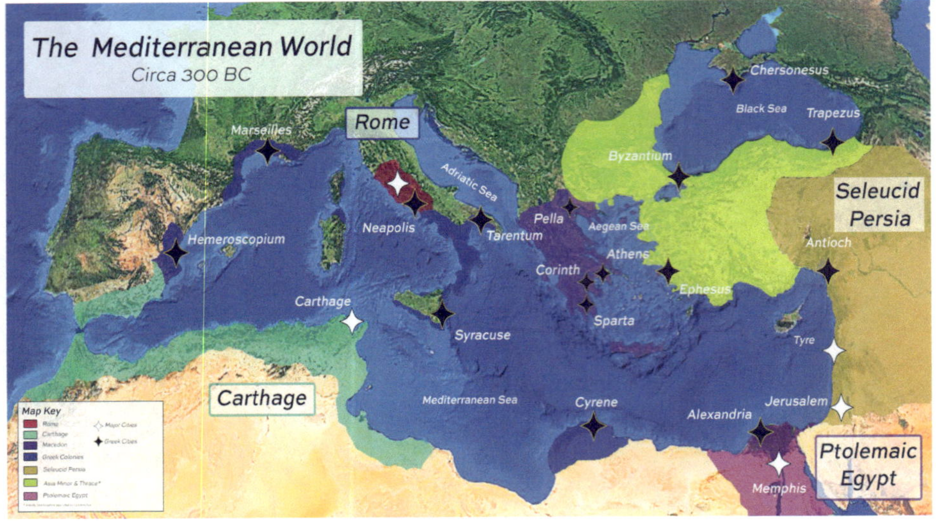

THE MEDITERRANEAN WORLD / ~ 300 BC

The Greeks had already established colonies across the Greek world, while the Macedonians (purple) established new Greek kingdoms in what once was Asia Minor, Thrace (both ruled by Lysimachos and in yellow) Egypt (violet), Seleucid Persia (gold). In time, the power of Greece and Carthage (green) would be conquered by the Romans (red), a small city-state located on the Italian peninsula.

of the Near East. The Greeks identified the gods of Egypt or India with the deities they already worshipped, just as Alexander claimed to be not just the son of Zeus but of Zeus-Ammon, a deity in both the Greek and the Egyptian pantheon of gods. This process of cultural assimilation and melding continued on through the Hellenistic age.

Moreover, the kingdoms ruled by Macedonians, and the colonies settled by the Greeks, helped establish new trade routes and commercial centers across the ancient world. Greek and Phoenician merchant ships sailed the Mediterranean coast, stopping at various ports to trade grain, wine, spices, precious metals, books, information, stories, and everything else imaginable. Goods from the steppes of Central Asia or the Indian subcontinent could travel across Seleucid Persia, too, while precious metals and aromatic resins, in addition to Egyptian grain, could travel up the Nile River to Alexandria or over the Arabian desert to Jerusalem or Antioch.

Through this cultural diffusion, Alexander inadvertently helped develop a new dialect of the Greek language called **Koine Greek**. The word *koine* is Greek for *common* or *fellowship* since Greeks from Boeotia, Attica, and Ionia serving alongside Macedonians needed a *common* language to speak to each other. As Greek colonies grew into cities, and Alexander's conquests stretched further into Asia, so too did the number of people who needed an accessible dialect to deal with these new Greek traders.

In time, Koine Greek became the **lingua franca** of the ancient world, the most widely-spoken language in a given time period. In the ancient world, the preferred language of diplomacy and trade, the language spoken from Spain to India, was Koine Greek—at least, until the coming of the Romans and their

Vocabulary

Magna Graecia
A collection of Greek cities and colonies spread across southern Italy and Sicily, with its most notably cities being Neapolis and Syracuse.

Koine Greek
Koine Greek is a dialect of the Greek language that developed in and among the soldiers of Alexander the Great. Koine Greek became the *lingua franca*, of the ancient world.

Lingua Franca
The term *lingua franca* refers to a language that is the preferred means of communication for trade and diplomacy.

own language, Latin. Indeed, the language of Koine Greek was so widely spoken that the writers of the New Testament chose Koine Greek to write in and not their native Aramaic. Writing in Koine Greek, the New Testament could be understood from Spain to India.

Then there were new schools of philosophy. Times of great prosperity make leisure, scholarship, and the discussion of great ideas possible. From the schools of Plato and Aristotle, two of the most significant Greek thinkers, came new philosophical systems that helped people understand the nature of the good life and put it into practice. Two of the most prominent schools of philosophy during the Hellenistic age were **Stoicism** and **Epicureanism**, both of which articulated how an individual may cultivate virtue, albeit in different ways.

As a broad, general summary, adherents of stoicism tried to keep their passions in check and urged people to serve the public good through virtue and self-sacrifice. Epicureans, on the other hand, believed the good life was characterized by the pursuit of pleasure with as little pain and discomfort as possible. The Stoics believed the universe was animated by a spirit, a *logos*, whereas the Epicureans denied the existence of spiritual substances and believed, instead, everything was made up of matter and nothing more. If everything was made up of matter, then there could be no soul and no gods, either.

Such philosophical schools influenced the era's leading citizens and authors, especially those who hailed from the city of Rome. But in time, they would wane in importance as a new religious tradition emerged from a relatively isolated corner of the Mediterranean world and spread with remarkably speed across the Mediterranean: Christianity, of which we will speak more in later volumes. As mentioned earlier, the language of Koine Greek spoken and understood from one end of the Mediterranean world to the other facilitated the spread of this new religion called Christianity.

MAGNA GRAECIA & THE ITALIAN PENINSULA / 390 - 264 BC

In the century that follows, the city of Rome would conquer the Italian peninsula, followed by the empire of Carthage and the kingdom of Macedon.

But perhaps the most breathtaking examples of Hellenistic culture come from the field of art. The wealth created by trade and commerce in cities like Antioch or Alexandria helped support a vast network of scholars, artists, and philosophers. Wealthy patrons and whole cities directed their resources towards the production of monumental works of art. While the earliest sculptures from ancient Greece were still beautiful, they were relatively simple. Figures stood in stiff, upright poses and, while they looked realistic, they displayed little emotion.

In contrast, Hellenistic art took the subjects of Greek mythology and epic, brought them forth from lifeless stone, and used them as vehicles to explore the uttermost depths of the human condition. The wealth of the Hellenistic world made it possible for talented individuals to study and practice the craft of the sculpture, resulting in realistic figures showing profound emotional sensibility. Check out the ***Closer Look at Greek Sculpture*** in this chapter for a more in-depth look at art across the ages of Greek history.

For now, we sadly have to turn to the end—the end not only of our study of Alexander the Greek and Hellenistic Greece but indeed the whole of the ancient Greek world. In time, the new power of **Rome** would come and conquer, one-by-one, Greek cities, leagues, and kingdoms planted across the Mediterranean world.

ZENO OF CITIUM & EPICURUS / STOICISM & EPICUREANISM

Zeno is considered the founder of the school of Stoicism, whereas Epicurus founded Epicureanism; Zeno lived from 343 to 262 BC, and Epicurus from 341 to 270 BC.

Rome had grown from a city-state on the banks of the Tiber to an empire seemingly without end, an empire that included Macedon, Greece, and everywhere else where Greek culture had once extended. So given the richness of this legacy, why were the Greeks not the lasting empire of the ancient world?

The End of It All

The Greeks' dynamic city-state culture certainly shaped the last few centuries of Antiquity. The Greeks reinvigorated the city-state, adorned the Mediterranean skyline with their temples, and endowed the Western canon with literary masterpieces from the likes of Homer, Plato, and Thucydides. More than that, the Greeks defeated the Persian Empire, a state that had brought the rest of the world into its dominion, drinking rivers dry and enslaving whole kingdoms in the process.

The courage of the Athenians and Spartans on the plains of Marathon or the hot gates of Thermopylae, respectively, made it possible for Greek ideas of freedom and liberty to spread from their remote corner of the Mediterranean to almost every corner of the globe.

Despite such achievements, the Greeks were never able to maintain their independence over the longterm. When confronting a common foe in the Persian Empire, the Greeks displayed a unity and resolve that has inspired generations of students, scholars, and leaders. A free people like the Greeks fighting to preserve their independence could triumph over the most powerful empire in the world.

Yet recall that the Greeks could not find the ground to work through their problems amongst themselves in the decades following the Persian Wars, resulting in a civil war between Athens, Sparta, and their respective allies in the Peloponnesian War that left the Greek *poleis* vulnerable to invasion from a new power like Macedon. The same sort of jealousy that often leads

Vocabulary.

Stoicism
Stoicism was a branch of philosophy popular in the Greco-Roman world which focused on controlling one's emotions, cultivating virtue, and trying to do good to one's city and family.

Epicureanism
Epicureanism was a branch of philosophy popular in the Greco-Roman world which focused on the pursuit of pleasure as the goal for which everyone should strive in life. Such pleasures were meant to be pursued in moderation, and intellectual pleasures were to be favored over physical ones.

Rome
Located on the Tiber River in central Italy, the city of Rome was the dominant power of the ancient Mediterranean world from the third century BC to the fifth century AD.

good friends to turn on each other led the Spartans and Athenians to wage a terrible war on each other. The resulting Peloponnesian War took all the benefits the Greeks had built up for centuries and cast them into the Aegean. Similar struggles between the Ptolemies and Seleucids weakened those states as well, making it even easier for the Romans to absorb them into their growing empire.

Moreover, the Greeks may have lost their way for the same reasons that other societies and peoples lose theirs. Simply put, the Greeks became too successful, and great success often keeps an individual or an entire country from doing the hard things that lead to strong character. The Greeks believed that the dangerous effects of success had happened to the Persians, whose rulers had grown increasingly corrupt and decadent. Rulers like Cyrus the Great may have been hardy, virtuous warrior-kings, but rulers like Xerxes and Darius III became cruel and lazy autocrats, kings more concerned with taking care of themselves than their people. Yet when Alexander conquered Persia, he began to act just like them, illustrating that universal truth that power so often corrupts the soul.

Indeed, once Alexander conquered Persia and captured the mammoth wealth the Persians had accumulated, he turned on friends and family members. Over time, the Greeks and Macedonians acted more and more like the Persians they had once fought so hard to expel from Greece. In this sense, Alexander the Great provides an object lesson to students of this once great and glorious age.In the end, the dynamic atmosphere of city-states across the Mediterranean world continued to produce astounding cultural and literary treasures.

As we bring our study of the Greeks to a close, we can be thankful for the rich, intellectual inheritance they have left for us. The accomplishments of even so significant a figure as Alexander the Great pale in comparison to the literary treasures of Plato's dialogues and Homer's epics. These great works (and others like them) allow us to better understand ourselves, the world, and our place in it. Such was the case with Herodotus and Thucydides and their monumental histories of the Persian and Peloponnesian Wars, respectively: wars may be terrible, but such struggles provide the opportunity for displays of human courage and valor that deserve to be preserved for posterity. The soaring temples of the Greeks may be crumbling at the edges, yet they still inspire us to build things that will last and not merely satisfy us for the immediate moment. Like the best of the Greeks, we ought to focus on building something that will last for ages.

Yet since we usually lack the opportunity to build a temple or found a city, or the inspiration to write an epic history, let us focus on forming our character and cultivating the habits of moral excellence those ancient Greek philosophers called *virtue*. That way, we may live lives worthy of imitation, love our families and neighbors, and accomplish deeds that truly reflect the nature of the good life. All in all, that we may attempt the great things the kind of which Herodotus celebrated in the opening lines of the *Histories*:

> *Thus Herodotus of Halicarnassos begins his inquiry, to the end that neither the deeds of men may be forgotten by lapse of time nor works great and marvellous, deeds having been produced by the Greeks and others by the barbarians, lose their renown...*

Reading Comprehension Questions

1. Define the term, "Hellenistic Age." What factors characterized Hellenistic Greece?

2. Where was Seleucid Persia? What factors made this kingdom so particularly wealthy?

3. What was the Maccabbean Revolt? Why did it start, and how did it end?

Reading Comprehension Questions

4. What was stoicism? Epicureanism?

5. Why were the Greeks ultimately not able to maintain their independence over the ensuing centuries?

6. Now that our study of the Greeks is over, what lessons should we learn from them?

A Closer Look at Greek Sculpture

PERHAPS THE MOST BREATHTAKING of Hellenistic culture come from the field of sculpture. The wealth created by trade and commerce in cities like Antioch or Alexandria helped support a vast network of scholars poets, artists and philosophers, and wealthy patrons and whole cities directed their resources towards the production of monumental works of art. Sculpture is a unique art form in that the artist transforms a block of cold lifeless stone into statue resembling the human form. (That marble, though, was famous in and of itself, often quarried in the mountains around Athens. Pentellic marble was a highly prized commodity well into the Renaissance.)

For this section, we will present a brief overview of sculpture in that era of Greek history, followed by reading comprehension questions. Then we have samples of Archaic, Classical, and Hellenistic art for students to identify based on the characteristics you see.

Sculpture in Archaic Greece

From the Greek world for *old*, the Archaic period lasted from 800 to 500 BC. In Greek history, the Archaic period was characterized by the growth of its most famous city-states, Athens and Sparta. While the earliest sculptures from ancient Greece were still beautiful, they were relatively simple. In sculpture, this period was dominated by a type of stiff, freestanding sculptures. Figures were carved in rigid, upright poses and while they looked realistic, they displayed little emotion. Some statues show a distinct Egyptian influence (such as braided hair, similar to the way kings in the ancient Near East were depicted in palace artwork.

For a sculptor, it is exceedingly difficult to carve the human form from a block of stone. The weight of the statue rests on the feet which, like our own feet, are much smaller relatively to the rest of the statue. As a result, it is difficult to give a statue a dynamic, energetic pose without taking the risk the statue would break apart. One can think of the sculptors of this period as learning how to carve marble in such a way as it give the statue both beauty and stability (Metropolitan Museum of Art).

Sculpture in Classical Greece

Lasting from 479 to 323 BC, the age of Classical Greece produced monumental architecture like the Parthenon and the Temple of Zeus at Olympia. During this period of Greek sculpture, artists carved their figures in grander and more energetic poses—at least compared to the Archaic period. They were more freestanding and natural—i.e., not stiff—although they were not so graceful and elegant the statues broke apart. Sculptors used tricks to try and provide the base with more support, such as carving small shrubs or bushes next to the statue's feet. Examples of sculptures from this period include the relief carvings on the Parthenon and the massive statue of Zeus, standing at over 41 feet tall, housed in the Temple of Zeus Olympia (Metropolitan Museum of Art).

Sculpture in Hellenistic Greece

In contrast, Hellenistic art took the subjects of Greek mythology and epic, brought them forth from lifeless stone, and used them as vehicles to explore the uttermost depths of the human condition. The wealth of the Hellenistic world made it possible for talented individuals to study and practice the craft of the sculpture, resulting in realistic figures showing profound emotional sensibility. These sculptures are far and away the most dynamic and portray the deepest and at times, the saddest emotions capable of being carved from stone.

Reading Comprehension Questions

1. Why is sculpture such a unique and beautiful art form?

2. What was sculpture like during the age of Archaic Greece?

3. What was sculpture like during the age of Classical Greece?

4. What was sculpture like during the age of Hellenistic Greece?

ACTIVITY

Closer Look at Greek Sculpture

Instructions: Each row contains a photograph of a particular Greek sculpture, one that could be either from *Archaic Greece, Classical Greece,* or *Helleneistic Greece*. In the space provided, identify the correct time period the sculpture was created based on the description given in the previous pages. There are two separate photos for each work of art—one for the head and torso, and another for the feet and legs—so be sure to look at both photos carefully before deciding on the time period it comes from. An answer key follows this section.

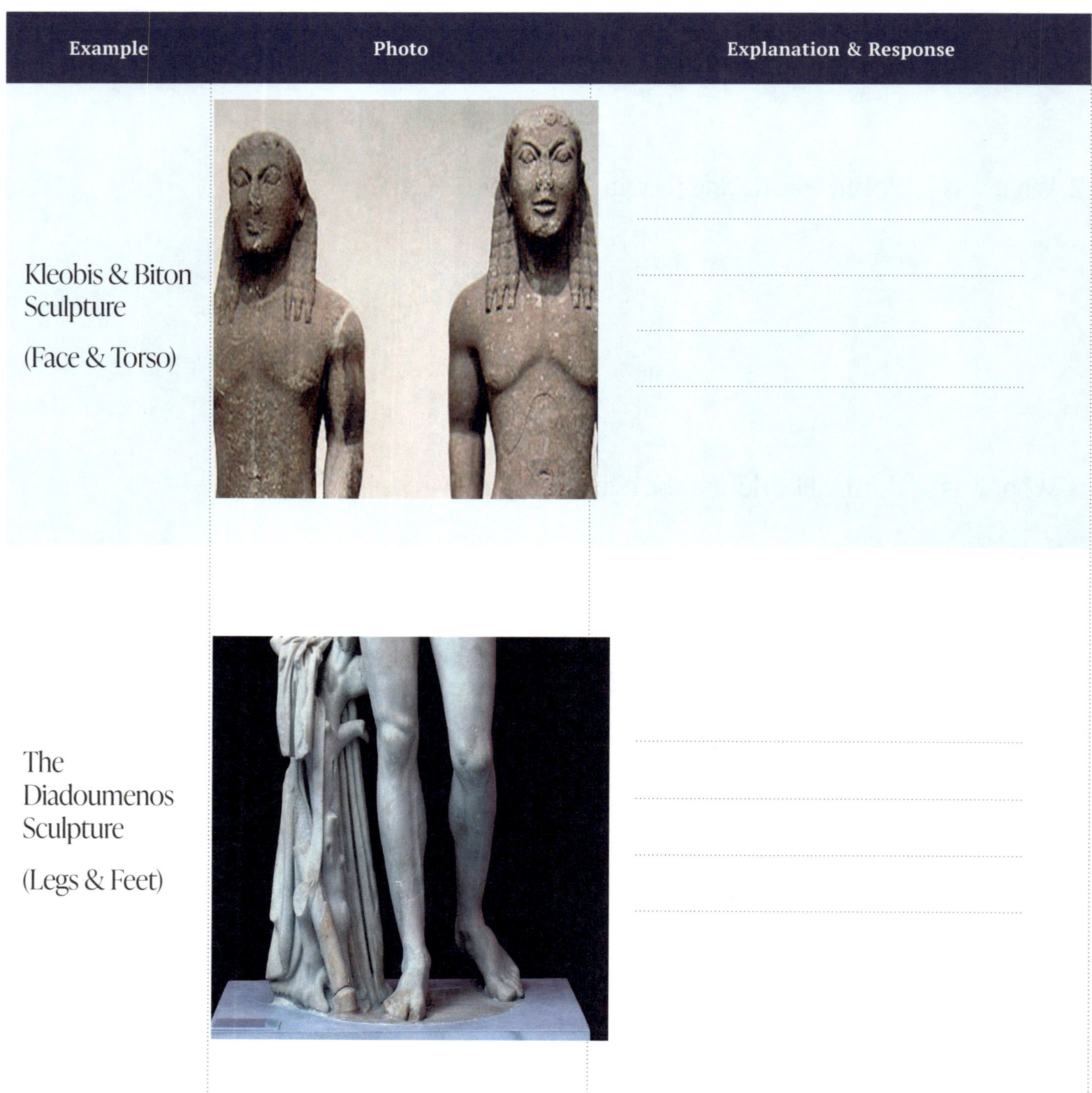

Example	Photo	Explanation & Response
Kleobis & Biton Sculpture (Face & Torso)		
The Diadoumenos Sculpture (Legs & Feet)		

Greek Sculpture (Continued)

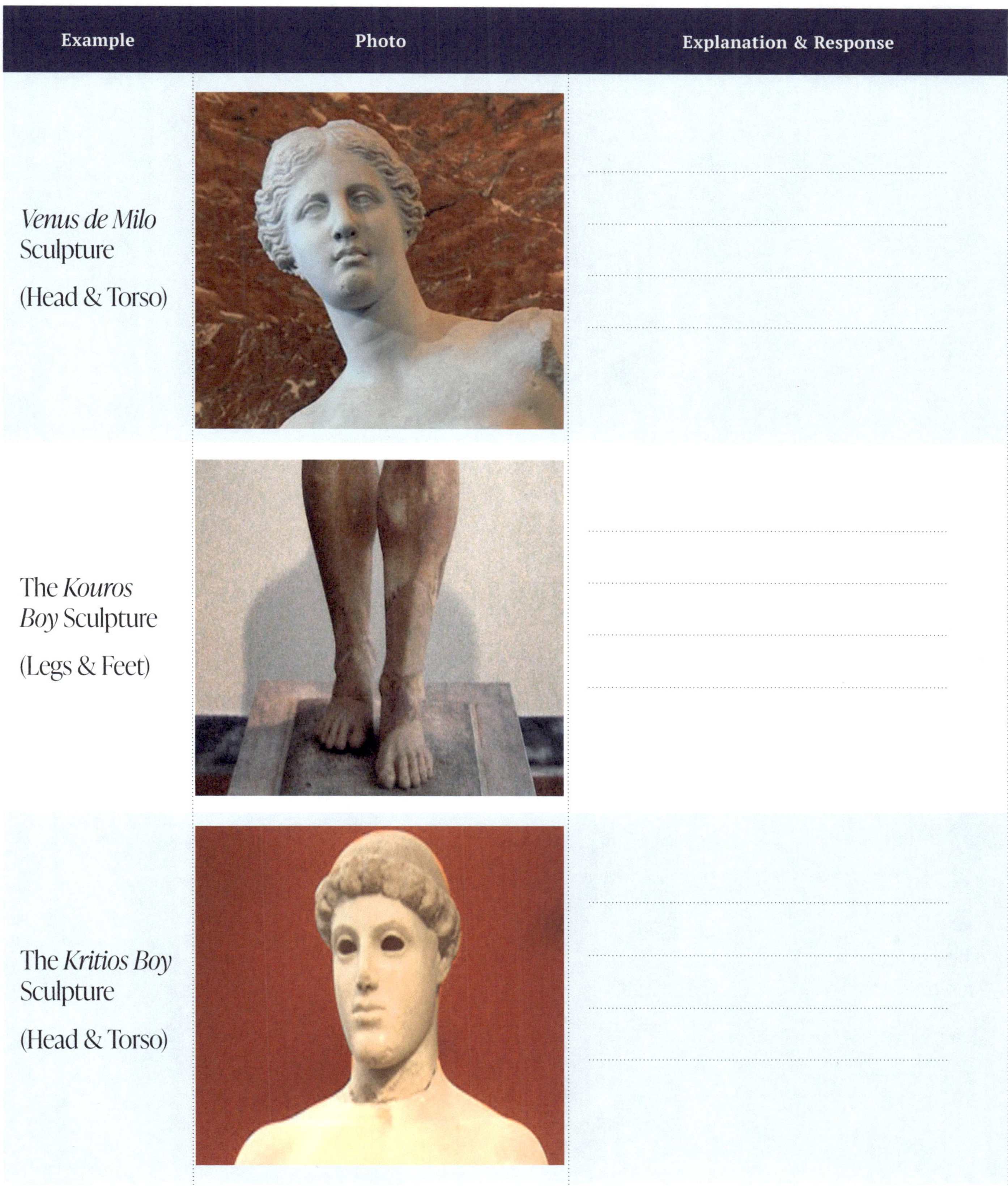

Example	Photo	Explanation & Response
Venus de Milo Sculpture (Head & Torso)		
The *Kouros Boy* Sculpture (Legs & Feet)		
The *Kritios Boy* Sculpture (Head & Torso)		

Greek Sculpture (Continued)

Example	Photo	Explanation & Response
Peplos Kore (Face & Torso)		
Laocoön and his Sons Sculpture (Face & Torso)		
The *Farnese Hercules* (Face & Torso)		

Closer Look at Greek Sculpture / Answer Key

Kleobis and Biton: *These two statues is from the Archaic period, having been dated to ~ 550 BC.*

Peplos Kore: *The statue is from the Archaic period, having been dated to ~ 530 BC.*

The Farnese Hercules: *This statue is a Roman copy, but the original was made during the Hellenistic age.*

The Diadoumenous Sculpture: *This statue is from Classical Greece and dates to around ~ 420 BC.*

The Kouros Boy: *The statue is from the Archaic period, having been dated to ~ 530 BC.*

The Kritios Boy: *The statue is from the Classical period, having been dated to ~ 480 BC.*

Laocoöna and His Sons: *The statue is from the Hellenistic period, having been dated to 200 BC.*

Venus de Milo: *The statue is from the Hellenistic period but its date is very much disputed.*

The act of creating a sculpture transforms cold, lifeless stone into something that resembles a human being. As such, a sculpture is a profound metaphor for the task of classical education which forms not only the mind by filling that mind with meaningful content, but also shapes the heart by showcasing the very best examples of human character and conduct.

ACTIVITY

Direct Instruction Review

The hardest part about history is memorizing all those facts, dates, and events. To make this process easier, we have included this short section called *Direct Instruction Review*. Direct Instruction (or DI) is a powerful pedagogical tool whereby teachers ask students a series of *call-and-response* questions, and students respond back with the aim of learning this material to *mastery*. Teacher's lines are in **bold**; student's lines in *italices*.

Where is Macedon? *Macedon is a kingdom to the north of Greece hemmed in by mountains to the north and the Aegean Sea to the south.*

How did the Macedonians live? *Macedon was a world almost in the Greek Dark Ages, living in small villages, farming and herding, and lacking the city-states that were the hallmark of Greek culture.*

What changed, that Macedon would ultimately come to conquer Greece? *Macedon enjoyed a series of kings who kept Macedon out of dangerous wars, encouraged their domestic industries and trade with southern Greece, and helped to organize Macedonian society into a strong, stable kingdom.*

Who was Philip II? *Philip II transformed Macedon into the dominant power in Greece, and he reigned as king of Macedon from 359 to 336 BC.*

Upon conquering Greece, what did Philip II establish? *Philip II established the League of Corinth, which was an alliance composed of the city-states he had just conquered.*

And what was the goal of the League of Corinth? *The League of Corinth had as their united goal the conquest of the Persian Empire.*

Did Philip II conquer the Persian Empire? *No! He was assassinated at the wedding of his daughter and his son, Alexander, inherited the throne of Macedon.*

What did Alexander do, once he became king? *Alexander put down a rebellion in Thebes and then prepared his invasion of the Persian Empire.*

What happened when Alexander invaded the Persian Empire? *Alexander crossed into Asia Minor, where he met a Persian army at the Battle of the Granicus River, fought in 334 BC.*

And did the Persians succeed in stopping Alexander at the Granicus River? *Almost! A Persian satrap almost killed Alexander in battle, but Cleitus the Black killed the satrap and saved Alexander's life.*

What about the next battle? *The next battle took place at Issus, a small town in Syria near the Mediterranean coastline, in 333 BC.*

ACTIVITY

Direct Instruction Review (Cont.)

And what happened at Issus? *Alexander defeated the Persian army and even captured the family of Darius III, who had fled the battlefield in disgrace.*

Did Alexander pursue Darius III and thus destroy the Empire of Persia? *No! Instead, Alexander went to Egypt and founded the city of Alexandria, which he named after himself.*

Why did Alexander go to Egypt? *Alexander marched his entire army to Egypt to ask the Oracle of Ammon if he was, in fact, a god—and the oracle confirmed he was the son of Zeus-Ammon.*

Upon finding out he was a god, what did Alexander do next? *In 331 BC, Alexander met the Persian Empire for one more battle, this time at Gaugamela near Babylon and defeated the Persians once and for all.*

Having defeated the Persian Empire, what did Alexander do next? *He hosted a massive feast in Persepolis, looted the Persian treasury, and burned the city to the ground, marking the end of the Persian Empire.*

Did Alexander enjoy his empire? *No, he died at the age of thirty-three after a massive banquet in the city of Babylon.*

What happened to his empire? *The Empire of Alexander the Great was divided up between four of his generals.*

What generals got which territory? *Ptolemy received Egypt; Lysander Macedon; Callimachus Asia Minor; and Seleucus Persia and Mesopotamia.*

So what event does the death of Alexander the Great mark? *The death of Alexander the Great is the dividing line between Classical Greece and Hellenistic Greece.*

What was Hellenistic Greece like? *Greek culture spread throughout the Mediterranean, and the Greeks and Macedonians in various kingdoms and city-states grew wealthy and prosperous.*

Did this prosperity last forever? *No! The Greeks would soon be eclipsed by a new power coming from the west.*

And what was the name of this new power that would soon conquer the Greeks? *Rome!*

ACTIVITY

Map Practice: The Empire of Alexander

Instructions: Carefully look over the map below, which are identical to maps provided in the rest of this chapter. However, there is one crucial difference: these maps have blanks in the place of the name of a sea, a region, or a site. Fill in the appropriate blank with the term list provided above each map.

The Empire of Alexander: Bodies of water such as the Indus River and the Mediterranean, the Aegean, the Caspian, and the Black Sea; the cities of Pella, Alexandria, Bactra, Susa, Ecbatana, Persepolis, Antioch, Babylon, and Jerusalem; mountains such as the Caucasus and the Hindu Kush; regions such as Bactria, Anatolia (or Asia Minor), the Libyan Desert, and Sogdiana; kingdoms of Seleucus, Ptolemy, Lysimachus, and Cassander; and landmarks such as the Oracle at Ammon, Granicus, Issus, Gaugamela, and the Hydaspes River.

Want to study this map online? Type in the link below or scan the QR code to access an interactive diagram: **https://bit.ly/3okSogF**

ACTIVITY

Timeline Practice / The Rise of Macedon

The hardest part about history is memorizing all those facts, dates, and events. To make this process easier, check out the timeline below—well, technically, there are *two* timelines. Some entries are missing dates, and others are missing the event that occurred on that date. With the information available from both timelines, fill in the missing blanks to get a better sense of the timeline for this chapter.

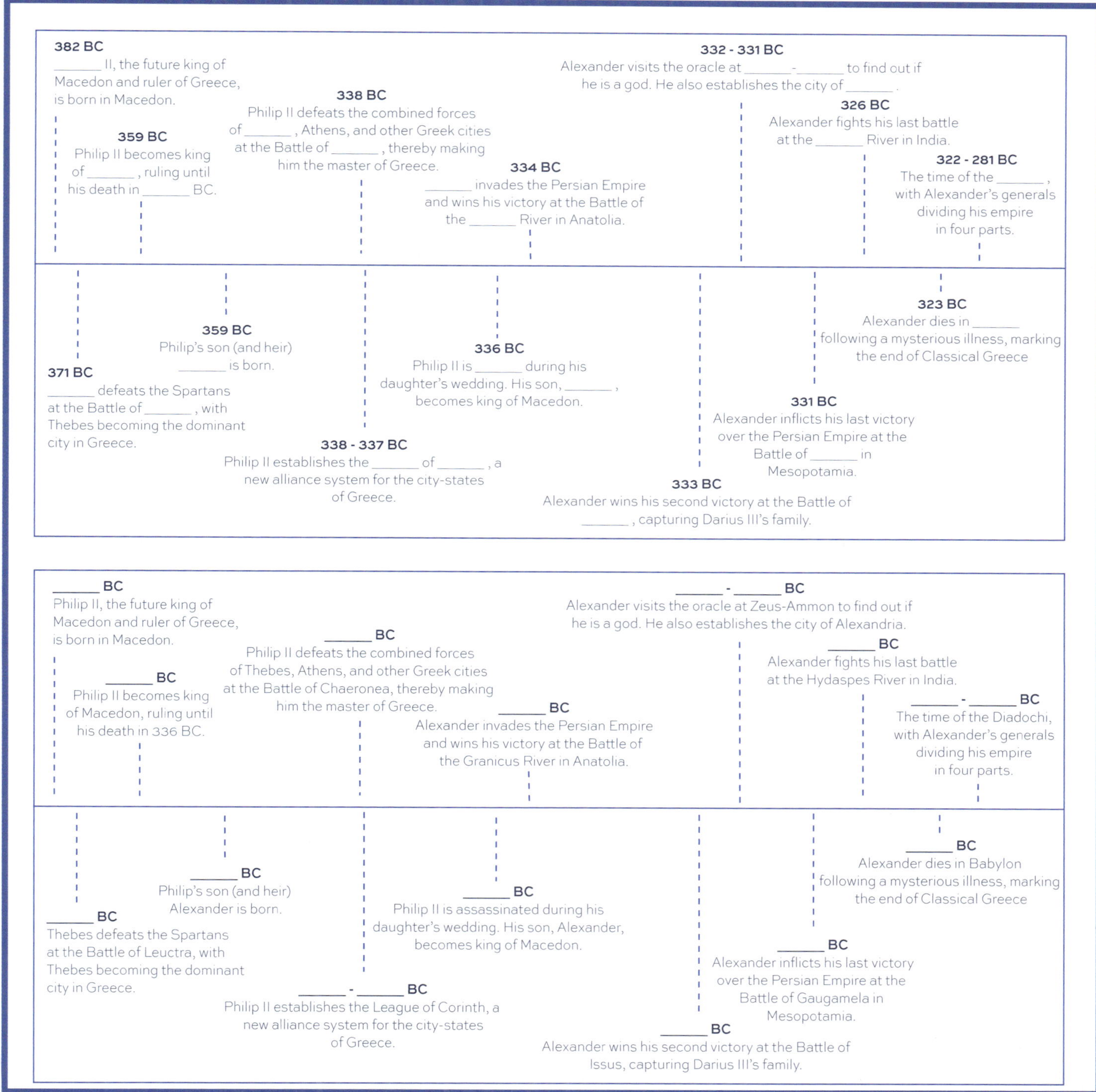

WRITING

Writing Prompt

Writing is thinking, so we will spend considerable time this year writing and thinking about history. In the space provided, write a short essay answering the question: ***Based on the life and accomplishments of Alexander the Great, what does real greatness look like? After all, if his success contributed to his demise, was that "greatness" worth it?***

Works Cited

Aristophanes. *The Clouds*. Translated by William James Hickie. Project Gutenberg, 2013. www.gutenberg.org/files/2562/2562-h/2562-h.htm

Aristotle. *The Athenian Constitution*. Translated by Frederic Kenyon, MIT Classics Archive, http://classics.mit.edu/Aristotle/athenian_const.1.1.html.

"The Art of Classical Greece (ca. 480–323 B.C.)." The Metropolitan Museum of Art, 1 Jan. 2008, https://www.metmuseum.org/toah/hd/tacg/hd_tacg.htm.

Britannica, The Editors of Encyclopaedia. "Draco". Encyclopedia Britannica, 12 Nov. 2008, https://www.britannica.com/biography/Draco-Greek-lawgiver. Accessed 26 January 2023.

Britannica, The Editors of Encyclopaedia. *"Hoplite"*. Encyclopedia Britannica, 23 Jan. 2023, https://www.britannica.com/topic/hoplite. Accessed 27 January 2023.

Britannica, The Editors of Encyclopaedia. *"Troy"*. Encyclopedia Britannica, 21 Oct. 2022, https://www.britannica.com/place/Troy-ancient-city-Turkey. Accessed 24 December 2022.

Cadoux, Theodore John. *"Solon"*. Encyclopedia Britannica, 7 Oct. 2022, https://www.britannica.com/biography/Solon. Accessed 26 January 2023.

Cooper, John, editor. *Plato: Complete Works*. Indianapolis: Hackett Publishing Co, 1997.

Corbett, Edward P.J. *Classical Rhetoric for the Modern Student.* Oxford University Press, 1971.

Chisholm, Lawrence James and Zupko, Ronald. "measurement system". Encyclopedia Britannica, 19 Nov. 2018, https://www.britannica.com/science/measurement-system. Accessed 26 July 2022.

"Greek Art in the Archaic Period." The Metropolitan Museum of Art, 1 Oct. 2023, https://www.metmuseum.org/toah/hd/argk/hd_argk.htm.

Editors of Encyclopaedia. "mina". Encyclopedia Britannica, 26 Apr. 2018, https://www.britannica.com/science/mina-unit-of-weight. Accessed 26 July 2022.

Herodotus. *The History Of Herodotus*. Translated by G. Macaulay, Project Gutenberg, https://www.gutenberg.org/files/2707/2707-h/2707-h.htm.

Hesiod. *Homeric Hymns, Epic Cycle, Homerica*. Translated by H. Evelyn-White, William Heinemann, 1914, Loeb Classical Library, https://www.theoi.com/Text/HesiodTheogony.html#15.

Humphreys, Justin. *"Aristotle."* Internet Encyclopedia of Philosophy, www.iep.utm.edu/aristotl/#H7.

Kennedy, George Alexander. *Quintilian: A Roman Educator and His Quest for the Perfect Orator.* Sophron, 2017.

Works Cited

Kraut, Richard. *"Plato."* Stanford Encyclopedia of Philosophy, Stanford University, 1 Aug. 2017, plato.stanford.edu/entries/plato/.

Mark, Joseph. "Alexander the Great." Ancient History Encyclopedia, 7 Nov. 2023, https://www.worldhistory.org/Alexander_the_Great/. Accessed 26 Apr. 2023.

Martin, Thomas. *An Overview of Classical Greek History from Mycenae to Alexander*. Yale University Press, 1996, The Perseus Project, https://www.perseus.tufts.edu/hopper/

Plato. *Phaedrus*. Translated by Benjamin Jowett. MIT Classics Archive. n.d. http://classics.mit.edu/Plato/phaedrus.html.

Quintilian. *Institutes of Oratory, or, Education of an Orator.* Edited by Curtis Dozier and Lee Honeycutt, translated by J. S. Watson, 2015.

Shields, Christopher. *"Aristotle."* Stanford Encyclopedia of Philosophy. Stanford University, 25 Sept. 2008, plato.stanford.edu/entries/aristotle/

Starr, Chester G. "Peisistratus". Encyclopedia Britannica, 4 Apr. 2019, https://www.britannica.com/biography/Peisistratus. Accessed 27 January 2023.

Thucydides. *The History of the Peloponnesian War*. Translated by Richard Crawley, E-book, https://www.gutenberg.org/files/7142/7142-h/7142-h.htm. Project Gutenberg.

Wasson, Donald L. "Ptolemy I." Ancient History Encyclopedia, 3 Feb. 2012, https://www.worldhistory.org/Ptolemy_I/.

Photography Credits

Cover & Table of Contents

The photograph of Achilles and Ajax playing dice is available in the public domain and is accessible at <https://www.wikiart.org/en/ancient-greek-pottery/exekias-amphora-achilles-and-ajax-engaged-in-a-game--530>.

The photo of the Roman Forum is available via an Unsplash license, was made by user Roman Wimmers, and is accessible at <https://unsplash.com/photos/krolC7VHgGc>.

Chapter 1: Minoan Crete & Mycenaean Greece

The photo of the Parthenon in Athens, Greece is available via an Unsplash license, was made by user Sergio Garcia, and is accessible at <https://unsplash.com/photos/8lKpEfyFSoY>.

The photo of the Acropolis is available via an Unsplash license, was made by user Roland Fényes, and is accessible at https://unsplash.com/photos/IooHbXUfOeA.

The photo of Uranos from the Pergamon Frieze is available via a Creative Commons license, was made by user Miguel Hermoso Cuesta on April 19, 2014, and is accessible at <https://en.wikipedia.org/wiki/Uranus_(mythology)#/media/File:Altar_Pérgamo_Urano_01.JPG>.

The picture of Prometheus and Zeus is available in the public domain and is accessible at <https://en.wikipedia.org/wiki/Prometheus#/media/File:Prometheus_and_Atlas,_Laconian_black-figure_kylix,_by_the_Arkesilas_Painter,_560-550_BC,_inv._16592_-_Museo_Gregoriano_Etrusco_-_Vatican_Museums_-_DSC01069.jpg>.

The photo of the Acropolis is available via an Unsplash license, was made by user Constantinos Kollias, and is accessible at <https://unsplash.com/photos/yqBvJJ8jGBQ>.

The photo of the ruins of Knossos is available via a Creative Commons license, was made by user Lapplaender on July 23, 2008, and is accessible at <https://en.wikipedia.org/wiki/Knossos#/media/File:Knossos_-_03.jpg>.

The diagram of the palace of Knossos is available from Brown University and is accessible at <https://www.brown.edu/Departments/Joukowsky_Institute/courses/greekpast/4796.html>.

The map of the ancient Greek world during the Persian Wars is available via a Creative Commons license, was made by user Bibi Saint-Pol on February 27, 2007, and is accessible at https://en.wikipedia.org/wiki/Ancient_Greece#/media/File:Map_Greco-Persian_Wars-en.svg.

The portico at Knossos is available via a Creative Commons license, was made by user Bernard Gagnon on October 18, 2011, and is accessible at https://en.wikipedia.org/wiki/Knossos#/media/File:Knossos_-_North_Portico_02.jpg>.

The photo of pithoi storage jars is available via a Creative Commons license, was made by user Agostino64 on Feburary 13, 2005, and is accessible at <https://commons.wikimedia.org/wiki/File:Pithoi_in_Knossos.jpg>.

The photo of the bull fresco at Knossos is available via a Creative Commons license, was made by user Deror_avi on September 24, 2011, and is accessible at https://en.wikipedia.org/wiki/List_of_Aegean_frescos#/media/File:Armon_Knossos_P1060086.JPG>.

The photo of the fresco of dolphins is available via a Creative Commons license, was made by user Armagnac-commons on July 16, 2010, and is accessible

Photography Credits

at https://en.wikipedia.org/wiki/List_of_Aegean_frescos#/media/File:Dauphins_de_knossos.jpg>.

The photo of the fresco of a group of women at Knossos is available via a Creative Commons license, was made by user cavorite on February 11, 2006, and is accessible at <https://en.wikipedia.org/wiki/List_of_Aegean_frescos#/media/File:Knossos_fresco_women.jpg>.

The photo of a close up of a griffin at Knossos is available via a Creative Commons license, was made by users Karl432 and Paginazero on May 3, 2016, and is accessible at <https://commons.wikimedia.org/wiki/File:Knossos_fresco_in_throne_palace.JPG>.

The photo of the priest-king at Knossos is available via a Creative Commons license, was made by user Leonard G. on April 21, 2007, and is accessible at https://en.wikipedia.org/wiki/Knossos#/media/File:KnossosFrescoRepro06827.jpg>.

The photo of the griffin from a far is available via a Creative Commons license, was made by user Chris 73 on June 18, 2005, and is accessible at https://en.wikipedia.org/wiki/Knossos#/media/File:Throne_Hall_Knossos.jpg>.

The photo of the ruins of Knossos is available via a Creative Commons license, was made by user Lapplaender on July 23, 2008, and is accessible at <https://en.wikipedia.org/wiki/Knossos#/media/File:Knossos_-_03.jpg>.

The photo of the North Portico at Knossos is available via a Creative Commons license, was made by user Bernard Gagnon on October 18, 2011, and is accessible at https://en.wikipedia.org/wiki/Knossos#/media/File:Knossos_-_North_Portico_02.jpg.

The map of ancient Greece is available in the public domain and is accessible at <https://en.wikipedia.org/wiki/Ancient_Greece#/media/File:Map_of_Greece,_Archipelago_and_part_of_Anadoli;_Louis_Stanislas_d'Arcy_Delarochette_1791.jpg>.

The map of Mycenaean Greece is available via a Creative Commons license, was made by users Alexikoua, Panthera tigris,and Reedside on August 5, 2017, and is accessible at <https://en.wikipedia.org/wiki/File:Mycenaean_World_en.png>.

The photo of the bust of Homer is available in the public domain and is accessible at <https://en.wikipedia.org/wiki/Homer#/media/File:Homer_British_Museum.jpg>.

The illustration of the Treasury of Atreus is available in the public domain and is accessible at https://en.wikipedia.org/wiki/Beehive_tomb#/media/File:Schatzhaus_des_Atreus,_Querschnitt.jpg.

The photo of the inside of tholos tomb is available via a Creative Commons license, was made by user Hpschaefer on October 17, 2006, and is accessible at <https://en.wikipedia.org/wiki/Beehive_tomb#/media/File:Sardinien_Orroli_Nuraghe_Arrubio_Scheinkuppel.jpg>.

The photo of Heinrich Schliemann is available via a Creative Commons license, was made available by the University of Heidelberg, and is accessible at https://en.wikipedia.org/wiki/Heinrich_Schliemann#/media/File:Heinrich_Schliemann_(HeidICON_28763)_(cropped).jpg>.

The photo of the walls of Troy is available via a Creative Commons license, was made by user CherryX on September 27, 2012, and is accessible at <https://en.wikipedia.org/wiki/Troy#/media/File:Walls_of_Troy_(2).jpg>.

Photography Credits

The photo of the Acropolis in Athens is available via an Unsplash license, was made by user Constantinos Kollias, and is accessible at <https://unsplash.com/photos/yqBvJJ8jGBQ>.

The photo of the Troy VI East Gate is available via a Creative Commons license, was made by user Bgabel on February 1, 2006, and is accessible at <https://en.wikipedia.org/wiki/Troy#/media/File:Troja-an-Stadtmauer.jpg>.

The photo of the Southwest gate of Troy II is accessible via a Creative Commons license, was made by user ccarlstead on October 7, 2006, and is accessible at <https://en.wikipedia.org/wiki/Troy#/media/File:Troy_II.jpg>.

The photo of the walls of Troy II is accessible via a Creative Commons license, was made by user Carole Raddato on April 17, 2011, and is accessible at <https://en.wikipedia.org/wiki/Troy#/media/File:Troy_(Ilion),_Turkey_(7446526244).jpg>.

The photo of the layers of settlement of Troy is accessible via a Creative Commons license, was made by user Winstonza on May 4, 2012, and is accessible at <https://en.wikipedia.org/wiki/Troy#/media/File:Layers_of_Troy.JPG>.

The walls of Troy I is available via a Creative Commons license, was made by Dennis Jarvis on October 20, 2005, <https://en.wikipedia.org/wiki/Troy#/media/File:Turkey-2941_(2216425111).jpg>.

The photo of the tower at the East Gate is accessible via a Creative Commons license, was made by user QuartierLatin1968 on February 6, 2007, and is accessible at <https://en.wikipedia.org/wiki/Troy#/media/File:Troy_walls_VII_and_IX.jpg>.

The photo of the Troy VI East Gate is accessible via a Creative Commons license, was made by user Bgabel on February 1, 2006, <https://en.wikipedia.org/wiki/Troy#/media/File:Troja-an-Stadtmauer.jpg>.

The map of Hisarlik and its archaeological excavations is available in the public domain and was made by user Bibi Saint-Pol; the map is accessible at <https://en.wikipedia.org/wiki/Hisarlik#/media/File:Section_Troy-Hisarlik-fr.svg>.

The photo of the Cyclopean masonry is accessible via a Creative Commons license, was made by user Berthold Werner on October 10, 2017, and is accessible at <https://en.wikipedia.org/wiki/Mycenaean_Greece#/media/File:Mykene_BW_2017-10-10_13-23-40.jpg>.

The photo of the Lion Gate at Mycenae is accessible via a Creative Commons license, was made by user Joyofmuseums on August 30, 2018, and is accessible at <https://en.wikipedia.org/wiki/Lion_Gate#/media/File:Lion_Gate_-_Mycenae_by_Joy_of_Museums.jpg>.

The photo of the archaeological plan of Troy is available in the public domain and was made by user Bibi Saint-Pol, and is accessible at <https://en.wikipedia.org/wiki/Hisarlik#/media/File:Plan_Troy-Hisarlik-en.svg>.

The map of the surrounding areas of ancient Athens is available in the public domain and is accessible at <https://en.wikipedia.org/wiki/History_of_Athens#/media/File:COX(1876)_p303_ATHENS_AND_ITS_NEIGHBOURHOOD.jpg>.

The map of Greek colonization is available in the public domain, was made by user Javierfv1212, and is accessile at <https://en.wikipedia.org/wiki/File:Ancient_colonies.PNG>.

The image of the Minotaur is available in the Creative Commons, was made by user Marie-Lan Nguyen on May

Photography Credits

13, 2008, and is accessible at <https://en.wikipedia.org/wiki/Minotaur#/media/File:Tondo_Minotaur_London_E4_MAN.jpg>.

The statue of Zeus is available in the public domain and is accessible at <https://en.wikipedia.org/wiki/Hera#/media/File:Hera_Campana_Louvre_Ma2283.jpg>.

The statue of Hera is available in the public domain and is accessible at <https://en.wikipedia.org/wiki/Hera#/media/File:Hera_Campana_Louvre_Ma2283.jpg>.

The statue of Posiedon is available via a Creative Commons license, was made by user Ricardo André Frantz on January 1, 2006, and is accessible at <en.wikipedia.org/wiki/Poseidon#/media/File:0036MAN_Poseidon.jpg>.

The statue of Hestia is available in the public domain and is accessible at <https://en.wikipedia.org/wiki/Hestia#/media/File:Hestia_Giustiniani.jpg>.

The statue of Hades is available via a Creative Commons license, was made by userCarole Raddato on October 17, 2016, and is accessible at <https://en.wikipedia.org/wiki/Hades#/media/File:Detail_of_Pluto-Serapis,_Statue_group_of_Persephone_(as_Isis)_and_Pluto_(as_Serapis),_from_the_Sanctuary_of_the_Egyptian_Gods_at_Gortyna,_mid-2nd_century_AD,_Heraklion_Archaeological_Museum_(30305313721).jpg>.

The statue of Poseidon is available via a Creative Commons license, was made by user Rama on September 17, 2010, and is accessible at <https://en.wikipedia.org/wiki/Aphrodite#/media/File:Turtle_Aphrodite_AO20126_mp3h9188.jpg>.

The statue of Athena is available in the public domain and is accessible at <https://en.wikipedia.org/wiki/Athena#/media/File:Mattei_Athena_Louvre_Ma530_n2.jpg>.

The photograph of the fresco of Hephasteus is available via a Creative Commons license, was made by userArchaiOptix on October 7, 2018, and is accessible at <https://en.wikipedia.org/wiki/Hephaestus#/media/File:Wall_painting_-_Hephaistos_producing_the_new_arms_for_Achilles_-_Pompeii_(IX_1_7)_-_Napoli_MAN_9529.jpg>.

The statue of Ares is available in the public domain and is accessible at <https://en.wikipedia.org/wiki/Ares#/media/File:Ares_Ludovisi_Altemps_Inv8602_n2.jpg>.

The statue of Hermes is available in the public domain and is accessible at <https://en.wikipedia.org/wiki/Hermes#/media/File:Hermes_Ingenui_Pio-Clementino_Inv544.jpg

The photo of the Pillars of Creation is available in the public domain and is accessible at <https://en.wikipedia.org/wiki/Pillars_of_Creation#/media/File:Pillars_of_creation_2014_HST_WFC3-UVIS_full-res_denoised.jpg

The photo of the Olympians is available in the public domain and is accessible at <https://en.wikipedia.org/wiki/Twelve_Olympians#/media/File:Greek_-_Procession_of_Twelve_Gods_and_Goddesses_-_Walters_2340.jpg>.

The photo of Hephasteus is available in the public domain and is accessible at <https://en.wikipedia.org/wiki/Twelve_Olympians#/media/File:Vulcan_Coustou_Louvre_MR1814.jpg

The photograph of Mount Olympus is from Ben Dumond, is available via an Unsplash license, and is accessible at <https://unsplash.com/photos/4ECvC48vzdI>.

The photograph of a black hole is available via a Creative Commons license, was made by user Event

Photography Credits

Horizon Telescope on April 10, 2019, and is accessible at <https://en.wikipedia.org/wiki/Hephaestus#/media/File:Wall_painting_-_Hephaistos_producing_the_new_arms_for_Achilles_-_Pompeii_(IX_1_7)_-_Napoli_MAN_9529.jpg>.

The statue of Heracles is available via a Creative Commons license, was made by user Marie-Lan Nguyen on June 14, 2014, and is accessible at <https://en.wikipedia.org/wiki/Farnese_Hercules#/media/File:Herakles_Farnese_MAN_Napoli_Inv6001_n01.jpg>.

The statue of Dionysus is available via a Creative Commons license, was made by user Marie-Lan Nguyen on January 1, 2009, and is accessible at <https://en.wikipedia.org/wiki/Dionysus#/media/File:Dionysos_Louvre_Ma87_n2.jpg>.

The image of Hephaestus presenting Achilles with his shield is available via a Creative Commons license, was made by user ArchaiOptix on October 7, 2018, and is accessible at <https://en.wikipedia.org/wiki/Hephaestus#/media/File:Wall_painting_-_Hephaistos_producing_the_new_arms_for_Achilles_-_Pompeii_(IX_1_7)_-_Napoli_MAN_9529.jpg>.

The photo of Crete is available via an Unsplash license and was made by user Stepan Unar, and is accessible at <https://unsplash.com/photos/wide-angle-photography-of-mountain-during-daytime-7gVz8-FrDRg>.

Chapter 2: Archaic Greece

The photo of the Athenian Theater and Athens is available via an Unsplash license, was made by user Kieran Everett, and is accessible at <https://unsplash.com/photos/Bd9M7zfsdg8>.

The photo of Corinth is available via an Unsplash license, was made by user Vassilis Terzo, and is accessible at <https://unsplash.com/photos/uFLIFfaXobM>.

The map of the Peloponnese is available via a Creative Commons license, was made by users Marsyas, Rowanwindwhistler, and Peter Gulyas on April 22, 2020, and is accessible at <https://en.wikipedia.org/wiki/Sparta#/media/File:Sparta_Territory.svg>.

The photo of the Spartan theater is available via a Creative Commons license, was made on April 13, 2007, and is accessible at <https://en.wikipedia.org/wiki/Sparta#/media/File:Ancient_sparta_theater.jpg>.

The photo of the Eurotas River in Sparta is available via a Creative Commons license, was made by user Aeleftherios on April 24, 2008, and is accessible at <https://en.wikipedia.org/wiki/Sparta#/media/File:Eurotas.JPG>.

The ruins of the Temple of Artemis Orthia is available via a Creative Commons license, was made by user George E. Koronaios on May 15, 2019, and is accessible at <https://en.wikipedia.org/wiki/Sparta#/media/File:The_remains_of_the_Temple_of_Artemis_Orthia_in_Sparta_on_15_May_2019.jpg>.

The photo of the Areopagus is available via an Unsplash license, was made by user Anna Kurmaeva, and is accessible at <https://unsplash.com/photos/EKoX8YrCFrE>.

The illustration of a hoplite soldier is available in the public domain and is accessible at <https://en.wikipedia.org/wiki/Hoplite#/media/File:Two_hoplites.jpg>.

The photo of hoplite soldiers fighting is available in the public domain and is accessible at <https://en.wikipedia.org/wiki/Hoplite#/media/File:Amphora_phalanx_Staatliche_Antikensammlungen_1429.jpg>.

Photography Credits

The photo of a Spartan hoplite soldier is available in the public domain and is accessible at <https://en.wikipedia.org/wiki/Hoplite#/media/File:Spartan_hoplite-1_from_Vinkhuijzen.jpg>.

The photo of the ruins at Corinth are available via a Creative Commons license, was made by user Chris Oxford on September 1, 2015, and is accessible at <https://en.wikipedia.org/wiki/Ancient_Corinth#/media/File:Ancient_Theater_in_Archeological_site_of_Ancient_Corinth.jpg>.

The photo of a hoplite on a Greek vase is available via a Creative Commons license, was made by user Jona Lendering on October 14, 2018, and is accessible at <https://en.wikipedia.org/wiki/Hoplite#/media/File:Hoplite_5th_century.jpg>.

The photo of hoplite armor is available via a Creative Commons license, was made by userDr. K on September 19, 2010, and is accessible at <https://en.wikipedia.org/wiki/Hoplite#/media/File:Hoplite_armour_exhibit_at_the_Corfu_Museum_closeup.jpg>.

The photo of an Athenian hoplite soldier is available in the public domain and is accessible at <https://en.wikipedia.org/wiki/Polemarch#/media/File:Datis_fighting_Kallimachos_at_the_Battle_of_Marathon_in_the_Stoa_Poikile_(reconstitution).jpg>.

The photo of the Macedonian phalanx is available in the public domain and is accessible at <https://en.wikipedia.org/wiki/Macedonian_phalanx#/media/File:Makedonische_phalanx.png>.

The photo of Peisistratus in his second coup attempt is available in the public domain and is accessible at <https://en.wikipedia.org/wiki/Pisistratus#/media/File:Return_of_Peisistratus_to_Athens_with_the_false_Minerva.jpg>.

The photo of the Theatre of Dionysus is available via a Creative Commons license, was made by user dronepicr on May 15, 2015 , and is accessible at <https://en.wikipedia.org/wiki/Theatre_of_Dionysus#/media/File:Athen_Akropolis_(18512008726).jpg>.

The photo of Ajax and Achilles Playing Dice is available in the public domain and is accessible at <https://commons.wikimedia.org/wiki/File:Akhilleus_Aias_MGEt_16757.jpg>.

The Dipylon Amphora, mid-8th century BC is available via a Creative Commons license, and is accessible at <https://en.wikipedia.org/wiki/Geometric_art#/media/File:Dypilon_vase_1.jpg>.

The photo of the miniature amphora (amphoriskos), or perfume vase, terra-cotta, Proto-Corinthian style, 575–550 BCE; is available via a Creative Commons license and is housed at the Metropolitan Museum of Art, New York City, and is accessible at <https://www.britannica.com/art/Proto-Corinthian-style>.

The photo of geometric-style krater with funeral scenes is available via a Creative Commons license and is accessible at <https://www.britannica.com/art/Greek-pottery>.

The photo of an amphora featuring Greek warriors is in the public domain and is accessible at <https://en.wikipedia.org/wiki/Red-figure_pottery#/media/File:Fight_Andokides_Louvre_G1.jpg>.

The photo of the Protogeometric amphora is available in the public domain and is accessible at <https://en.wikipedia.org/wiki/Pottery_of_ancient_Greece#/media/File:Amphora_protogeometric_BM_A1123.jpg>.

The photo of the "Embassy to Achilles" is available in the public domain and is accessible at <https://

Photography Credits

en.wikipedia.org/wiki/Achilles#/media/File:Akhilleus_embassy_Staatliche_Antikensammlungen_8770.jpg>.

The photograph of the Odeon of Herodes Atticus is available via a Creative Commons license, was made by user Salvador Calyso on October 30, 2023, and is accessible at <https://en.wikipedia.org/wiki/Odeon_of_Herodes_Atticus#/media/File:"Herodeon"_-_Odeon_of_Herodes_Atticus.jpg>.

The theatre at Epidaurus is available via a Creative Commons license, was made by Carole Raddato on January 16, 2015, and is accessible at <https://en.wikipedia.org/wiki/Theatre_of_ancient_Greece#/media/File:The_great_theater_of_Epidaurus,_designed_by_Polykleitos_the_Younger_in_the_4th_century_BC,_Sanctuary_of_Asklepeios_at_Epidaurus,_Greece_(14015010416).jpg>.

Chapter 3: The Persian Wars

The photo of the bust of Herodotus is available in the public domain and is accessible at < https://commons.wikimedia.org/wiki/File:Cropped-removebg-herodotus-historian.png>.

The map of the Persian Wars is available via a Creative Commons license, was made by user Bibi Saint-Pol on February 27, 2007, and is accessible at <https://en.wikipedia.org/wiki/Battle_of_Plataea#/media/File:Map_Greco-Persian_Wars-en.svg>.

The photograph of the bust of Thucydides is available via a Creative Commons license, was made by user shakko on January 1, 2008, and is accessible at <https://en.wikipedia.org/wiki/Thucydides#/media/File:Thucydides_pushkin02.jpg>.

The map of the Battle of Marathon is available via a GFDL license, was made on July 13, 2005, and is accessible at <https://en.wikipedia.org/wiki/Battle_of_Marathon#/media/File:Battle_of_Marathon_Initial_Situation.png>.

The photo of the terrain at Marathon is available via a Creative Commons license, was made by user Seisma on June 10, 2016, and is accessible at <https://en.wikipedia.org/wiki/Battle_of_Marathon#/media/File:Marshlands_of_Marathon,_with_Pentelikon_mountains_in_the_background.jpg>.

The photo of Xerxes I is available via a Creative Commons license, was made by user Darafsh on June 17, 2005, and is accessible at <https://en.wikipedia.org/wiki/Xerxes_I#/media/File:National_Museum_of_Iran_Darafsh_(785).JPG>.

The illustration of Xerxes whipping the Hellespont is available in the public domain and is accessible at <https://en.wikipedia.org/wiki/Dardanelles#/media/File:Xerxes_lash_sea.JPG>.

The photo of Themistocles is available via a Creative Commons license, was made by user Rijksdienst voor het Cultureel Erfgoed, originates from a photo on on October 1, 1926, and is accessible <https://en.wikipedia.org/wiki/Themistocles#/media/File:Beeld,_Themistocles_-_Unknown_-_20408396_-_RCE.jpg>.

The map of the Persia Empire at its greatest extent is available via a Creative Commons license, was made by user Cattette on December 8, 2021, and is accessible at <<https://en.wikipedia.org/wiki/Achaemenid_Empire#/media/File:Achaemenid_Empire_500_BCE.jpg>.

Chapter 4: Classical Greece

The picture of the Acropolis is available via an Unsplash license, was made by user Victor Malyushev, and is accessible at <https://unsplash.com/photos/WVrrQgjH6y4>.

Photography Credits

The photo of the Theatre and Sanctuary of Dionysus is available via a Creative Commons license, was made by user dronepicr on May 15, 2015, and is accessible at <https://en.wikipedia.org/wiki/Theatre_of_Dionysus#/media/File:Athen_Akropolis_(18512008726).jpg>.

The photo of the hillside of Taormina is available via an Unsplash license, was made by user Freysteinn G. Jonsson, and is accessible at <https://unsplash.com/photos/kmBg8ElP8Pc>.

The photo of Stonehenge is available in the public domain and is accessible at <https://en.wikipedia.org/wiki/Post_and_lintel#/media/File:Stonehenge_Inside_Facing_NE_April_2005.jpg>.

The illustration of the Temple to Zeus at Olympia is available in the public domain and is accessible <https://en.wikipedia.org/wiki/Temple_of_Zeus,_Olympia#/media/File:Olympia-ZeusTempelRestoration.jpg>.

The floor plan of the Parthenon is available via a Creative Commons license, was made by userIo Herodotus on February 15, 2017, and is accessible at <https://en.wikipedia.org/wiki/Parthenon#/media/File:Parthenon_plan.png>.

The statue of the Varvakeion Athena is available via a Creative Commons license, was made on November 4, 2015, and is accessible at <https://en.wikipedia.org/wiki/Athena_Parthenos#/media/File:NAMA_Athéna_Varvakeion.jpg

The Temple of Concord in Sicily is available via a Creative Commons license, was made by user Wolfgang Pehlemann on December 28, 2015, and is accessible at <https://commons.wikimedia.org/wiki/File:Concordiatempel_Tempio_della_Temple_of_Concordia_de_la_Concorde_Tal_der_Tempel_Valle_dei_Templi_Agrigento_Sizilien_Foto_Wolfgang_Pehlemann_DSC07490.jpg>.

The photo of the Parthenon is available via an Unsplash license, was made by Amir Hanna, and is accessible at <https://unsplash.com/photos/TXWbwRlIdnY>.

The photo of the Parthenon is available via an Unsplash license, was made by Sergio García, and is accessible at <https://unsplash.com/photos/8lKpEfyFSoY>.

The photo of a bust of Aristotle is available in the public domain and is accessible at < https://en.wikipedia.org/wiki/File:Aristotle_Altemps_Inv8575.jpg>.

The Temple of Juno in Agrigento, Sicily is available via a Creative Commons license, was made by user Berthold Werner on October 7, 2012, and is accessible at <https://en.wikipedia.org/wiki/Temple_of_Hera_Lacinia#/media/File:Agrigent_BW_2012-10-07_12-24-45.JPG>.

The illustration of Aristotle and Plato from Raphael's School of Athens (1509) is available in the public domain and is accessible at < https://en.wikipedia.org/wiki/Aristotle#/media/File:Sanzio_01_Plato_Aristotle.jpg>.

The photo of Socrates is available via a Creative Commons license, was made by user Berthold Werner on October 7, 2012, and is accessible at <https://en.wikipedia.org/wiki/Socrates#/media/File:Socrate_du_Louvre.jpg>.

The photo of the Paestum in southern Italy is available via an Unsplash license, was made by Antonio Sessa, and is accessible at <https://unsplash.com/photos/cVP68YK4Evg>.

The photo of the Acropolis in Athens is available via an Unsplash license, was made by user Igor Wang, and is accessible at <https://unsplash.com/photos/sVV5uawtsaM>.

Photography Credits

The photo of the Acropolis is available via a Creative Commons license, was taken by Carole Raddato on April 18, 2014, and is accessible at <https://en.wikipedia.org/wiki/Acropolis_of_Athens#/media/File:The_Acropolis_of_Athens_viewed_from_the_Hill_of_the_Muses_(14220794964).jpg>.

The photo of the Parthenon is available via an Unsplash license, was made by Sergio García, and is accessible at <https://unsplash.com/photos/8lKpEfyFSoY>.

The photo of West side of the Erechtheion is available via a Creative Commons license, was made by user Jebulon on October 26, 2015, and is accessible at <https://en.wikipedia.org/wiki/Erechtheion#/media/File:Erechtheum_Acropolis_Athens.jpg>.

The photo of the Erechtheum from the Acropolis of Athens by C. Messier on November 6, 2017, and is accessible at <https://en.wikipedia.org/wiki/Ancient_Greek_temple#/media/File:Ερέχθειο_4984.jpg>.

The photo of the Temple of Garni is available via a Creative Commons license, was made by user Gnvard in September 7, 2013, and is accessible at <https://en.wikipedia.org/wiki/Temple_of_Garni#/media/File:Garni_Temple_02.JPG>.

The north porch of the Erechtheum in Athens is available via a Creative Commons license, was made by user Vicenç Valcárcel Pérez on March 3, 2008, and is accessible at <https://en.wikipedia.org/wiki/Ionic_order#/media/File:Temple_de_l'Erecteon_(421-406_aC),_Acròpolis_d'Atenes.jpg>.

The photograph of the ruins of a temple is available via an Unsplash license, was made by user, T. Selin Erkan and is accessible at <https://unsplash.com/photos/fmtYssAZCgE>.

The photograph of the bust of Thucydides is available via a Creative Commons license, was made by user Shakko on January 1, 2008, and is accessible at <https://en.wikipedia.org/wiki/Thucydides#/media/File:Thucydides_pushkin02.jpg>.

The painting of the "Scene at the Constitutional Convention" is available in the public domain and may be accessed at <https://en.wikipedia.org/wiki/Constitutional_Convention_%28United_States%29#/media/File:Scene_at_the_Signing_of_the_Constitution_of_the_United_States.jpg>.

The reconstruction of an Athenian trireme, called the "Olymias," is available via a Creative Commons license, was made by user Da jackson on June 12, 2022, and is accessible is <https://en.wikipedia.org/wiki/Trireme#/media/File:"Olympias",_Nachbau_einer_Triere_im_Schiffsmuseum_Trokadero_Marina,_Paleo_Faliro,_Athen.jpg>.

The diagram of an Athenian trireme is available via a Creative Commons license, was made by user Eric Gaba on October 1, 2005, and is accessible at <https://en.wikipedia.org/wiki/Trireme#/media/File:Trireme_cut-fr.svg>.

The painting of the Plague in an Ancient City by Michiel Sweerts is available in the public domain and may be accessed at <https://en.wikipedia.org/wiki/Plague_of_Athens#/media/File:Plague_in_an_Ancient_City_LACMA_AC1997.10.1_(1_of_2).jpg>.

The photo of Philip II of Macedon is available in the public domain and is accessible at <https://en.wikipedia.org/wiki/Philip_II_of_Macedon#/media/File:Philip_II_of_Macedon_Ny_Carlsberg_Glyptotek_IN2263.jpg>.

Chapter 5: The Rise of Macedon

The photo of Staro Nagoircane in North Macedonia is available via an Unsplash license, was taken by user Tomica S., and is accessible at <https://unsplash.com/photos/SWeiUS_cV9k>.

The photo of the bust of Philip II is available in the public domain and is accessible at <https://en.wikipedia.org/wiki/Alexander_the_Great#/media/File:Philip_II_of_Macedon_Ny_Carlsberg_Glyptotek_IN2263.jpg>.

The photo of the Roman medallion of Olympias is available via a Creative Commons license, was made by user Fotogeniss on April 12, 2013, and is accessible at <https://en.wikipedia.org/wiki/Alexander_the_Great#/media/File:Coin_olympias_mus_theski.JPG>.

The illustration of Philip II being assassinated is available in the public domain and is accessible at <https://en.wikipedia.org/wiki/Philip_II_of_Macedon#/media/File:Assassination_of_Philip_of_Macedon.jpg>.

The photo of the bust of Philip II is available in the public domain and is accessible at <https://en.wikipedia.org/wiki/Alexander_the_Great#/media/File:Philip_II_of_Macedon_Ny_Carlsberg_Glyptotek_IN2263.jpg>.

The photo of the coin of Archelaus is available in the public domain and is accessible at < https://en.wikipedia.org/wiki/Archelaus_I_of_Macedon#/media/File:Didrachm_of_Archelaos_I_King_of_Macedonia.jpg>.

The painting of Alexander the Great being tutored by Aristotle is available in the public domain and is accessible at <https://commons.wikimedia.org/wiki/File:Alexander_and_Aristotle.jpg>.

The photo of the coin of Perdiccas III is available in the public domain and is accessible at <https://en.wikipedia.org/wiki/Perdiccas_III_of_Macedon#/media/File:Coin_of_Perdiccas_III_with_figure_of_Herakles.jpg>.

The photo of the Macedonian phalanx is available in the public domain and is accessible at <https://en.wikipedia.org/wiki/Macedonian_phalanx#/media/File:Makedonische_phalanx.png>.

The illustration of Philip II being assassinated is available in the public domain and is accessible at <https://en.wikipedia.org/wiki/Philip_II_of_Macedon#/media/File:Assassination_of_Philip_of_Macedon.jpg>.

The photo of the bust of Philip II is available in the public domain and is accessible at <https://en.wikipedia.org/wiki/Alexander_the_Great#/media/File:Philip_II_of_Macedon_Ny_Carlsberg_Glyptotek_IN2263.jpg>.

The photo of the Roman medallion of Olyumpias is available via a Creative Commons license, was made by user Fotogeniss on April 12, 2013, and is accessible at <https://en.wikipedia.org/wiki/Alexander_the_Great#/media/File:Coin_olympias_mus_theski.JPG>.

The image of Alexander from the House of the Faun in Pompeii is available in the public domain and is accessible at <https://en.wikipedia.org/wiki/Alexander_the_Great#/media/File:Alexander_the_Great_mosaic_(cropped).jpg>.

The image of Alexander is available in the public domain and is accessible at <https://en.wikipedia.org/wiki/Alexander_the_Great#/media/File:Alexander_the_Great_Ny_Carlsberg_Glyptotek_IN574_n1.jpg>.

The painting of Spihtridates and Cleitus is available in the public domain and is accessible at <https://en.wikipedia.org/wiki/Battle_of_the_Granicus#/media/

Photography Credits

File:Spithridates_attacking_Alexander_from_behind_at_the_Battle_of_Granicus.jpg>.

The map of Magna Graecia is available in the public domain and is accessible at <https://en.wikipedia.org/wiki/Magna_Graecia#/media/File:Magna_Graecia_ancient_colonies_and_dialects-en.svg>.

The illustration of Cleitus the Black is available in the public domain and is accessible at <https://en.wikipedia.org/wiki/Cleitus_the_Black#/media/File:The_killing_of_Cleitus_by_Andre_Castaigne_(1898-1899)_reduced.jpg>.

The statue of the Kleobis and Biton is available via a Creative Commons license, was made by user Ricardo Andre Frantz on January 1, 2005, and is accessible at <https://en.wikipedia.org/wiki/Archaic_Greek_Sculpture#/media/File:Kouroi2.jpg>.

The statue of the Kritios Boy is available via a Creative Commons license and was made by user Tetraktys on January 1, 2005, and is accessible at <https://en.wikipedia.org/wiki/Kritios_Boy#/media/File:009MA_Kritios.jpg>.

The statue of the Venus de Milo is available via a Creative Commons license and was made by user Livioandronico2013 on October 24, 2016 , and is accessible at <https://en.wikipedia.org/wiki/Kritios_Boy#/media/File:009MA_Kritios.jpg>.

The staute of Laocoön and his sons is available in the public domain and is accessible at <https://en.wikipedia.org/wiki/Laocoön_and_His_Sons#/media/File:Laocoon_Pio-Clementino_Inv1059-1064-1067.jpg>.

The photo of a Kouros boy is available in the public domain and is accessible at <https://en.wikipedia.org/wiki/Kouros#/media/File:Kouros_anavissos.jpg>. Hemingway, Seán.

The Athenian statue of a diadoumenos is available via a Creative Commons license, was made by user Tilemahos Efthimiadis on January 18, 2009, and is accessible at <https://en.wikipedia.org/wiki/Diadumenos#/media/File:Youth_binding_his_hair._About_450-425_BC_(3209630605).jpg>.

The photo of the Peplos Kore is available via a Creative Commons license and is accessible at <https://en.wikipedia.org/wiki/Peplos_Kore#/media/File:ACMA_679_Kore_1.JPG>.

The Farnese Hercules is available via a Creative Commons license, was made by Marie-Lan Nguyen on June 14, 2014, and is accessible at <https://en.wikipedia.org/wiki/Farnese_Hercules#/media/File:Herakles_Farnese_MAN_Napoli_Inv6001_n01.jpg>.

The photo of the Roman Forum is available via an Unsplah license, was made by user Roman Wimmers, and is accessible at <https://unsplash.com/photos/krolC7VHgGc>.

The illustration of Alexander the Great's tomb is available in the public domain and is accessible at <https://en.wikipedia.org/wiki/Tomb_of_Alexander_the_Great#/media/File:Mid-nineteenth_century_reconstruction_of_Alexander's_catafalque_based_on_the_description_by_Diodorus.jpg>.

The illustration of the Lighthouse of Alexander is available in the public domain and is accessible at <https://en.wikipedia.org/wiki/Lighthouse_of_Alexandria#/media/File:Lighthouse_-_Thiersch.png>.

Glossary of Terms

A

Abydos: Abydos is a city in Asia Minor, close to the Hellespont.

Academy: The Academy was the school started by Plato.

Acropolis: The highest part of a Greek city that contained a citadel and supplies capable of withstanding a siege.

Aegean Sea: The sea of the Greek world, populated with Greek islands, criss crossed with Greek trading routes, and filled with stories of Greek gods and heroes.

Aegospotami: The Battle of Aegospotami was fought in 405 BC near the Hellespont, the straits that connect the Aegean to the Black Sea. The Spartan navy ensured Athens could no longer control the Aegean Sea, thus ending the Peloponnesian War.

Agamemnon: The king of Mycenae and the leader of all the Greeks assembled at Troy. Here, Thucydides argues Agamemnon was the leader because he possessed the largest fleet of ships.

Age of Pericles: At times, the world of Classical Greece is called the Age of Pericles because so many of Athens' great accomplishments and institutions were conducted thanks to this influential Athenian politician.

Alcibiades: Alcibiades was an Athenian politician during the Peloponnesian War. He was a relative of Pericles and a student of Socrates, but he is most remembered for his plans to invade the island of Sicily, which ended in disaster. He lived from 450 to 404 BC.

Alexander: Alexander is an alternate name for Paris, the Trojan prince who abducted Helen of Sparta. These actions initiated the Trojan War.

Alexander: Alexander was the son of Philip II and Olympias who, as prince and later the king of Macedon, would conquer the known world. Today, we know him as Alexander the Great, and he lived from 356 to 323 BC.

Alexander I: Alexander I was the first strongly-attested king of Macedon, whose reign lasted through the Persian Wars. He initially took an oath of loyalty to the Persian king Xerxes and helped him in his invasion of Greece, but he may have also given the Athenians and Spartans intelligence about Persian battle plans. He reigned from 497 to 454 BC.

Alexandria: Located at the mouth of the Nile River, Alexandria was perhaps the most prosperous and successful port city in the ancient world. Alexander founded the city in 331 BC, naming the city after himself.

Amphora: A large jar used for transporting commodities in the ancient world.

Anarchy: A form of government wherein there is no government.

Anatolia: A peninsula surrounded by the Aegean, the Black Sea, and the Mediterranean; the region is also referred to as Asia Minor. Today it corresponds to the Republic of Turkey.

Antioch: Founded by Seleucus I, Antioch was one of the most prosperous cities and commercial centers of the Hellenistic world. Antioch is located in Syria on the Mediterranean coastline.

Antipater: Antipater was a Macedonian general and a close friend of Philip II, who decisively brought Alexander before the Macedonian army to proclaim him king before any rivals could appear and challenge Alexander's claim.

Glossary of Terms

Apology: In Greek, this word referred to a well-reasoned argument in defense of some action, decision, or doctrine.

Arbitration: Arbitration is the formal process by which two sides reach a compromise through negotiation rather than outright fighting.

Archaic Greece: A period in Greek history from approximately 750 BC to the invasion of the Persian Empire in 480 BC. During this period, the city-states of Athens, Sparta, and Thebes, among others, became especially prominent.

Archelaus: The king of Macedon who built the capital of Pella and encouraged Hellenization amongst the Macedonian nobility. He reigned as king of Macedon from 412 to 400 BC.

Archon: An Athenian leader who served as the head of the Athenian assembly.

Areopagus: Greek for the Hill of Ares, this place was the heart of Athenian civic government and sat atop the Athenian Acropolis.

Argeads: The royal family of Macedon, who claimed descendancy from Heracles.

Aristocracy: A form of government in which the very best individuals rule. Presumably, the best individuals are those who are the best fighters or those capable of giving the best advice on political issues.

Aristotle: A Greek philosopher whose writings on Politics, Poetics, Physics, Metaphysics, and Rhetoric form the basis for much of the Western canon. He lived from 384 to 322 BC.

Artemisium: Fought in 480 BC, this battle was a naval battle between the Athenian navy, commanded by Themistocles, and the Persian fleet. A storm destroyed much of the Persian fleet before the battle.

Aspis: A large shield used in Greek phalanxes that covered half of the bearer's bpdy and half of the body of his neighbor on his right.

Athenian Black-Figure Pottery: In use from 700 to 500 BC, this style of pottery is known for its bright orange background and the realistic black figures decorating these pots.

Athenian Red-Figure Pottery : In use from 530 BC onwards, this style of pottery is known for its dark black background and the realistic red figures decorating these pots.

Athens: One of the three most important cities in ancient Greece. The city of Athens was famous for its civic and political freedoms, its wealth, and its navy.

Athos: Athos is a mountain in northern Greece, around which Xerxes built a canal.

Attica: Attica is a region in mainland Greece of which Athens is the principal city.

B

Bacchiadae: The Bacchiadae were the rulers of Corinth.

Bactria: Bactria was a former satrap of the Persian Empire Alexander populated with Greeks and Macedonians. As a result, Bactria became famous as a melting pot region of Central Asian, Greek, Indian, and Persian culture.

Barbarians: Herodotus is following Greek custom which separates the world into civilized Greeks and everyone else—the barbarians.

Basileus: The name of the king in ancient Greece following the collapse of the Bronze Age.

Glossary of Terms

Boeotia: A region in central Greece west of Athens and north of Corinth.

Bucephalus: The name of Alexander the Great's horse.

C

Capital: Capital refers to the possession of economic resources capable of producing goods at relatively low cost. A single olive tree in one's backyard is just a tree; an orchard of productive olive trees is capital.

Capital: The top of a column where the column meets the roof of the temple.

Cecrops: Cecrops is the mythical founder of Athens, a king who founded the city, forged its relationship with Athena, and organized the demes surrounding Athens.

Chaeronea: Taking place in Boeotia, the Battle of Chaeronea saw Macedon crush the combined forces of Athens and Thebes.

City Dionysia: The City Dionysia was a religious festival held each year in Athens to honor the god Dionysus. Since Dionysus was the god of wine, comedy, revelry, and the theater, the City Dionysia featured plays written by Athenian playwrights.

City-State: A city-state is an independent commercial center responsible for drafting and maintaining its own laws, infrastructure, military, and other services we might expect of modern-day states.

Classical Greece: Lasting from 479 to 323 BC, the age of Classical Greece produced philosophers such as Socrates, Plato, and Aristotle; playwrights like Sophocles and Aeschylus; and monumental architecture as grand as the Parthenon.

Cleitus: Cleitus came from a noble family and served as a cavalry commander. His sister was also the nurse of Alexander. He famously saved Alexander's life at the Granicus River, but later, Alexander killed him in a drunken brawl.

Colony: A colony is an outpost or settlement inhabited by residents who originally came from a distant country or region.

Constitution: The word constitution refers to the order of a state and the way in which power is distributed amongst different institutions and people.

Corcyra: Corcya was founded as a colony by the city of Corinth but had formed with Corinth's rival Athens.

Corinth: A Greek city-state whose location on the Peloponnese, near the Isthmus of Corinth, which made it especially wealthy through commerce and trade, as well as their job in dragging ships overland to the Saronic Gulf.

Corinthian: The most decorative and elaborate of the three orders, the capital of a Corinthian column was carved to look like acanthus leaves pushing through a basket.

Corinthian Pottery: In use from 725 to 600 BC, this style of pottery used flowers, animals, trees, etc. for decoration.

Council of Four Hundred: A subset of the Athenian Assembly that set the legislative agenda for the Assembly. Everyone in Athens could serve in the Council of Four Hundred except for the poorest residents in Athens.

Crete: An island in the eastern Mediterranean that supplied convenient ports for their wealthy trading partners like Egypt and Phoenicia.

Crocus Field: Fought in 352 BC, Philip II defeated Phocis and gained mastery of almost all of northern Greece.

Glossary of Terms

Cyclades: The Cyclades are a chain of islands in the eastern Mediterranean.

Cyrus the Great: Cyrus the Great was the founder of the Persian Empire and one of the most successful military and political leaders of all time. He reigned from 559 to 529 BC.

D

Darius I: Under Darius' rule, the Persian Empire reached the apex of its territorial expansion, stretching from the Indus River Valley to northern Greece, and achieving its peak of commercial, political, and economic power. Darius I reigned from 522 BC to 486 BC.

Darius III: Darius III was the last king of Persia, having been defeated by Alexander the Great. He lived from 381 to 330 BC.

Delian League: The Delian League was an alliance between the Greek city-states for protection against Persia. Under the leadership of Athens, the Greek fleet patrolled the Aegean and kept it clear of Persian ships. The members of the alliance contributed either ships to the fleet or money to help maintain the fleet.

Delos: Delos is an island in the Aegean Sea that contained the treasury for the Delian League.

Demagogue: From the Greek demos for "people" and agogos for "driver", a demagogue was a leader who uses their rhetorical and public speaking abilities to advance their own interests and not those of the broader community.

Demes: The Greek word for political units in Attica, the region of which Athens is the largest city, as well as the twelve political divisions into which Athens organized the people of Attica.

Democracy: A form of government in which political power is vested in the people. The word democracy comes from the Greek word demos for "people" and kratos for "rule".

Demosthenes: Demosthenes was a famous Athenian orator who tried, unsuccessfully, to slow down Philip II's conquest of Greece. He lived from 384 to 322 BC.

Diadochi: Upon the death of Alexander the Great, his great empire was divided between four of his most prominent generals. The wars leading to this division are the Diadochi, or the Successor Wars.

Dialogue: A literary work where two or more speakers discuss a topic of philosophical significance.

Diplomacy: Diplomacy is the practice of maintaining good relations between countries.

Division of Labor: As communities grow in population, less people need to be directly engaged in farming and agriculture. More food means more people, and more people means more "activities" can be done that are directly related to farming. At times, this is known as "job specialization."

Dorians: A race of people claiming descent from the Greek hero Heracles; they may have invaded mainland Greece at the end of the Bronze Age.

Doric Order: The Doric order is one of the three architectural orders of Greek temples, is marked by a simple but commanding style, and is named for the Dorians, the people of the Peloponnesus known for their reserved, stern character.

Draco: An Athenian aristocrat who wrote down the first set of laws for ancient Athens. The laws were so strict and severe, however, they were quickly repealed.

Glossary of Terms

E

Ekklesia: From the Greek words for called out ones, the Ekklesia was the Athenian assembly.

Ephors: The elders in ancient Sparta, who met together as a council, advised the Spartan king on important issues, and made sure that Spartan traditions were followed.

Epicureanism: Epicureanism was a branch of philosophy popular in the Greco-Roman world which focused on the pursuit of pleasure as the goal for which everyone should strive in life. Such pleasures were meant to be pursued in moderation, and intellectual pleasures were to be favored over physical ones.

Epidamnus: Epidamnus was founded as a colony by the city of Corcyra, which itself was founded by Corinth. The conflict between Epidamnus and Corcyra, and by extension with Corinth and Athens, led to the outbreak of the Peloponnesian War.

Erythraian Sea: The Erythraian Sea is known as the Gulf of Aden today and is located off the coast of the Arabian Peninsula.

Ethiopia: The Greeks were aware of the kingdom of Ethiopia, sometimes called Cush. Ethiopia was connected to the Mediterranean world via the Nile River which, because the Nile flowed south to north, is above Egypt although it is south of Egypt.

Europa: Europa was a Phoenician princess, whom Zeus abducted after he transformed himself into a bull. Tyre was one of the more significant cities among the Phoenicians.

Euxine Sea: The Euxine Sea is an alternative name for the Black Sea.

F

First Peloponnesian War: The First Peloponnesian War was a relatively short conflict fought between Athens and Corinth, but is not the same Peloponnesian War immortalized by Thucydides.

Forms: This word refers to ideas such as truth, beauty, and goodness that, for Socrates and Plato, exist in an independent realm called the World of Forms.

Fresco: A fresco is a type of painting done on wet plaster, so that the painting and plaster dry together. The word is Italian for fresh since the painting must be done relatively quickly before the plaster has a chance to dry.

G

Gaugamela: Fought in 331 BC at the town of Gaugamela, this battle saw Alexander the Great defeat the Persian Empire for the third and final time.

Geometric Pottery: In use from 1000 to 700 BC, this style of pottery used geometric designs and shapes for decoration.

Golden Age: The term golden age refers to a time period of great cultural and artistic achievements, as well as great material and economic prosperity.

Good Life: A life spent in contemplation of ideas like justice, virtue, and beauty.

Gordian Knot: Local legend said that whoever untied the Gordian Knot would become ruler of Asia. Alexander cut the knot with his sword.

Granicus: Fought in 334 BC at the Granicus River in Anatolia, Alexander the Great defeated the Persian army and established a foothold in Anatolia.

Greek Dark Ages: The Greek Dark Ages lasted from 1100 to 750 BC, or from the end of the Mycenaean

Glossary of Terms

civilization to the rise of Athens, Sparta, and other prominent city-states of Archaic Greece. The centuries in between saw a notable lack of writing and literary documents which accounts for the period's "darkness."

H

Hegemon: In Greek, the word hegemon refers to a single military or political leader. In political theory, the word hegemon refers to the dominant superpower in a regiom, similar to the position Macedon held after the Battle of Chaeronea.

Hellas: The word Hellas and Hellenes is actually the word the Greeks used to refer to themselves and their culture. The word Greek is a misnomer that was popularized by the Romans.

Hellenes: The name the Greeks used to refer to themselves.

Hellenic League: The Greek city-states that fought against the Persian Empire, with Athens, Corinth, and Sparta being the foremost cities in the League. The league formed in 481 BC.

Hellenistic Greece: Lasting from the death of Alexander the Great in 323 BC to the death of Cleopatra VII in 30 BC, the age of Hellenistic Greece saw the spread of Greek culture, Greek language, and other expressions of Greek (or Hellenic) spread across the Mediterranean world and beyond.

Hellenization: Hellenization is the process of adapting, imitating, and spreading Greek culture beyond the borders of Attica and the Peloponnese.

Hellespont: The Hellespont is a strait that separates Europe from Asia; today, it is known as the Dardanelles.

Helots: The helots were the class of slaves in ancient Sparta.

Herodotus: A Greek historian sometimes called the father of history, Herodotus' major work is the Histories, which tells the story of the Persian Wars. He lived from 484 to 425 BC.

Homer: The blind poet and author of the oral poems the Iliad and the Odyssey, two epic poems about the events in and around the Trojan War. He was born in the eighth century BC.

Hoplite: The word hoplite refers to a soldier in ancient Greece who fought with a hoplon shield.

Hoplite Revolution: The term Hoplite Revolution refers to the greater political and civic privileges that hoplite soldiers could demand of their city-state. If a soldier risked his life for his polis, then that soldier should have a say in the political affairs of that polis.

Hydaspes River: Fought in 326 BC, the battle at the Hydaspes River saw Alexander defeat King Porus. The battle is famous for its location, which was further east than any Greeks had ever gone before, the battle's use of war elephants, and that it was Alexander's last battle.

I

Idol: A statue made of wood, stone, or in the case of many ancient Greek idols, ivory and gold. In the ancient world, such objects were worshiped by people who believed they represented the god or goddess it imaged. Only Jews and Christians did not engage in this practice.

Immortals: The Immortals were a group of elite soldiers in the Persian army, whose name derived from the fact that their numbers always equaled 10,000 soldiers.

Indus River: One of the two major river systems on the Indian subcontinent.

Glossary of Terms

Io: Io was a Greek princess from Argos, located in the Peloponnese. In Greek mythology, the Greek god Zeus abducted Io, then transformed her into a cow to hide Io from his wife, Hera.

Ionia: The west coast of Asia Minor that had been colonized by Greek city-states.

Ionian Revolt: Lasting from 499 to 493 BC, the Ionian revolt saw the Greek-city of Asia Minor revolt against Persian rule.

Ionic Order: An order characterized by the appearance of a volute, a scroll-like ornament found at the top of the column.

Issus: Fought in 333 BC at the town of Issus, Alexander the Great defeated Darus III, captured Darius' family, and all-but ensured that the Macedonians would triumph over Persia.

Isthmus: An isthmus is a land bridge that connects two larger land areas. The isthmus of Corinth and the isthmus of Panama are two of the most significant such land bridges.

Isthmus of Corinth: The Isthmus of Corinth connects the Peloponnesian peninsula to the regions of Attica and Boeotia.

K

Kiln: An oven used to make pottery.

King Minos: In Greek mythology, Minos was the king of Crete. He built a labyrinth beneath his palace, where he kept a cruel beast called the Minotaur.

Knossos: The chief city of Minoan Crete, famous for its palace.

Koine Greek: Koine Greek is a dialect of the Greek language that developed in and among the soldiers of Alexander the Great. Koine Greek became the lingua franca, of the ancient world.

Kraters: A huge drinking vessel.

L

Lacedaemon: An alternate name for Sparta used in ancient Greece.

Laconia: A region in the southern Peloponnese, of which Sparta was the dominant city.

Late Bronze Age: The Late Bronze Age refers to the last thousand or so years of the Bronze Age, characterized by huge trading networks and international diplomacy. The Bronze Age lasted until approximately 1200 BC, when the period collapsed suddenly and without warning.

League of Corinth: Led by Philip II of Macedon, the League of Corinth was a new alliance system, whereby all the Greek city-states pledged to work together for the common defense of Greece.

Leonidas: The king of Sparta, whose most famous accomplishment was leading the band of Spartan hoplites at Thermoplyae. He lived from 540 to 480 BC.

Leuctra: Fought in 371 BC, the Thebans defeated the Spartans and became masters of Greece.

Linear A: The writing system of Minoan Crete that remains largely indecipherable today.

Linear B: The writing of ancient, Mycenaean Greece.

Lingua Franca: The term lingua franca refers to a language that is the preferred means of communication for trade and diplomacy.

Long Walls: The Long Walls were a series of defensive that connected Athens to the port of Piraeus, located

Glossary of Terms

on the Saronic Gulf. The Long Walls made sure Athens would still have access to the sea during a siege and make Athens all but impossible to conquer.

Lycurgus: Lycurgus is the legendary founder of Sparta, credited with writing the city's laws and constitution to produce a class of highly disciplined soldiers.

Lysander: Lysander was a Spartan admiral who helped secure the funds needed to build a Spartan navy. With that navy, Lysander defeated the Athenian navy at the Battle of Aegospotami.

M

Maccabean Revolt: In 167 BC, the Jewish priest Judas Maccabeus led a revolt in and around Jerusalem against the Seleucid king Antiochus IV Epiphanes and his demands that the Jews worship Zeus, among other pagan practices. The successful revolt saw the creation of an independent Jewish kingdom that lasted until the coming of the Romans in the first century BC.

Macedon: Macedon was a kingdom located to the north of Greece. Following the Peloponnesian War, Macedon became organized and powerful enough to conquer the entirety of Greece.

Magna Graecia: A collection of Greek cities and colonies spread across southern Italy and Sicily, with its most notably cities being Neapolis and Siracusa.

Marathon: Fought in 490 BC, Athens defeated a much-larger army of Persian soldiers and was the first upset in a series of upsets by the Greeks over the Persians. The Athenians considered their victory over Persia to have preserved their city, their way of life, and the unique civic freedoms and opportunities that life in Athens gave to its citizens.

Mardonius: The Persian general in charge of the invasion of Greece.

Medea: Medea was the daughter of King Aeëtes of Colchis and, in Greek mythology, she helps Jason steal the Golden Fleece. Again, Herodotus takes a story popular in Greek myth and cites an alternative version to the story. Colchis was a kingdom located on the east coast of the Black Sea.

Mediterranean Sea: From the Latin for "in the middle of the land", the Mediterranean Sea is the principal body of water for the ancient world. The Mediterranean is surrounded by the modern-day countries of Spain, France, Tunisia, Egypt, and Israel, among others.

Megara: A city near Athens which had long been Athens' rival. However, in the years following the Persian Wars, Megara made an alliance with Athens to protect itself from Corinth.

Megarian Decree: In 432 BC, in response to Megara's incursion on land sacred to the goddess of Artemis, the city of Athens forbade any Megarian merchants and traders from operating in any ports Athens controlled.

Messenia: A Greek city-state that Sparta conquered in the eighth century BC. Sparta then forced much of its population to live as helots.

Metropolis: From the Greek for mother city, a metropolis is city that founds a colony or settlement in a distant place.

Miltiades: Of of the ten Athenian strategoi in command at Marathon, Miltiades urged his colleagues to attack the Persians as soon as possible.

Minoan Crete: The name given to a period in Greek history during the Late Bronze Age when the island of Crete was independent and wealthy.

Glossary of Terms

Minos: Minos was a famous king of Crete in Greek mythology. Here, Thucydides claims that Minos controlled a navy that allowed him to project his power outwards from his palace at Knossos.

Monarchy: A form of government wherein one person rules, and that one person cares for the needs of his or her subjects.

Museum: Named for the Muses of Greek mythology, the Museum was the name of massive library the Ptolemaic kings built at Alexandria.

Mycale: Fought in 479 BC, the Athenian navy destroyed the remaining ships of the Persian fleet.

Mycenae: The Greek city of Mycenae, located near the isthmus of Corinth. Mycenae flourished during the Late Bronze Age in the thirteenth to the eleventh centuries BC.

O

Oligarchy: The rule by the few, wherein a relatively small number of people rule. They are more concerned with themselves than with the common good.

Olive Trees: The soil of Attica is particularly good for growing olives, which are used for food and for making oil.

Olympias: Olympias was a Molossian princess, wife of Philip II, and the mother of Alexander the Great. She lived from 375 to 316 BC.

Olympic Games: Held in honor of Zeus, the Olympics were competitive games that brought all the Greek-speaking world together. The first Olympics were held in 776 BC.

Opis Mutiny: In the Opis Mutiny, Alexander's soldiers rebelled when he introduced a group of Iranian soldiers into his army and told his veteran troops they would be going home.

Order: The word refers to different conventions of Greek architecture.

Ostracism: In Athens, the Assembly could vote to ostracize, or exile, any citizen who appeared ambitious and had designs on becoming a tyrant. The policy is named for the broken pieces of pottery called ostraka upon which a person's name may be written.

P

Panegyric: Panegyric is the formal Greek term for a funeral oration.

Panhellenism: Derived from the words pan, meaning "all", and Hellenes, the word the Greeks used to refer to themselves, this word refers to all the Greeks and the common culture, language, and customs they all share.

Parthenon: The Parthenon is a temple built on the Athenian Acropolis and dedicated to the goddess Athena. Construction began in 447 and was completed in 432 BC.

Pausanias: Pausanias was a Spartan general who commanded Greek forces in Asia Minor following the Battle of Plataea, but he was accused by his fellow Greeks of acting too "Persian" and that he was conspiring with the Persian king Xerxes I.

Peace of Nicias: Issued in 421 BC, the Peace of Nicias ended hostilities between Athens and Sparta, but fighting resumed shortly thereafter.

Peisistratus: Peisistratus seized power in a coup and ruled Athens off and on until his death in 527 BC. Peisistratus was technically a tyrant, and he did build large public buildings and expand Athenian trade across the Mediterranean world.

Glossary of Terms

Pella: Pella was the capital of the ancient kingdom of Macedon.

Peloponnese: A large peninsula in southern Greece that contained the prominent cities of Sparta, Argos, and Corinth.

Peloponnesian LeaguevThe Peloponnesian League was an alliance system composed of states from the Peloponnesian Peninsula, with Sparta being the dominant city-state in the league.

Peloponnesian War: The Peloponnesian War lasted from 431 to 404 BC and was between Athens and Sparta and their respective allies.

Pelops: In Greek mythology, Pelops helped establish the house of Atreus, the ruling family of Mycenae. Agamemnon and Menelaus are descendants of Pelops.

Peninsula: A peninsula is a piece of land surrounded on three sides by water and is thus "almost an island".

Pentelic Marble: A marble of high quality mined in Mount Pentelikon, north of Athens. This marble was famously used in the Parthenon and other famous sculptures from Antiquity.

Perdiccas: Perdiccas was a Macedonian general and a close friend of Alexander the Great, serving as a regent of Alexander's vast empire until Alexander's son came of age. He lived from 355 to ~320 BC when his soldiers revolted and murdered him.

Perdiccas II: The king of Macedon during the Peloponnesian War who made it a matter of policy to support neither Sparta nor Athens in the war but instead, to sell them as many goods as they needed, and thus profit off of the war. He reigned from 454 to 412 BC.

Pericles: Pericles was an Athenian *strategos* and politician during the age of Classical Greece. As the most influential politician in Athens, Pericles oversaw the building of the Parthenon, the transformation of Athens into an empire, and its early strategy in the early years of the Peloponnesian War. He lived from 495 to 429 BC.

Perioikoi: The perioikoi were the craftsmen and merchants of ancient Sparta.

Perseus: The Greeks believed Perseus, the hero who killed Medusa, also founded the nation of Persia.

Persian Wars: Lasting from 499 to 449 BC, the Persian Wars are so-named because the Persian Empire invaded mainland Greece. In a series of shocking upsets, the Greek city-states defeated the Persian Empire and held onto their independence.

Pezhetairoi: The "foot companions" of the king, referring to a Macedonian soldier.

Phalanx: The phalanx was a military formation used in ancient Greek warfare. Soldiers would fight in organized, close-knit ranks, forming a shield wall and stabbing at the enemy with spears.

Pharos: The 300-foot-tall lighthouse at the harbor of Alexandria.

Phidias: Phidias was a Greek sculptor and architect who built the massive statue of Zeus at Olympia and the statue of Athena in the Parthenon. He lived from 480 to 430 BC.

Philip II: Phillip II was the king of Macedon who transformed Macedon into the dominant power in Greece. He reigned from 359 to 336 BC.

Philosophy: Literally, the “love of wisdom”; philosophy is the academic subject that treats certain overarching, unanswerable questions of the human condition.

Phoenicians: The Phoenicians had been impressed into the Persian army to serve as sailors, as well as in

Glossary of Terms

other tasks in which they had more specialized knowledge than did the Persians.

Plataea: Plataea was the name of a small village in Boeotia that earned much glory for itself during the Persian Wars. First, hoplites from Plataea were the only other people to aid Athens at the Battle of Marathon in 490 BC, and Plataea was the site of the final victory over Persia in 479 BC.

Plato: An Athenian philosopher whose writings serve as the basis for much of Western philosophy. He wrote dialogues that explored the fundamental nature of reality and morality and the value of believing in ideas like truth, goodness, and beauty.

Polemarchos: The head of the army in ancient Athens.

Polis: The Greek word for city-state.

Porus: Porus was king of the lands around the Hydaspes River in northern India.

Post and Lintel: An architectural system composed of horizontal beams resting on vertical supporting beams. Large gaps exist in between the vertical beams.

Potidaea: Potidaea was a Corinthian colony that, given its location on the Aegean Sea, had entered into an alliance with Athens to protect them from Persia.

Pottery: A vessel used for drinking and eating or storing for food made from clay that is fired in a kiln until it hardens.

Ptolemy: The Macedonian general Ptolemy triggered the wars of the Diadochi. Ptolemy ruled Egypt as his own kingdom, and he lived from 366 to 282 BC.

R

Realist Theory: In politics and international relations, states pursue their own rational self-interest. At times, this self-interest may seem amoral at best but the state is concerned with its own survival.

Relief Effect: A relief carving is done on a flat surface, where unwanted material is removed to leave only the person or thing being depicted.

Republic: From the Latin res publica, meaning the property of the people", a republic is a form of government that mixes elements of a monarchy, aristocracy, and democracy.

Rome: Located on the Tiber River in central Italy, the city of Rome was the dominant power of the ancient Mediterranean world from the third century BC to the fifth century AD.

Roxane: A princess from the region of Sogdiana who married Alexander the Great.

Salamis: Fought in 480 BC in the narrow straits between the island of Salamis and mainland Greece, the Athenian navy crippled the Persian fleet.

S

Sardis: The capital of Lydia which, after it was conquered by Cyrus the Great, was made into the administrative capital of the far eastern reaches of the Persian Empire.

Sarissa: A sarissa was a twenty foot spear carried by soldiers in a Macedonian phalanx.

Satraps: The administrators of a particular province in the Persian Empire, akin to a governor.

Scientific History: History is a narrative about past events; scientific history is an effort to recreate the past as accurately as possible in terms of dates, source material, and other pieces of evidence available to the historian.

Glossary of Terms

Scorched Earth Tactics: At times, a country being invaded may destroy its own crops, resources, and infrastructure to make it as difficult as possible for the invading army to survive.

Sea Peoples: While their exact identity remains uncertain, the Sea Peoples is a catch-all term to the various groups of people that invaded kingdoms around the ancient Near East.

Seleucus: Seleucus ruled over Mesopotamia and Persia and established the Seleucid dynasty that lasted until the first century BC. He lived from 358 to 281 BC.

Septuagint: The Greek translation of the Hebrew Bible, completed at the request of King Ptolemy II.

Seven Wonders of the Ancient World: The Seven Wonders of the Ancient Wonder are architectural masterpieces.

Sicily: Sicily is an island in the middle of the Mediterranean Sea that, thanks to its rich farmland and long coastlines, has long been a rich prize for neighboring empires.

Syracuse: Syracuse is a port on the island of Sicily which, thanks to its fertile plains and deep harbor, became one of the wealthiest cities in the ancient world.

Sisyphus: In Greek mythology, Sisyphus founded the city of Corinth. He was also famous for cheating death; in Tartarus, Sisyphus was condemned to push a boulder up a hill, and when the boulder reached the top, it would fall back down.

Socrates: A Greek philosopher and gadfly of Athens whose incessant questioning about the nature of the good life led to his execution in 399 BC.

Solon: Solon was an Athenian archon and poet. He stands among the Seven Sages of Greece on account of the wise and moderate reforms he gave to Athens in the sixth century BC. These reforms helped alleviate much of the tension between social classes in Athens. He lived from 630 to 560 BC.

Sparta: One of the three most important cities in ancient Greece. The city of Sparta was famous for its strict, highly regimented society and its highly disciplined soldiers.

Sphere of Influence: A sphere of influence refers to territory controlled by a larger, more powerful state, who consider it a necessity to guard their territory from rivals.

Stoicism: Stoicism was a branch of philosophy popular in the Greco-Roman world which focused on controlling one's emotions, cultivating virtue, and trying to do good to one's city and family.

Strategoi: The generals in charge of the Athenian army, of which there were ten in total. One strategos was elected from each of the ten tribes of Athens.

Synoecism: Made of the Greek preposition syn for "with" and oikos for "household", this term refers to the process of the Greek countryside identifying with a Greek city-state.

T

Temperance: Temperance is one of the four cardinal virtues; the idea of temperance refers to moderation in all things.

Temple to Zeus at Olympia: The Temple to Zeus at Olympia was a Doric temple built near Mount Olympus.

Thebes: Thebes was the dominant city in the region of Boeotia and a rival of Sparta, Athens, and Corinth.

Glossary of Terms

Themistocles: A Greek politician and general who led Athens during the Persian Wars. He argued that the proceeds from the silver mines at Laurium be used for constructing a naval fleet. He lived from 524 to 459 BC.

Thermopylae: Fought at a narrow passage called Thermopylae in 480 BC, an army of 7,000 Greek troops managed to hold off a Persian army of 120,000 to 300,000 troops.

Theseus: Theseus was an Athenian hero who brought the demes under the authority of Athens. He also slew the Minotaur, a monstrous half-man, half-bull creature who lived on the island of Crete.

Tholos Tombs: From the Greek word for beehive, these tombs were the grave sites of Mycenaean kings.

Thucydides: An Athenian general and historian whose most famous work is The History of the Peloponnesian War, which describes a conflict fought between Athens and Sparta. Thucydides lived from 460 to 400 BC and is credited as the Father of Scientific History.

Tiryns and Pylos: Tiryns and Pylos were two of the most prosperous cities in Greece during the Late Bronze Age.

Trireme: A Greek warship so-named for the three banks of oars that powered them. They also were equipped with a bronze prow used for ramming enemy ships.

Tyranny: A form of government wherein one person rules, but that one cares only for him or herself.

Tyrant: In ancient Greece, a tyrant was not necessarily a cruel leader, but a leader who did not receive his power from ancient, traditional heredity and was not bound by a constitution.

Tyre: Tyre was one of the more prominent cities in Phoenicia.

V

Vassal: The word vassal refers to someone who has taken an oath of obedience to a more powerful ruler.

Virtue: From the Latin vir for "manliness", the word virtue refers to a series of habits of moral excellence individuals should strive to develop for themselves.

W

Wanax: The Mycenaean word for king.

X

Xanthippus: Pericles supported democratic institutions in Athens, but he also came from the Alcmaeonid family, one of the wealthiest and most established families in Athens.

Xerxes I: Xerxes I was the son of Darius and Atossa and the grandson of Cyrus the Great. He is most famous for mounting a second invasion of Greece, an invasion that was ultimately unsuccessful when Xerxes and his forces were stopped at the battles of Plataea and Salamis. He lived from 518 to 465 BC.

NEVER ✦ CEASE
LEARNING

Made in the USA
Columbia, SC
08 April 2025

56370765R00159